*The Radical Republicans and Reform
in New York during Reconstruction*

The Radical Republicans and Reform in New York during Reconstruction

James C. Mohr

Cornell University Press | ITHACA AND LONDON

First published 1973 by Cornell University Press.
Published in the United Kingdom by Cornell University Press Ltd.,
2-4 Brook Street, London W1Y 1AA.

International Standard Book Number 0-8014-0757-5
Library of Congress Catalog Card Number 72-12404

PRINTED IN THE UNITED STATES OF AMERICA

*Librarians: Library of Congress cataloging information
appears on the last page of the book.*

To Elizabeth

Contents

Preface

Historians of Reconstruction have described in extraordinary detail how the victorious North dealt with the defeated Southern states after the American Civil War. Yet historians seem largely to have ignored the ways in which the victors tried during the same period to alter their own state and local institutions. Political developments in the postwar North, especially at the state level, are frequently dismissed as little more than a prologue for the "Great Barbecue" and the "Gilded Age." Readers would hardly guess that the period was one of promising starts, far-reaching reforms, and significant legislative precedents.

In view of the attention American historians have traditionally paid to reform movements, how may the neglect of Northern state politics immediately after the Civil War be explained? Why has the Republican Party at the national level during this period been so often and so meticulously analyzed, while the party at the state level has been relatively ignored? Why have so few historians looked at the activities of the so-called Radicals in the Northern states who provided the local political base? At a time when they were trying to change completely the social institutions of the former Confederate states, what were the Radicals' policies at home?

The dearth of detailed studies of state politics in the mid-

1860's partly reflects the dearth of studies of state activities in any period of American history. Some first-rate state histories have appeared, and New York has probably been the subject of as many of these as any other state. But American historians have nevertheless tended to concentrate upon national politics, especially when dealing with reform movements, and this emphasis on the national government has sometimes obscured an understanding of the fate of widespread and significant political reform at secondary levels. Scholars have suggested, for example, that this may have been the case in some studies of the 1920's.[1] Likewise, America's historical attention has been focused for many years on the dramatic events of Southern Reconstruction, constitutional amendments, and a presidential impeachment, while the history of the postwar North during the 1860's has been for the most part bypassed. As late as 1965, David Donald stated flatly, "There are no good books on the politics of any Northern state during Reconstruction."[2]

There were some articles, however, including the work of Ira Brown and David Montgomery on Pennsylvania. The subsequent publication of Montgomery's cross-state study of the Radicals and the labor question has filled additional gaps.[3]

---

[1] Arthur S. Link, "What Happened to the Progressive Movement in the 1920's?" *American Historical Review*, LXIV (1959), 833–851; Paul W. Glad, "Progressives and the Business Culture of the 1920's," *Journal of American History*, LIII (1966), 75–89.

[2] *The Politics of Reconstruction* (Baton Rouge, La., 1965), p. xi.

[3] Ira V. Brown, "Pennsylvania and the Rights of the Negro, 1865–1887," *Pennsylvania History*, XXVIII (1961), 45–57, and "William D. Kelley and Radical Reconstruction," *Pennsylvania Magazine of History and Biography*, LXXXV (1961), 316–329; David Montgomery, "Radical Republicanism in Pennsylvania, 1866–1873," *Pennsylvania Magazine of History and Biography*, LXXXV (1961), 439–457, and *Beyond Equality: Labor and the Radical Republicans, 1862–1872* (New York, 1967).

Erwin S. Bradley, who also treats Pennsylvania, and Felice A. Bonadio, who examines the situation in Ohio, have also made substantial contributions in recent years.[4] Yet even the focus of these two volumes remains primarily on the relationship between party problems at the local level and decision-making at the national level. The significant impact of the Radical Republicans on specific Northern states remains largely unexplored.

Another probable reason for the relative neglect of Northern state politics during the immediate postwar period stems from the long-standing characterization of that era as a time of corruption and spoils, but of little else. Except to those historians particularly fascinated with human corruption, the period appeared barren and depressing. As perceptive a scholar as Richard Hofstadter wrote off the years between the Civil War and the dawn of the Progressive era as "an age of cynicism."[5] This characterization may be traced in large measure to the preconceptions of some of the earliest writers who did look closely at Northern state politics during the late 1860's.

Foremost among the early analysts of postwar New York were two of the most gifted political commentators the United States has ever produced: the brothers Henry Adams and Charles Francis Adams, Jr. Their articles about the Erie Railroad and about the financial buccaneers of postwar America, which began appearing in the *North American Review* in 1869 and the *Westminister Review* in 1870, set the tone for writing about this period of American history in general and

[4] Bradley, *The Triumph of Militant Republicanism: A Study of Pennsylvania and Presidential Politics, 1860–1872* (Philadelphia, 1964); Bonadio, *North of Reconstruction: Ohio Politics, 1865–1870* (New York, 1970).

[5] *The American Political Tradition and the Men Who Made It* (New York, 1948), chap. vii, "The Spoilsmen: An Age of Cynicism,"

about this period of New York State history in particular. Their stories of the political manipulation of Erie Railroad stock and the attempt to corner the gold market still seem lively and are still well known. But too often historians see these events as comprising the whole history of the period. Governor Reuben E. Fenton, the man who signed the infamous Erie Railroad Act, emerges as either a fool or a bought man, or perhaps as both.[6]

Moreover, by the end of the nineteenth century there arose among historians something of a pro-Southern attitude regarding settlement of the nation's postwar problems. The Civil War itself seemed just and righteous, but the Reconstruction which followed was a dismal scheme imposed by zealots and fanatics. Along with this pro-Southern attitude came an anti-Republican bias, which was significantly reinforced during the first two decades of the twentieth century in the writings of William A. Dunning and his students at Columbia University. Their monographs were of high quality but helped to perpetuate the impression that postwar politics in the Northern states consisted simply of venal contests among self-serving extremists over public spoils. The Dunning school was either unwilling to admit that measures of enduring value could emerge from the base motives it attributed to the Radicals or so conscious of the venality of the era that it was blind to any idealism that may have coexisted with the corruption.[7]

---

[6] Charles Francis Adams, Jr., "A Chapter of Erie," *North American Review*, CIX (July 1869), 30–106, and "An Erie Raid," *ibid.*, CXII (April 1871), 241–291; Henry Adams, "The Gold Conspiracy," *Westminister Review*, XCIV (1870), 411–436. Cornell University Press has made these articles available in a convenient book, *Chapters of Erie*, ed. Robert H. Elias (Ithaca, 1956).

[7] Don E. Fehrenbacher, "Disunion and Reunion," in John Higham,

Among the monographs produced by Dunning's students is the only full-length, detailed analysis of the period of Radical rule in New York State: Homer A. Stebbins' *A Political History of the State of New York, 1865–1869*. Although this work is now nearly sixty years old, it remains the standard account of the era, and it continues to leave readers, as Stebbins himself put it, thoroughly imbued with Dunning's "scholarly grasp of the Reconstruction period." Stebbins lumped Fenton and "Boss" William M. Tweed together as similar political types and saw high tragedy in the failure of a conservative alliance to emerge. Without the Radicals, he concluded, Reconstruction "would have followed more natural lines." For half a century this "Dunning school of the North" has clung to an inordinately prominent position.[8]

The purpose of the present study is to look again at the Radical Republicans in New York, to examine the kinds of legislation they fought to enact while they controlled the state, and to suggest the reasons for their relatively rapid decline. To understand the Reconstruction era, one must know that though Reuben Fenton signed the Erie bill in 1868, as the Adams brothers pointed out, he had earlier struggled for three years to hold together a reform coalition and had consistently vetoed bill after bill designed to enrich the state's railroad corporations at public expense. Though he was a thoroughly political type, as Stebbins argued, the Radical governor was no Tweed, and the machine manned by Fenton's allies passed significant civil and institutional reform measures for New York State. The Radicals' activities may be viewed as a reconstruction at home undertaken at the state

---

ed., *The Reconstruction of American History* (New York, 1965), pp. 98–118.

[8] *A Political History of the State of New York, 1865–1869* (New York, 1913), pp. 9, 407–413.

level; the course of that reconstruction is the subject of this book.

I owe my greatest scholarly debt to the late David M. Potter, who guided my early research, encouraged this project at every stage, and gave generously of his precious time and invaluable insight. I am also indebted to Don E. Fehrenbacher, whose interest in politics at the state level first led me to explore this subject, and to Carl N. Degler, who read an early version of this manuscript and offered positive suggestions. The careful critical assessments by the readers and editors at Cornell University Press helped me to clarify several important points. I wish to thank them as well.

Historians have no finer allies than good librarians. I was fortunate to have the assistance of several. I want to extend my gratitude to Florence Chu and the staff of the Stanford University Library; to Virginia Loovis, Marjorie Davis, Mary Louise Meadow, Binnie Braunstein, Tuan-Sue Kao, and the staff of the University of Maryland, Baltimore County, Library; to Susan B. Grills of the Fenton Historical Society; to Jonathan Addelson of the Boston Athenaeum Library; and to the staffs of the Library of Congress, the New York Public Library, the Butler Library of Columbia University, the New-York Historical Society, the New York State Library at Albany, the Buffalo and Erie County Historical Society, the Chautauqua County Historical Society, and the Johns Hopkins University Library.

To the New-York Historical Society I am grateful for permission to use, in a section of Chapter 6, my article "New York State's Free School Law of 1867: A Chapter in the Reconstruction of the North," *New-York Historical Society Quarterly*, LIII (1969), 230–239. For permission to quote from documents I am grateful to the following: the New-

York Historical Society, from its collection of campaign pamphlets; Cornell University Libraries, from the Andrew Dickson White Papers; the Milton S. Eisenhower Library, the Johns Hopkins University, from the Daniel Coit Gilman Papers; and the New York State Library, from the Reuben Fenton Papers.

Grants from the Department of History, Stanford University, and the Bailey Fund, Stanford University Library, aided my earliest research; an award from the University of Maryland, Baltimore County, allowed me to make important final revisions. Jessie Applegarth, Marian Guentner, and Mary Dietrich helped type my manuscript. I also appreciate the aid of two student assistants, James and Joanne Giza.

For the support and understanding of my wife there can be no proper acknowledgment.

Baltimore, Maryland JAMES C. MOHR

*The Radical Republicans and Reform
in New York during Reconstruction*

1

Rise of the Radical Coalition

I

Prior to the Civil War the Republican Party in New York followed a well-known pattern of development. Coming together in protest against the Kansas-Nebraska Act, the state's Republicans had been more united in opposition to the expansion of slavery than in devotion to any positive program. The old Whig organization in New York under William H. Seward and Thurlow Weed provided a large degree of stability and most of the leadership within the new party during the late 1850's and early 1860's. Moreover, Governor Edwin D. Morgan can be made without much trimming to fit the Whiggish conservative mold which was typical of most Eastern Republican governors on the eve of the Civil War.[1]

A combination of political factors, however, encouraged the Republicans of New York to undertake a program of civil and institutional reform as the Civil War drew to a close. Not all of those "idealistic youths eager to give themselves to

[1] George H. Mayer, *The Republican Party, 1854–1966* (New York, 1967), pp. 3–47; Margaret Shortreed, "The Antislavery Radicals: From Crusade to Revolution, 1840–1868," *Past and Present*, XVI (Nov. 1959), 65–74; James A. Rawley, *Edwin D. Morgan: Merchant in Politics* (New York, 1955); William B. Hesseltine, *Lincoln and the War Governors* (New York, 1948), pp. 17–34.

a cause, political aspirants with an eye to the main chance,
able tyros itching to have a chance at personal leadership,"
who had come into the Republican fold during the 1850's,
were content to see their new party drift along in this lei-
surely half-Whig direction.[2] Two groups in particular were
growing restive. The first included most of those politicians
who had come into the Republican Party from the Free Soil
Democracy. Owing to the peculiar intensity of the old Barnburner movement in upstate districts, New York's Republican
Party probably contained more former Democrats than most
other state organizations, perhaps 25 percent.[3] From the origins of the Republican Party these ex-Democrats formed "a
self-conscious faction, proud of their antecedents, insistent on
proper recognition in offices and patronage, and above all,
determined that the party not become a mere reconstruction
of Whiggery."[4] Reuben Fenton, who had organized and pre-

[2] Hesseltine, *War Governors*, p. 10.

[3] Herbert D. A. Donovan, *The Barnburners* (New York, 1925),
pp. 116–120; Eric Foner, *Free Soil, Free Labor, Free Men: The Ideology of the Republican Party before the Civil War* (New York,
1970), p. 165. The former Democrats in New York State's Republican Party reached the height of their influence as a group in the
1867 legislature. Of the 110 Republicans who sat in that legislature
49.5 percent had formerly been Whigs, 20.7 formerly Democrats,
14.4 young enough to have always been Republicans, only 5.4 Know-
Nothing, 3.6 Liberty and Free Soil (as distinguished from Free Soil
Democrat), and one man was old enough to have been an Anti-
Mason. There were also 16.2 percent (or 18) of the Republicans old
enough to have had non-Republican, but undetermined, antecedents.
If the established percentages held for those with unknown antecedents, then the 25 percent estimate, which is also Foner's figure,
would prove fairly accurate. It is possible, of course, that among
rank-and-file Republicans the percentage of former Democratic voters
may have exceeded 25, but reliable data on that possibility would be
very difficult to obtain.

[4] Foner, *Free Soil*, p. 167.

sided at the first Republican convention in the state of New York, was one of these former Democrats. He and others like him chafed under the continuing iron grip of their former Whig opponent, Thurlow Weed, and Weed knew it.[5]

A second group of disaffected Republicans was made up of a number of men who had joined the party from a sense of independent commitment to the antislavery crusade in particular and to what they considered the more liberal of the two major parties in general. They held high expectations that the Republican Party might become a swift and powerful vehicle of social change. The young professor Andrew Dickson White, who was persuaded to run for the state senate in 1863, typified the Republicans that fit into this mold. Men like White, who were socially conscious, ideologically rationalistic, and reform oriented, also became upset with the general drift of their party during the early years of the war.[6]

Republicans of both the Fenton type and the White type wanted to see a more vigorous prosecution of the war by the national government and less conservative nit-picking on the part of their own Republican leadership at home. The conduct of Morgan's administration, especially the Governor's reticent attitude toward emancipation, disappointed these men.[7] By 1862, in fact, the number of party workers upset with Morgan's policies had grown larger than the number who were still pleased with his cautious brand of Whiggish Republicanism. At the party's Syracuse convention that year the Governor made a virtue of necessity and gracefully bowed

---

[5] Thurlow Weed to the Editor, Albany *Evening Journal*, Feb. 15, 1866, p. 2.

[6] Foner, *Free Soil*, pp. 103–148; Shortreed, "Radicals"; Andrew Dickson White, *Autobiography of Andrew D. White* (New York, 1905), I, 3–99.

[7] Rawley, *Morgan*, pp. 126–132; Glyndon G. Van Deusen, *Thurlow Weed, Wizard of the Lobby* (Boston, 1947), p. 301.

out, leaving the *ad hoc* alliance of restless former Democrats and disenchanted would-be reformers free to nominate a man of their own choosing. Major General James S. Wadsworth, their choice to succeed Morgan, proved a satisfactory nominee in the eyes of both of the most important groups comprising this coalition of discontented Republicans. To the former Democrats he was, like themselves, a man who had risked his political career in the Barnburner revolt against the national Democratic Party and then found vindication in the success of the Republicans. He had worked against Seward's nomination for President in 1860 and constantly against Whiggery in the Republican organization. To emphasize the point a preponderant number of former Democrats were placed on the state ticket along with the General. In the eyes of the liberal idealists Wadsworth was a patrician reformer and the military governor who had hampered enforcement of the Fugitive Slave Law in the District of Columbia.[8]

Few terms in all of American history are more difficult to pin down with precision than the word "Radical." The nomination of Wadsworth demands a brief consideration of the term, nonetheless, if only because almost every historian who has dealt with the Republican Party in New York State cites the 1862 gubernatorial nomination as marking the rise of the Radicals to party control.[9] In some ways the use of the term

[8] De Alva Stanwood Alexander, *A Political History of the State of New York* (New York, 1909), III, 31–52; Alexander C. Flick, ed., *History of the State of New York* (New York, 1933–1937), VII, 104; Hesseltine, *War Governors*, pp. 93, 268; Rawley, *Morgan*, p. 182; Henry Greenleaf Pearson, *James S. Wadsworth of Geneseo* (New York, 1913), *passim*.

[9] Hesseltine, *War Governors*, pp. 268–269; Rawley, *Morgan*, p. 182; James Sullivan, *et al.*, eds., *History of New York State, 1523–1927* (New York, 1927), IV, 1730–1737; Flick, ed., *New York*, IV, 113; Van Deusen, *Weed*, pp. 301–302.

"Radical" on the state level may be misleading, since those who have made the most rigorous attempts to define the term precisely have insisted that a politician could only be a Radical in his attitude toward the South, and particularly in his attitude toward the way in which the freedmen were being treated in the South. Even by these standards, however, the line between a Radical and a non-Radical Republican is far from sharp. Historians have regularly disagreed over which bills should be considered Radical measures when dividing federal legislators into various camps on the basis of roll-call votes.[10] And the situation is further complicated by the debate over the "radicalism" of the "Radicals." The Democratic press, hoping to persuade voters that the Republicans were all fanatics and zealots, blurred the distinction between "radical" and "Radical" at every opportunity, and by the time Fenton became governor the Democrats had also abandoned all distinction between "Radical" and "Republican," using the terms interchangeably.

Historians, of course, must concern themselves with distinctions that the popular partisan press can afford to minimize. Thus, in the interest of some precision, this study will preserve the most widely accepted definition of what distinguished a

---

[10] Donald, for example, selects six key procedural votes taken between December 12, 1864, and February 22, 1865, as his indicators of factional allegiance (*Reconstruction*, pp. 29–30); W. R. Brock, on the other hand, relies on a single crucial roll call taken January 28, 1867 (*An American Crisis: Congress and Reconstruction, 1865–1867* [New York, 1963], pp. 71–72). Allan G. Bogue, "Bloc and Party in the United States Senate: 1861–1863," *Civil War History*, XIII (1967), 221–241, selects a large number of votes, but arrives at the depressing conclusion that the distinctions are almost impossible to make in a precise fashion: "We will profit, I believe, in the future by treating the houses of Congress during the Civil War as political systems in which a variety of determinants of voting behavior were interacting."

Radical Republican from any other Republican: a Radical was one who publicly and politically expressed a hard line toward the South and, when he had the opportunity, defended the right of the freedman to full civil liberties.[11] Obviously, this definition still involves difficulties of interpretive judgment and matters of degree. Furthermore, it adds to the burden since politicians at the state level did not participate directly in the decision-making process at Washington and instead simply voiced their sentiments whenever they seemed appropriate. This traditional definition is also unsatisfactory insofar as it begs the question whether it might not have been much easier to voice Radical sentiments at the state level than it was to fight for Radical measures in the national Congress. Still, the old standard of Radicalism is not without application at the state level, and by that standard the coalition of former Free Soil Democrats and forward-looking young reformers which began to assert itself in the New York State Republican Party in 1862 may be labeled "Radical." Wadsworth conducted his campaign on the necessity of a more vigorous prosecution of the war against the evil Confederacy and on his desire to implement the President's preliminary emancipation proclamation as fully as possible. By comparison, the Weed-Seward-Morgan wing of the Republican Party attempted to generate a fusion ticket based upon moderation in conducting the war and a sort of chilly formality toward the emancipation proclamation.[12]

The nascent Radical alliance of 1862, however, was not strengthened by the results of the election. Wadsworth was

[11] Hans L. Trefousse, *The Radical Republicans: Lincoln's Vanguard for Racial Justice* (New York, 1969), pp. 4–5.

[12] Pearson, *Wadsworth*, pp. 150–166; Alexander, *New York*, III, 31–52; Hesseltine, *War Governors*, p. 268; Van Deusen, *Weed*, pp. 301–302.

defeated by the able state-rights Democrat, Horatio Seymour. In the state assembly the Democrats captured exactly half of the 128 seats, and the congressional delegation which went off to Washington consisted of 17 Democrats and only 14 Republicans. Many factors entered into the Republican defeat in New York, which was characteristic of the poor showing made by the party in other states that year. Not the least of these was the fact that no provision to vote by absentee ballot had been made for the one hundred thousand New York State volunteers then serving in the Union Army. But Wadsworth's backers chose to blame his defeat on the lack of support he received from many of the old Whigs in the outgoing Republican administration, thereby further increasing the friction between the various political blocs clustered together under the Republican umbrella. Blood eventually grew so bad over the results of this election that the Radical press began to refer to the Weed-Morgan portion of their own party as the "assassins" of General Wadsworth.[13] Thurlow Weed had to abandon his dream of retiring to a farm outside Rochester because his former friends in that upstate urban center blamed him personally for the defeat of Wadsworth, the Genesee valley's most prominent citizen.[14]

The defeat of 1862 proved only a temporary setback for the Radical alliance. Weed was able to reassert his control

[13] The word "assassins" had a *double-entendre* because Wadsworth, who returned to his field command after his gubernatorial defeat, was wounded during the Battle of the Wilderness and died in a Southern field hospital on May 8, 1864. The Radicals, of course, felt that he would have been serving as governor in Albany at that time had the Weed-Morgan wing of the party supported him in 1862. See New York *Tribune*, Feb. 3, 1866, p. 4; New York *World*, Feb. 15, 1866, p. 4 (hereafter cited as *Tribune* and *World*).

[14] Alexander, *New York*, III, 57–58; Henry W. Clune, *The Genesee* (New York, 1963), pp. 290–292.

over the Republican (now Union) central committee in 1863 and in 1864, but events of the Seymour administration seemed to be pushing many people into more extreme positions than they might otherwise have assumed. The best-known and most dramatic of these events was, of course, the New York City draft riot, which occurred during the summer of 1863. But many less sensational problems, such as the failure of the state government to halt competitive bidding by various towns and villages for volunteers to fill their troop quotas, were probably just as important in exacerbating popular frustrations. By 1864, Weed, as tactician for the Whiggish Republicans, decided to concede the state nominations to the Radicals and to concentrate his dwindling influence on holding New York for Lincoln. The Radicals responded by "load[ing] the ticket with old Democrats, all anti-Weed men."[15]

II

The Radical alliance of idealistic independents and politically aggressive former Democrats gave the 1864 gubernatorial nomination to the forty-five-year-old, five-term Congressman from Jamestown, Reuben E. Fenton. Both his personal background and his previous political career made Fenton typical of the more politically oriented members of the emerging Radical coalition. A native of Chautauqua County in the extreme western section of the state, Fenton left the family farm and made a fortune for himself in real estate and lumber. Like so many of their western New York and Ohio neighbors, the Fentons had come originally from rural New England to farm the new lands of the Lake Erie plain. After only a few years in the academies of his home county, a combination of poor health and financial straits ended Fenton's formal schooling while he was still in his early teens. As governor, Fenton would

[15] Alexander, *New York*, III, 87–94; Van Deusen, *Weed*, p. 310.

remember this well and help lead the fight which made New York State's elementary schools free to all children without fees of any kind.[16]

Fenton had first been elected to Congress in 1852 as a Free Soil Democrat, even though all of the other offices in his district went to Whigs. Significantly, it was the endorsement of the local Abolitionist Party which secured his election, for his intense hatred of slavery was well known.[17] At thirty-four years of age he was the youngest member of the thirty-third Congress. Running again as a Free Soil Democrat in 1854, he was narrowly defeated by a Know-Nothing opponent. In 1855 he served as president of the first Republican convention in New York State history, and in 1856 he was easily re-elected to Congress under his new party label.[18] Until 1862, he was regularly re-elected in his strongly Republican district, and he was still a member of New York's congressional delegation in 1864 when nominated to run against Seymour.

If there was any specific cause that Fenton conspicuously championed while in the House of Representatives, it was the welfare of American soldiers. His first act as a congressman in 1854 had been the introduction of a bill to grant relief to surviving invalids of the Revolution and the War of 1812. The outbreak of the Civil War afforded a splendid opportunity to enhance his reputation as a "friend of the soldier," and among the bills that he helped maneuver through the House of Representatives from his position on the powerful Ways

[16] *A Sketch of the Life of Governor Fenton* (New York, George R. Nesbitt & Co., 1866), p. 4, in Special Collections of Butler Library, Columbia University, New York; Helen Grace McMahon, "Reuben Eaton Fenton" (M.A. thesis, Cornell University, 1939), pp. 9–10, 14.

[17] McMahon, "Fenton," pp. 25, 43; Alexander, *New York*, II, 212.

[18] Fenton's first election as a Republican was a landslide. Only Elihu B. Washburne in Illinois received a higher percentage of the vote in his district (McMahon, "Fenton," p. 32).

and Means Committee were laws to "facilitate furloughs and discharges to disabled soldiers," to "facilitate payment of bounties and arrears of pay due wounded and deceased soldiers," to provide for the payment of a bonus to soldiers honorably discharged because of wounds or sickness, and to "simplify the form of application for pensions."[19] Unspectacular as this legislation was, Fenton's active support of the Union soldier strengthened his standing among those who wished to see the war conducted in a more vigorous manner and probably exempted him from that virtual prerequisite among prominent postwar Republican candidates: an active commission in the Union army.[20] The only other piece of legislation associated with Fenton's name was a pork-barrel harbor for the Lake Erie town of Dunkirk in his home district.

Even if his congressional career was lacking in drama or brilliance, however, Fenton's credentials as a Republican of forthright opposition to both slavery and secession were impeccable. He had been the first member of the House to attack the proposed Nebraska bill with its provision to repeal the Missouri Compromise. He urged President Franklin Pierce to veto the bill, and when Pierce refused, Fenton helped lead the Free Soil Democrats in their break with the administration. During the winter of the secession crisis Fenton counseled rigid opposition to any compromise on the question of extending slavery. In a speech which he had reprinted for

[19] Fenton's congressional career is sketched in New York *Times*, Sept. 19, 1864, p. 5 (hereafter cited as *Times*).

[20] Fenton was occasionally referred to as "Colonel" but the rank had been conferred by the New York State militia. Fenton was only twenty-one years old when he received this rank as the result of election by his local militia unit (McMahon, "Fenton," p. 9). After the first Battle of Bull Run, Fenton declined a regimental command, deferring to professional soldiers. See Fenton to D. E. Sil, Aug. 16, 1861, quoted in McMahon, "Fenton," p. 66.

circulation during his gubernatorial campaign he quoted from Thomas Jefferson and Hinton Helper to emphasize the moral justice of the Republican Party's position regarding slavery. The Republican cause, he concluded in the heavy-handed rhetoric of the day, would "no more be turned aside than the cause of the winds or the onsweeping tide of the ocean." Presumably Republican policy had a bit more precise substance than the wind or the ocean, but Fenton had forthrightly maintained his standing among the hardliners in the party.[21]

During the first months of the Civil War, Fenton combined his strong interest in the welfare of the American soldier with his dominant political themes of progress and reform by asking to serve on a special House committee to investigate alleged fraud in the letting of army contracts. Galusha Grow, whose election as Speaker of the House had been managed by his good friend from Chautauqua County, granted the request. Although this committee's weighty volumes of indictment and evidence were for the most part ignored, Fenton's action prefigured a political course which he would subsequently pursue more intensely at the state level as the leader of New York's Radical Republicans.[22]

Fenton's years in Washington indirectly afforded him another important advantage in securing the nomination for governor in 1864: he had managed to avoid much of the bitter

[21] "Sketch of the Life of Reuben Fenton," in Fenton Papers, New York State Library, Albany; Henry Wilson, *The History of the Rise and Fall of the Slave Power in America* (Boston, 1872), *II*, 382–383, 410; McMahon, "Fenton," pp. 44–60; *Speech of Hon. Reuben E. Fenton, of New York, delivered in the House of Representatives, February 16, 1860* p. 8, pamphlet in Special Collections of Butler Library.

[22] McMahon, "Fenton," pp. 63–64; Fred Nichlason, "The Civil War Contracts Committee," *Civil War History*, XVII (1971), pp. 232–245.

internal dissension that boiled up within the New York State
Republican Party during the war years.[23] Other members of
the Radical coalition in New York were surely better known
than the congressman from Jamestown, but the intensity of
the hatreds which they had managed to generate at the state
level eliminated their chances of nomination. Horace Greeley,
a prime example of one deeply embroiled in local feuds, recognized the great advantage of Fenton's detached position
and fell into line behind the congressman as the next best
candidate after himself. Urging Beman Brockway to become
Fenton's private secretary, Greeley wrote: "Knowing the
lobby men of the State as you do, you ought to be able
to warn him against all thieves but such as you choose to
[boost?]. *He* does not know Albany well—*can't* know it—
whereas you do, having spent more years than an honest man
should in that Sodom."[24] Moreover, Fenton's relative isolation
also allowed him to retain at least the personal regard of many
of the old Whiggish leaders in the party, and these relationships helped prevent their open bolt in the face of an entirely
Radical state ticket in 1864. Weed's paper, though hardly
ecstatic about the state nominations, described Fenton as "radical in his views, yet moderate in the expression of them; identified with no clique and committed to no Jacobinal theories,"
and endorsed him for governor.[25]

Finally, Fenton was known to be a canny politician, and
this was very important to the Radicals, for they hoped to be
able to preserve their dominant position in the party. Many
even considered him the managerial equal of the Whiggish

[23] Chauncey M. Depew, *My Memories of Eighty Years* (New York,
1922), p. 34.
[24] Greeley to Brockway, Nov. 15, 1864, The Papers of Horace
Greeley, Library of Congress, Washington, D.C.
[25] Albany *Evening Journal*, Sept. 8, 1864, p. 2; Alexander, *New
York*, III, 115.

wizard Thurlow Weed, with the crucial difference that Fenton had been successful without having to compromise his basic principles. Those who nominated him realized, indeed probably hoped, that Fenton might try to forge a new political machine in New York State.[26] This would be welcomed, however, not feared, because a Fenton machine would elect ever more Radicals and would be built upon idealism and a faith in progress, rather than upon calculating expediency. "With the establishment of constitutional authority upon the firm foundation of Humanity and Justice," Fenton declared in his acceptance speech, "we shall go forward into a career of prosperity and wealth, that no people have hitherto enjoyed."[27] So far, idealism had always paid off for Fenton politically, and this was close to the essence of Radical Republican politics.

The Radicals in New York conducted all phases of the campaign of 1864 entirely on the basis of national issues. The resolutions of the Republican state convention, which had been called for the sole purpose of nominating state-level candidates, were entirely national in their scope: they defended the war, attacked slavery, advocated a "discriminating" confiscation of Southern land for Union soldiers, and applauded recent Union victories. Rallies in Binghamton and Brooklyn alike focused exclusively on national questions. In a letter to the largest Republican rally of the campaign Fen-

[26] Alexander, *New York*, II, 212.

[27] See *Times*, Sept. 19, 1864, p. 5. The same theme had dominated his earliest recorded speech and recurred frequently in later years as well. See "Speech to Chautauqua County Agricultural Society," Sept. 28, 1853; "Address" delivered at the cornerstone ceremonies for the Gustavus Adolphus orphanage in Jamestown (n.d., but probably during his tenure as United States senator); and "Speech at St. John's School" (n.d., but probably, from internal evidence, 1879 or 1880), all in Fenton Papers, New York State Library.

ton urged people to vote for him as a supplement to the war efforts which they had already made. The Radicals' gubernatorial candidate was staking the greatest political opportunity he had ever had, not upon his credentials as a potential governor of the state of New York, but upon the vigor of his opposition to the Confederacy. The prime importance of his election, Fenton wrote, lay in the "moral support" it would provide for the Union cause.[28]

The Radicals also devoted a great deal of effort to winning the vote of New York State's soldiers, and this may have decided the outcome. The Republican-dominated legislature of 1864 had forced through an amendment to the state constitution providing for the vote by proxy of soldiers in the field; the Republicans well remembered that the absence of military votes in 1862 had probably cost them Wadsworth's election. A great furor of charge and countercharge arose when some of the commissioners sent down to arrange for these proxies were discovered returning false ballots. Although only Democrats were actually convicted and jailed for voting frauds, the Republican commissioners may have done their share of forging as well. Whatever the indiscretions committed, however, the vote of the state's soldiers did prove decisive in electing to the office of governor of New York the man who had so assiduously presented himself as a "friend to the soldier," Reuben E. Fenton. Without military votes Fenton, and Lincoln too, would almost certainly have lost New York State; even with them the final outcome was close enough to be in doubt for several days.[29]

[28] *Tribune*, Sept. 8, 1864, pp. 1, 5; Albany *Evening Journal*, Sept. 9, p. 2; 23, 1864, pp. 1, 5, 8; Fenton to Republican Committee, *Times*, Sept. 30, 1864, p. 2.

[29] Alexander, *New York*, III, 124, suggests that the indiscretions were predominantly on the Democratic side, while Hesseltine, *War Governors*, p. 381, implies that the Republicans may have gained

The certified returns eventually confirmed election of the entire Republican state ticket and indicated that men calling themselves Unionists would outnumber Democrats in the new state assembly, 76 to 52. In the state senate, whose members were elected for two-year terms in odd-numbered years, the Republicans already enjoyed a 21 to 11 advantage as a result of the previous November's elections. Moreover, one of the 11 Democrats had been challenged by his Republican opponent and now, after a year's investigation of the original returns, the Republicans had mustered enough of a case to reverse the old result. Consequently, the Republicans gained an additional seat in the senate, even though members of the upper house had not stood for election. The new man, Henry R. Low, was another former Democrat and an outspoken ally of the ascendant Radicals.[30]

III

New York Republicans actively committed to the Radical coalition could feel reasonably satisfied as the state legislature gathered in Albany to begin its 1865 session. They had rid the state of the despised Horatio Seymour, thus freeing their Republican legislature from the constant threat of a veto.

---

more votes by forgery than their opponents, who were unfortunate enough to get caught because they were operating in Republican-held Washington, D.C. Flick, ed., *New York*, VII, 121, however, supports Alexander's view that the Democrats were doing most of the vote stealing. The Republican version of the story is in the *Tribune*, Oct. 27, 28, 29, 30, and Nov. 1, 2, 3, 4, 5, 1864.

[30] *Journal of the Senate of the State of New York at Their Eighty-eighth Session, 1865* (Albany, 1865), pp. 32, 34, 40, 45, 49, 55, 61, 65, 66; Albany *Evening Journal*, Jan. 9, 1865, p. 2; *The Evening Journal Almanac, 1865* (Albany, 1865), p. 66; S. R. Harlow and H. H. Boone, *Life Sketches of the State Officers, Senators, and Members of the Assembly of the State of New-York, in 1867* (Albany, 1867), pp. 115–118.

They had also opened up the rich patronage of the governor's office to their fellows, many of whom had been forced to come a long, tortuous way to this reward since their days under Silas Wright and Martin Van Buren in the old Democratic Party. The war in which they so strongly believed was at last showing signs of being won, and, since the passage and pocket veto of the Wade-Davis bill some six months before, political discussions had begun to shift toward the problems of a postwar settlement. New York State, too, could begin to look forward to an end of the frustrations, the human and material losses, and the countless disruptions of normal life engendered by the Civil War.

Not far below the surface of this optimistic appraisal, however, lay more sobering considerations for the victorious Radical politicians. The conclusion of the war would also end their single most important vote-getting issue: opposition to the Confederacy and all that it stood for. Since the party's very inception, Republicans had been more united in their common antagonisms than in any common commitment to specific programs, and the ascendancy of the Radical coalition within the Republican Party made this traditional lack of a positive program even more apparent than it had been in 1860, when the old Whig leaders then directing the party held, at least in principle, some consistent views about the kinds of legislation they wished to see enacted. The new Radical leaders by comparison had defined themselves almost exclusively in negative terms and had campaigned entirely on the basis of their vehement opposition to the secessionists.[31] In short, the Radicals had won the election of 1864, but they had won it on issues that were fast becoming extinct. Some positive program had to be found.

[31] Shortreed, "Radicals," pp. 66–67; Campaign Pamphlets, 1864, New-York Historical Society, New York.

In addition to the anticipated disappearance of their most crucial issues, the Republicans in New York State were also at a loss for guidance from the national party. Despite their victory at the state level, the Radicals could count on no help from Washington in forcing the party's other factions to recognize that they had been eclipsed. If anything, the exact opposite was the case. Seward clung to a strong position within Lincoln's cabinet, and Weed was able to preserve a good deal of his influence in the allocation of federal patronage even though Fenton made it clear to him that his long-held position as a power behind the throne in Albany had come to an end.[32]

The historian William B. Hesseltine suggests that from 1860 to 1864 Republican Party leadership shifted from the states and the governors to the President; in 1864 Lincoln "was master of his party, and the governors depended upon him for their elections."[33] The situation in New York, however, does not appear to have been quite this straightforward. For one thing, because Fenton ran ahead of Lincoln in the election, the assertion that Lincoln and his national advisors "elected" the Governor seems open to debate. Second, the continued squabbles over federal patronage would suggest that "direction" from the White House was not very clear to those at the state level. Finally, one can accept fully Hesseltine's argument and still be left with a serious difficulty after April 1865. For if the creation and the continued maintenance of a truly national Republican Party depended upon the existence of a strong and skillful chief executive at its head, then the elevation of Andrew Johnson to party leadership would

---

[32] La Wanda Cox and John H. Cox, *Politics, Principle, and Prejudice, 1865–1866: Dilemma of Reconstruction America* (New York, 1969), pp. 1–67; Van Deusen, *Weed*, p. 312.

[33] *War Governors*, p. 361.

necessarily reverse the logic of the Hesseltine position. The lack of coordinated central direction under Johnson, especially after the President began to interest himself actively in the possibility of an entirely new political party, caused the national Republican organization to revert to its former state-by-state structure.[34] In New York, where the direction from above had been confusing even under Lincoln, Fenton and his Radical allies at the state level were left to formulate their own policies. Consequently, the need during the immediate postwar years for some sort of program upon which they might consolidate their position of power was even more acute than it might have been under a well-defined national policy and a skillful President who was willing consistently to apply that national policy to particular situations in each state.[35]

Partially stemming from this lack of direction from above was another political consideration which helped to convince the Fenton Republicans that they should begin to work out a positive program of their own. This consideration was the extreme fluidity of the political situation in the United States as the Civil War ended. Many political analysts were predicting the probable demise of the Republican Party as soon as the unifying issue of the war was removed. Even before the death of Lincoln, for example, just when New York's Radicals were trying to decide what to do with their newly won power, *Harper's Weekly* featured a story entitled "New Par-

[34] Cox and Cox, *Politics, Principle, and Prejudice,* pp. 68–87.

[35] Eric McKitrick, *Andrew Johnson and Reconstruction* (New York, 1960), overwhelmingly demonstrates that Johnson was not the skillful politician that Lincoln had been during his lifetime. Donald, *Reconstruction,* pp. 17–25, suggests that circumstances may have made Johnson's position impossible and that he actually followed the politically shrewd alternative. But the outcome resulted in a break-down of leadership at the top of the Republican Party, regardless of where blame is placed.

ties: We Are At the End of Parties." It would be difficult to capture more concisely the political instability of the immediate postwar years:

Of the parties that existed when the war began the name "Democratic" alone remains. The Constitutional Union Party survives only in John Bell drinking success to the rebellion in bad whiskey. The Republican Party as such has secured its great object of limiting the extension of slavery. The necessities of the case, in a nation waging a civil war, divide us all into two bodies: those who support the administration in its war policy and those who do not. But the old party lines do not separate us. The Party of the Administration is composed of men as different as the late Edward Everett, General Butler, John A. Griswold, Thurlow Weed and Charles Sumner, who were respectively leaders of the Bell-Everett, the Breckinridge, the Douglas parties and both wings of the Republican Party before the war. We are at the end of parties.[36]

A month later the Albany *Knickerbocker* ran a similar article declaring that there were "no issues left for the Republican Party, [and] that its object [the eradication of slavery] ha[d] been accomplished." The article went on to suggest that a new alliance of conservatives, reaching across old party lines, might be needed to keep "the Radical contagion" in check.[37] Only in light of this kind of speculation does the urgency of the Radicals' need for a cohesive counterprogram become apparent. They might continue to campaign on entirely national issues, as in 1864, but they could not ignore the fact that the end of the war would make these issues much less dramatic. In a state as politically close as New York had

[36] *Harper's Weekly*, IX (Feb. 25, 1865), 114.
[37] This article was quoted with glee on the front page of the Democratic *World*, March 24, 1865, p. 1; the national implications of this logic are the subject of Cox and Cox, *Politics, Principle, and Prejudice*.

just demonstrated itself to be, even in a supposedly "Republican year," those issues might not suffice much longer. Nor
could the Radicals count on a collapse of the opposition to
assure the future of their newly acquired political position.
Fenton and his allies needed a political strategy which would
at once hold together the coalition they had formed within
the Republican Party and also cut into the strength of their
well-organized Democratic opposition.

The New York State Republicans of 1865 found an answer
to their political problems in a legislative program of civil
and institutional reform. This program, gradually worked out
over three legislative sessions in Albany, fulfilled their requirements almost perfectly. Because it addressed itself to the
postwar problems arising from urbanization and industrialization as well as to the rights of the Negro, it appealed to the
independent reformers who had entered the Radical coalition
for liberal and idealistic motives. Because it sought to make
political inroads into the state's largest urban concentrations,
especially those clustered about New York City, where the
Democrats had just registered an almost two-to-one advantage at the polls, it appealed to the partisan interests of the
more politically oriented members of the Radical alliance. Because it would eventually deal with several problems not attacked seriously on the national level for over thirty years, it
prefigured many of the reform principles and political strategies usually associated with the later Progressive era. Because
it wrought substantive, far-reaching changes, it warrants the
label of a "reconstruction at home."

2

The Politics of Fire Protection

I

Many of the problems which faced postwar New York State were concentrated in New York City. Urbanization there had been rapid during the war, and so few housing starts had been made that residential crowding had grown serious.[1] The drifting of indigent and discharged soldiers into the city not only exacerbated this problem, but also created a situation in which the press feared a breakdown of "law and order." In January 1865, the *Times* noted with disgust that it was "safer to take a stroll on the picket lines of the James than to walk through some of the streets of New-York after nightfall."[2] The resumption of considerable immigration during the last years of the Civil War worsened the already chronic difficulties encountered by the city in trying to educate its young people and provide work for its unskilled laborers. Sanitation and health facilities were archaic; foraging hogs shared many of the side streets with pedestrians, while filth and sewage pro-

---

[1] On the housing shortage, see *Times*, Dec. 12, 1864, p. 4, which reported that people could not continue to live with the "crowding and gouging" forced by the landlords of the city; and *World*, Feb. 11, p. 4, "House Hunting Panic," March 16, p. 4, and March 25, 1865, p. 8.

[2] Jan. 7, 1865, p. 4.

vided a perpetual blanket for the city's cobblestoned streets. Despite three decades of aqueduct and reservoir construction, the problem of supplying enough fresh water for Manhattan's million people remained a major headache.[3] In short, New York City was experiencing many of the growing pains of a modern urban center, but was almost wholly lacking in even the most rudimentary facilities to relieve them.[4]

No wonder that New York City provided an absorbing focus of attention for the new Republican administration in Albany, especially since this huge center of social problems was also the center of Democratic Party strength in the state. During the recent campaign the Republicans had begun to believe that they might make some inroads into the New York City vote, and they had begun to suggest the direction which their later efforts might take. In reply to questions concerning the expenditures and the corruption of the Tammany city government, Fenton acknowledged a desire to look into the situation as soon as he was in a position to do something about it. "I hold it to be the duty of the legislative and executive departments of the Government," he asserted in a public letter, "to exercise a watchful care over the interests of the people, and to protect them from unnecessary burdens."[5] Earlier in the campaign the Radicals' leading paper, the *Tribune*, had called for "a completely new departure" based upon civil reform to unify the Republicans of New York City and to win converts from the Democratic Party there.[6] A Republican victory at the state level would provide an opportunity to launch such a new departure from above, and the implications

[3] Nelson M. Blake, *Water for the Cities* (Syracuse, 1956), pp. 121–171.

[4] Seymour J. Mandelbaum, *Boss Tweed's New York* (New York, 1965), pp. 1–26.

[5] *Times,* Oct. 28, 1864, p. 4, letter dated at Jamestown, Oct. 24, 1864.

[6] Sept. 9, 1864, p. 4.

of state action against local municipal problems could only make the Democrats in New York City wince.

Following the Republican triumph, the *Times* began to hint even more broadly at what this new departure might entail. Reprinting an article from *Wilkes' Spirit of the Times,* the *Times* argued the case for city reform at the state level. Since the city functioned under a charter granted by the state, the state had the right—indeed the duty—to step in and fill the needs of the people whenever the city authorities demonstrated their own inability to do so. This was clearly the case in New York City, continued the editorial, where "nothing less than the uprooting of the whole system springing from City Hall" could rescue the people. Most significantly, the argument concluded with the assertion that support for state action at the local level would be forthcoming not only from the Republicans in the city, but also from "thousands within the pale of the Democratic Party . . . whom an inexorable discipline has shut of their voices, and reduced to the condition of political slaves."[7] Nothing could better please the Republicans than to prove this political prediction accurate, and, considering the lopsided vote in New York City, the Republicans had very little to lose by trying.

A precedent for state intervention already existed in the form of the Metropolitan Police Act, passed in 1857 when a combination of Republicans and Know-Nothings had lashed out at Fernando Wood.[8] Though many believed the police to have been a special case, a more extensive new departure based upon that precedent now seemed worth the risk, and the Fenton administration prepared to wade into the sociopo-

[7] Dec. 3, 1864, p. 4.

[8] James F. Richardson, "Mayor Fernando Wood and the New York Police Force, 1855–1857," *New-York Historical Society Quarterly,* L (1966), 5–40.

litical quagmire of New York City. With the election of a state legislature that was two-thirds Republican and a governor who would not veto the needed reforms, New York City might yet be saved from itself.[9]

Even in an era of wooden frame buildings and open-flame lighting, however, reformation of a city's fire department might not appear at first glance to be a very dramatic way to launch a "new departure" or to "free political slaves." And yet, when William Laimbeer, Jr., a first-term Republican from New York City, stood up in the state senate on its first working day and formally announced his intent to submit a bill that would reorganize the fire department of his home district, he was addressing himself directly to the hopes of the Republicans for political gains in New York City.[10] He was also touching off what became the most significant political battle of the 1865 legislative session at Albany, for the metropolitan fire department bill proved to be the first real test of the Republican Party's postwar program of civil and institutional reform in New York State. Both the Republicans and their Democratic opponents realized the symbolic importance of the measure, and both realized also that it was not only a substantive reform in itself, but equally important as an indication of future Radical direction. The bill had no sooner been proposed than the Democratic *World* began to howl that its real purpose was "to reduce, if possible, the great Democratic majority in the City of New-York."[11] Since the battle over the fire department bill set the tone for postwar politics in New York State and revealed the patterns, alliances, and legislative strategies for the next three sessions, it is worth following in some detail.

[9] *Times*, Dec. 3, 1864, p. 4.
[10] *Senate Journal, 1865*, p. 25.
[11] Jan. 6, 1865, p. 1.

II

Laimbeer's proposal mentioned specifically a "paid" fire department, and the word "paid" was important. As the Civil War drew to a close, New York City still maintained a wholly voluntary fire department. New York was by no means unique; less than half a dozen major cities had yet replaced their old volunteer systems with paid professionals. Cincinnati had established a paid fire department in 1853, one of the earliest cities in the western world to do so, and Baltimore followed in 1858. Other cities having professional departments by 1865 included Boston, St. Louis, and Paris, France. But paid firemen were the exception rather than the rule in 1865.[12]

Although nearly a million people lived on Manhattan Island by 1865, the city fire department still functioned under a plan originally put into effect in 1798. Fire insurance rates in New York were the highest anywhere in the United States or Europe, and the fire insurance companies blamed these high rates on the inefficacy of the city's volunteer department. Citizens complained bitterly in letters to the press about the fire alarm systems of the city, which necessitated bell ringing, trumpet blasting, and a general clamor, often in the middle of the night, in order to alert the neighborhood volunteers. The introduction of more technically advanced equipment, particularly the horse-drawn and steam-powered pumper, could now eliminate the need to mobilize great numbers of men to form bucket brigades, pull equipment about the city, and supply energy for the manual pumpers. A system of volunteers might be both adequate and effective in most of the villages, towns, and smaller cities of nineteenth-century America, but postwar New York City had outgrown its old volunteer fire department.

[12] *Times*, Jan. 26, 1865, p. 1.

The establishment of a paid fire department promised, in addition to better and more effective fire protection, an actual reduction in the cost of that protection to the city's taxpayers. Increased efficiency would eliminate the expense of equipping and maintaining the extremely large number of fire companies which were needed under the volunteer system of district jurisdictions. Laimbeer's bill was based in part on the anticipation that a force of less than a thousand firemen with mobile equipment could adequately do the work of the existing body of more than four thousand locally organized volunteers. The entire weight of objective argument, then, seemed to support the Republican proposal to reorganize the New York City fire department.

In order to effect this eminently rational reform, however, the Republicans had to attack the very structure of New York City politics, for the old volunteer fire department had gradually become an important adjunct of the Democratic Party. Since the mid-1850's, when the city's Irish population first began to help man the fire lines, the local fire companies had been doubling as Democratic ward organizations in their neighborhoods. On election day the Democrats depended upon the firemen not only to get out the vote, but to vote themselves, as the saying went, both early and often. The so-called "bunking" system, whereby a certain number of the volunteers were allowed to live in the various firehouses at public expense in order to be on hand for any emergency, provided a means of rewarding the party faithful with free room and board for a year in return for delivering their wards. Engine companies were named for the city's Democratic mayors, and more revealingly, one was named for the Democratic city comptroller, who distributed funds to the fire department.[13]

13 *Ibid.*, March 23, 1865, p. 2.

Indicative of the intimate ties between the fire department and the Democratic Party was the rise of the most powerful Democrat in the city during the postwar era: William Marcy Tweed himself. Tweed had helped organize the "Americus" fire company as a young man and discovered that the ladder up through the fire department stood so close beside the one which led up through the Democratic Party that he had no difficulty in transferring his power from the fire department to the more formal party machinery.[14] One of the leading scholars on the subject of politics in the city of New York during this postwar period has argued recently that the success of the Democratic Party under Tweed depended upon an informal system of graft and payoff, which provided the only possible means of keeping open the vital channels of communication and control in an otherwise hopelessly decentralized political structure.[15] The volunteer fire department provided one of the most crucial links in this informal system of control; any attempt to alter or destroy the old department would necessarily represent a threat to the Democratic hold on the city.

The Republicans, of course, recognized the importance of the fire department in the scheme of Democratic control and never ceased berating the fire companies for their role in local elections. The Republican press also delighted in bringing to public attention some of the more glaring flaws in the volunteer fire department. The quality of the department's personnel, for example, had deteriorated considerably during the war years, and in some wards the fire companies had become interlocked not only with the Democratic Party but also with

[14] Denis T. Lynch, *"Boss" Tweed* (New York, 1927), pp. 51–66; Matthew P. Breen, *Thirty Years of New York Politics Up-to-date* (New York, 1899), pp. 45–49, 68–82.

[15] Mandelbaum, *Boss Tweed's New York*, p. 58 and *passim*.

some of the notorious street gangs of New York City.[16] Frequent brawling and substantial looting at the scene of fires resulted. The police department actually accused the volunteers of setting some of the city's fires themselves in order to provide an opportunity for such looting.[17]

Attempts to implicate the fire department in the draft riots of 1863 were not particularly convincing, but several firemen's riots since 1863 had been bad enough. A number of deaths occurred, and among the victims were several of the policemen who had tried to break them up. Like so many of the fire department's other difficulties, these riots could usually be traced back to the political role of the department, since they generally started as a result of internal feuds within the Democratic Party. During the immediate postwar years the most bitter infighting involved a splinter group, known after its meeting place as Mozart Hall, which was led by the city's former mayor, Fernando Wood. When a company of Mozart men responded to an alarm that was being answered simultaneously by a company of Tammany men, the result was often a pitched battle fought by the light of the fire which they had been summoned to extinguish. Lest this situation appear merely comic, it is worth noting that these battles were not good-natured brawls; clubs and guns were used freely. As late as August 1865, the press reported a fight between engine company number 6 and engine company number 41. The former was one of the least reputable companies in the city and completely controlled the seventh ward for the Democrats. The latter was considered open-minded on the question of a paid fire department, a position tantamount to heresy

[16] For a melodramatic look at New York City's street gangs and their infiltration into the fire department, see Lloyd Morris, *Incredible New York, 1850–1950* (New York, 1951), pp. 31–43.

[17] *Tribune*, Feb. 10, 1865, p. 5.

or treason. Wrenches and pipes were swung, over eighty
shots were fired, and "the firemen were dashing trumpets,
brickbats and bludgeons into each other's faces." At least two
men were killed and five precincts of police were required
to break it up. Needless to say, the building which they had
come to save burned to the ground.[18]

Here then was one of those classic situations in the drama
of American reform: on the one hand an institution desperately in need of alteration, and on the other hand a well-en-
trenched political organization with a vested interest in maintaining that institution unchanged. The missing weight in this
balance, a rival political organization with something to gain
by reforming the institution, was provided by the Fenton Republicans when they decided to make the fire department issue
the first major trial of their new program of institutional and
civil reform. The Republicans felt that they had chosen their
ground well for this first attack. Reform of the fire department not only appeared to be an issue around which the Radicals might muster a good deal of otherwise Democratic support, but it would be at the same time a telling blow against
one of the most important and most successful vehicles of
Democratic control in New York City. And the people of
New York City might actually receive better fire protection.

III

The Fentonites decided to concentrate their initial effort
in the upper house, where all but a few of the Republican
members had already cast their lots with the now dominant
Radical coalition. Seventeen of the twenty-one Republican
state senators, for example, signed a public letter in 1864 urging postponement of the Baltimore convention; they had

[18] *Times,* Aug. 21, 1865, p. 8. For the report of an earlier riot, see
Tribune, Dec. 14, 1864, p. 4.

wanted additional time to organize support for a more Radical candidate than Lincoln.[19] Many were currently reaffirming their Radicalism during debates over ratification of the Thirteenth Amendment.[20] Moreover, the Radical position had just been strengthened further by the substitution of Low for one of the Democrats who sat during 1864. Leadership, committee assignments, and legislative seniorities were already established from the previous year, and this prior organization would help the Governor's allies maintain party discipline in the senate. Having chafed under Seymour for one session, the Radical senators were now given an opportunity not only to strike back at the party they had considered virtually treasonous during the darkest days of the war, but also to get on with a new departure of their own at the state level. It took the senate only two weeks to give the fire department bill two of its required three readings and refer the measure to the standing Committee on Cities and Villages.[21]

Public interest in the fire department bill ran high from the outset. The firemen, the old New York City Board of Fire Commissioners, the Democratic Party, and the Democratic press on the one side traded insults, investigations, public rallies, and editorials with the insurance companies, the Citizens' Association, the Republican Party, and the Republican press on the other side. Each of these groups played a major role in the battle over the fire department. The firemen themselves took an active hand in trying to influence both the public and the legislature. At one point during the early weeks of the 1865 session the *Tribune*'s Albany correspondent quipped that

[19] Alexander, *New York*, III, 88–89.
[20] Albany *Evening Journal*, Feb. 3, 1865, p. 1.
[21] *Senate Journal, 1865*, p. 56; *Documents of the Senate of the State of New York at Their Eighty-eighth Session, 1865* (Albany, 1865), VI, Doc. No. 21, p. 2; *World*, Feb. 20, 1865, p. 5.

there were so many firemen in the capital city trying to run the machinery of state that not enough firemen could possibly be left either in Brooklyn or in New York City to put out a fire.[22] The old Board of Fire Commissioners also sent representatives to Albany to "see what was being done in the matter, take such measures as they might deem proper, and keep the department generally advised as to what action was being taken or likely to be taken by the Senate relative to [the fire department] Bill."[23] The board's agents included John Decker, chief engineer of the fire department, James Baremore, a member of the city council, and John R. Platt, president of the volunteer department.

These opponents of Laimbeer's bill had no monopoly on the lobby, however, since a number of New Yorkers also journeyed to Albany to voice support for the measure. One of these men was Dorman B. Eaton, a remarkable young attorney whose name reappears in later reform battles. He was sent as the official representative of the Citizens' Association, a group of wealthy civic-minded New Yorkers whose membership included George Templeton Strong, Peter Cooper, William E. Dodge, and Robert B. Roosevelt. The Citizens' Association in many ways prefigured the mugwump and "good government" organizations of a later period, which so often have been chided by American historians for their failure to appreciate how the "game of politics" was actually played.[24] Such criticism may be justified for a later period—probably for any time after New York City was ruled by the

[22] Jan. 26, 1865, p. 5.

[23] *Times,* Jan. 22, 1865, p. 8.

[24] Hofstadter, *American Political Tradition*, chap. vii, and Hofstadter, *The Age of Reform* (New York, 1955), *passim*; John A. Garraty, *The New Commonwealth, 1877–1890* (New York, 1968), pp. 214–219; Matthew Josephson, *The Politicos, 1865–1896* (New York, 1938), *passim*.

so-called Committee of Seventy in 1870—but in 1865 the Republican Party was the organization actually "playing the game," and the Citizens' Association was an effective pressure group working on the sidelines.

More difficult to assess is the role played by the insurance companies in the Albany lobby. In the past the fire insurance business had been characterized by cutthroat competition, which had led at various times to extremely low rates that in turn resulted in a very high incidence of bankruptcy and failure whenever serious fires ravaged the city. In 1835, when one of the worst fires in New York's history occurred, only three of the city's twenty-six fire insurance companies escaped ruin.[25] Yet by 1837 there were once again twenty-one firms in the field, and a new rate war was under way.[26] Agreements to set standard rates broke down in the early 1840's, and the so-called Broad Street fire of 1845 brought about a repetition of the failures of a decade before. By 1865 this pattern was repeating itself once again, and no fewer than seventy new companies were writing fire insurance in the city of New York since the rates had gone back up following the losses of 1845.

The situation for the fire insurance companies was made particularly acute by the steep increase in American fire losses during the latter years of the Civil War. For the nation as a whole these losses jumped from $29,000,000 in 1864, the worst year ever, to $43,000,000 in 1865. Coupled with the apparent

[25] There are a large number of contemporary descriptions of the great holocaust of 1835, but it was still remembered in later years, as Beman Brockway, Governor Fenton's private secretary for a time, felt compelled to include an account of the fire in his largely political memoirs written in 1891 (*Fifty Years in Journalism, Embracing Recollections and Personal Experiences, with an Autobiography* [Watertown, N.Y., 1891], pp. 5–6).

[26] Sullivan, *et al.*, eds., *New York*, V, 2189.

inability of the industry to regulate itself regarding safe rates, a continued loss of this proportion would once again send the weaker companies under. The result would be to increase the burden on the larger firms, decrease public faith in fire insurance, and leave a substantial number of private businesses in New York holding fire insurance which was no longer any good. Thus, despite their long history of bitter infighting, the companies saw an advantage in anything which would help check the alarming rate of fire loss and possibly save both themselves and the city from still another repetition of the events of 1835 and 1845.[27]

Toward this end a number of New York City's fire insurance companies had been cooperating since the spring of 1864 in gathering evidence against the volunteer fire departments.[28] There is some reason to believe that they brought their evidence to Laimbeer prior to the opening of the 1865 legislature and may therefore have been partially responsible for planting the idea of fire department reform in the minds of the Republicans at Albany.[29] Whether or not this was the case, the insurance companies certainly came to the defense of the proposal once it was introduced. An informal "Committee of Insurance Companies" sent an official representative to the legislative hearings which were eventually held on the fire department bill, and several petitions were introduced into the

[27] Harry Chase Brearley, *The History of the National Board of Fire Underwriters: Fifty Years of a Civilizing Force* (New York, 1916), pp. 3–26; Cecil F. Shallcross and Thomas A. Ralston, *The History of the New York Board of Fire Underwriters* (New York, 1917), p. 8.

[28] Lowell M. Limpus, *History of the New York Fire Department* (New York, 1940), pp. 241–242, dates the effort from the formation of a "Committee of Eight" for this purpose by the City Board of Fire Underwriters, March 17, 1864.

[29] *Ibid.*, p. 242. Laimbeer also served on the Committee on Insurance Companies; see *Senate Documents, 1865,* VI, No. 21, p. 2.

assembly which registered the approval of the city's insurance companies for the proposed reform.[30]

Despite the presence in Albany of these various pressure groups, however, the paramount considerations in the fire department bill remained political. The Democratic Party had an economic stake in the bill roughly comparable to that of many of the insurance firms, since the volunteer fire departments accounted annually for over a million dollars in public expenses which would be lost to party distribution. Furthermore, the fire department bill was the Radical coalition's first significant piece of domestic legislation, and all sides realized that its fate could greatly affect the subsequent legislation of the postwar period.

IV

On January 24, 1865, the senate Committee on Cities and Villages began public hearings on the proposed fire department bill, and these hearings provided an opportunity for the pressure groups to make public their respective arguments. A spokesman for the insurance committee, Mr. Norwood of the Lorillard Company, argued that both the economy and the morality of the city would benefit from the establishment of a professional fire department and the disbanding of the volunteer system. His economic arguments were based upon a comparison with the expenses incurred by cities like Baltimore and Cincinnati, which had already adopted salaried fire departments; his argument relative to the morality of the city was an allusion to the widespread belief on the part of many citizens in New York that several of the fire stations were little more than bawdy houses.[31]

Norwood's concern with the immorality of the city is in

[30] *Tribune*, Feb. 9, 1865, p. 4.
[31] *Times*, Jan. 26, 1865, p. 1.

some ways more interesting than his primary argument about the relative expense of volunteer and paid fire departments, for it reveals something about the social preconceptions of the men he was addressing. Norwood presumably made his argument hoping that it would strike home with the ruling Radicals and their constituents, and there is evidence that he was correct, since the state's leading Radical paper later re-emphasized his point in a major editorial on the fire department bill:

Because associations of young men from the class that supplies volunteer firemen in a great city are removed from the restraints of family and well-ordered society, they become proud of vices, and popular with their fellows because they possess them. Being organized and acting under a semblance of command, they feel a degree of strength that impels them too often to defy the law and disturb public order. Their calling as volunteer firemen requires them to turn out at any hour of the day and night, and is incompatible with any steady pursuits of industry, and renders impossible the earning of an honest support by labor. For this reason they are driven by their wants to exercise their wits to supply the deficiency of wages.[32]

In common with virtually every other reform group in nineteenth-century America, the Radicals in New York State after the Civil War maintained a strongly moralistic outlook. Home and order, work and regularity, were important to them. The Radicals were interested in making such institutional and civil reforms as would allow them to deal with the world of the city and the factory in a rational and a moral manner; they were interested in adjusting and perhaps in manipulating that world, but not in tearing it down or in restructuring its social order. Even though many of these men would eventually lose their political power in large measure because of their com-

[32] *Tribune*, Feb. 28, 1865, p. 4.

mitment to equal political rights for black New Yorkers, they cherished the traditional social values of their era.

Chief Engineer John Decker followed Norwood to the stand, but he could do very little to defend the volunteers. Sidestepping completely the morality argument, he contented himself with unsubstantiated denials of Norwood's statistical information concerning the relative cost of the Democratic volunteers in New York as against salaried professionals in other cities. Decker was wholly unprepared for the closely researched presentation that Norwood had made; Decker did not even have a copy of his own annual report, which Norwood had offered in evidence. Feeling the pinch, Decker managed to obtain a postponement of the hearings in order to gather some data of his own,[33] which somewhat diminished Norwood's initial advantage.

It is again worth noting a parallel between Radical Republican tactics after the Civil War and Progressive tactics at the turn of the century: the use of experts and statistical data. Decker and the Democrats had come to Albany expecting another committee hearing like the ones they were used to, involving a little name-calling and some political vagaries. Instead they encountered a well-prepared expert capable of speaking authoritatively on financial matters and armed with a long array of damning statistics. This use of experts and statistical data to influence both the legislators and the public would increase in the subsequent reform battles fought by the Radical Republicans and their allies in the postwar era. By the time health reform and school reform became the issues, they had perfected this technique to an extent rarely surpassed by the Progressives, even though the latter are probably better known for employing it.

[33] *Times*, Jan. 26, 1865, p. 1.

The senate committee hearing reconvened two weeks later amid intense public interest. As the *World* pointed out:

The chamber was filled to suffocation, about half the lower house being in attendance, notwithstanding the Bounty Bill was under consideration [in the state assembly]. For several years a like scene of interest has not been witnessed before a committee in this city. One would have thought that a peace measure was under consideration, and that the fate of the nation depended upon the result.[34]

This time William Hitchman, a Tweed lieutenant sent to Albany by the existing New York fire department, took over the defense from Decker.[35] Hitchman made a weak effort to controvert the statistics offered at the previous session by the insurance committee; this time he at least had the city comptroller's report for 1863 with him. It was rapidly apparent, however, that the volunteers could not match figures with the insurance men, so they retreated to a compromise. Hitchman asked the legislature to drop the Laimbeer proposal and in its stead to legalize a fire department reform bill which had been rushed through the New York City Council in record time when the city's Democrats had caught wind of the Radical plan to introduce a reform bill in Albany. New York's Democratic mayor, C. Godfrey Gunther, had signed the emergency act on Christmas Eve, only four weeks before the present hearings had begun. John R. Platt then took the stand and defended the department's ability to clean its own house. The charges of immorality in the fire stations and of graft in the

[34] *World*, Feb. 9, 1865, p. 4.

[35] William Hitchman was subsequently elected to the assembly, where he served as speaker in 1869 and again in 1870. In both of these years Tammany controlled the lower house and Hitchman was considered Tweed's mouthpiece (Alexander, *New York*, III, 224, 228).

operation of the system, he claimed, needed only to be substantiated to be acted upon.[36]

Abraham R. Lawrence, who claimed to represent "certain citizens who were large owners of property in the City of New-York," responded to the firemen with the single most cogent summary of the case offered on behalf of Laimbeer's bill during the course of the hearings.[37] He began with an attempt to justify state intervention in what might easily be considered an almost wholly local problem. This argument no doubt helped assuage the sensibilities of those upstate Republicans who favored the bill on political grounds, but still had serious qualms about meddling in someone else's local affairs. Action in this case could be justified, Lawrence believed, because it would

vastly promote the interests not only of the City of New-York and of the City of Brooklyn [the two cities which comprised the bulk of the "metropolitan district" to which the official title of the bill referred], but also of the entire state. For, after all, everything which tends to secure the safety of property in those cities, tends to promote the interests of the people of the whole State; because, as the commerce of the State centers in those cities in a greater or less degree, the people of the whole State are therein represented; and, when a fire breaks out, it is not only the property of the individual citizen of New-York or Brooklyn, but the property of gentlemen who live along the line of our canals and in the interior of the State at times.[38]

While this argument might appear tenuous, the demographic

[36] Limpus, *New York Fire Department,* p. 243; *Tribune,* Feb. 9, 1865, p. 4.

[37] For a brief sketch of Lawrence, a prominent New York City political figure, see *Times,* Feb. 15, 1917, p. 11.

[38] This and subsequent references to Lawrence's testimony are from a transcript in *Tribune,* Feb. 9, 1865, pp. 4–5.

and economic patterns of New York State had for some time been shifting toward more concentrated units of population, and these units were in turn becoming more and more interdependent both upon one another and upon New York City. As early as 1835 the state as a whole had realized its interest in helping New York City recover from the great fire.[39] In 1865 it was effective politics to remind the rapidly growing upstate urban centers of their possible nonpolitical stake in the reform of New York City's fire department.

Lawrence continued by suggesting that a system created in 1798 to serve a city of 58,000 people might be incapable of dealing with the situation that existed in 1865. Running quickly over the remarkably few alterations which had been made in the original plan, Lawrence pointed out that even these few changes had been mere stopgap measures. "The great commercial metropolis of the United States," he stressed, a municipal center containing "fourteen hundred thousand people in round numbers," was badly served by a patched-up system "which might do for a large village."

A third point made by Lawrence was the suggestion that discipline in the volunteer fire department might be lax not simply because its members were weak or evil characters themselves, but because the institutional structure of the department was inherently faulty. This argument must have been particularly effective with the Radicals, for it explained the observation that the form of an institution could influence the functioning and even the behavior of the people involved in that institution. Many of the Radicals had made the same general argument on the much larger question of the institution of slavery. Lawrence reasoned that the hierarchical

[39] Nathan Miller, *The Enterprise of a Free People: Aspects of Economic Development in New York State during the Canal Period, 1792–1838* (Ithaca, 1962), pp. 192–193.

arrangement of the fire department, in which the firemen
themselves elected all of their own leaders, including those
charged with punishing irregularities, necessarily resulted in
having extremely lax disciplinarians at the helm. Although the
city council had an official check upon the activities of the
department, he continued, this check was not effective in
practice, since the council simply rubber-stamped anything
that its comrades in the fire department chose to do. "I undertake to say there is no check, there is nothing which would
lead to a proper superintendence of the Department." Only
the proposed Laimbeer bill would rectify the situation, for in
it "the officers are entirely independent of the men whom they
control. They are not like the Fire Commissioners who sit in
judgment upon firemen, who are themselves liable to be removed by a board of representatives. They are not like my
friend, the Chief Engineer [Decker], who has to be elected
by those same firemen. They are to hold a term of eight years,
which will make them independent of any consideration except what their duty would make them take a cagnizance
[sic] of. They are not in any way responsible to the firemen."
The proposed fire commissioners would be appointed by the
governor and confirmed by the senate. Even if the Republicans could not always count on a friendly governor like Fenton to appoint either neutral or Republican fire commissioners, they knew that Republican control of the senate had
remained unbroken since the party's formation.[40]

The remainder of Lawrence's testimony was spent in adding to the detailed statistical data previously introduced by
Norwood. In every case where a paid fire department already
operated, both the expense of maintaining that department
and the cost of fire insurance were proportionately lower than
in New York City. In Baltimore, for example, where the

[40] Alexander, *New York*, III, 227–228.

change had been made in 1858, the losses by fire were supposedly reduced from $2,175,000 for the period 1855–1858 to $803,000 for the period 1859–1862; the number of men required to provide the city with this increased protection had also been reduced by the introduction of advanced equipment. Baltimore's insurance rates had fallen between 21 and 30 percent below those of New York City. Summing up the case for a paid fire department, Lawrence claimed: "An opportunity presents itself in the passage of this bill to obtain at once both a decrease in our expenditures and a fire system which will afford a greater security to property."

Thomas C. Acton, president of the New York City Board of Police Commissioners, testified next. Acton was concerned much less with the statistics of finance or the justifications for institutional reformation than he was with the conduct of the volunteers. He began by citing examples of fraudulent voting by members of the fire companies and rapidly warmed to his subject; within a few short sentences he was blaming the volunteer firemen for inciting the draft riots of 1863. Democratic Senator Thomas Fields of New York City, who had been frustrated earlier in an attempt to cut short the testimony of Lawrence, could control himself no longer and threatened to walk out if Acton's wholesale charges were permitted to stand as legitimate testimony. Chairman George Andrews restored order, and Acton continued his testimony against a running counterpoint of questions and denials from Senator Fields. Eventually Acton claimed that the fire department had deteriorated to such an extent that he would ask the legislature for an increase of "1,000 to 1,500" new policemen for the specific purpose of controlling the volunteers, many of whom had taken to walking the street fully armed.

Police Inspector Carpenter, Police Superintendent Kennedy, and several precinct captains then proceeded to substantiate the charges that Acton had leveled against the volunteers, which included vote frauds, larceny at the scene of fires, frequent rioting and misconduct, and occasional murder. Carpenter, who had been a member of the fire department at one time, testified that in his opinion the quality of the volunteers had deteriorated badly during the war years; the public "rowdyism" of the present engine companies combined with the private debauchery of the firehouses now made the department both a blight and a threat. Kennedy and the lower ranking officers all testified to specific instances of criminal conduct by members of the fire department. Throughout the rest of the afternoon and into the evening Senator Fields continued to act as a sort of defense attorney for the old fire department and tried repeatedly to put the long line of hostile witnesses off stride. When the day's session had ended, however, it had become increasingly obvious that the supporters of the proposed reform were more than holding their own against the Democrat from New York City.[41]

When the committee resumed its hearings on the following afternoon, Hitchman and Decker both returned to the stand to reassert the good intentions of the city council and to plead for an opportunity to let the fire department reform itself. Dorman B. Eaton had just commenced testimony in rebuttal when Senator Fields returned from his evening meal. Apparently his gradually building frustrations had gotten the better of him for he "entered in a condition of gross intoxication, and after staggering to his chair" began to interrupt Eaton and to badger him. Soon Eaton found it impossible to continue over Fields' interjections, which included a boast "that he [Fields] would bet two hundred and eighty thousand dollars that he would beat the bill." The legislature would later come back to boasts like this one, but for the time being

[41] *Tribune*, Feb. 10, 1865, p. 5.

Chairman Andrews could do nothing except declare adjournment; Fields was too drunk to respond to a call to order. While the senator from New York City railed on, the rest of the committee filed out of the chamber leaving, as the *Tribune*'s headline put it, "Mr. Fields with the Field to Himself."[42]

This incident aptly symbolized the frustration of the Democratic Party in the New York State legislature. Beaten in 1864 by the anti-Southern rhetoric of the Radical Republicans, they must have begun to feel like surrogate Southerners themselves. Two weeks after the Fields outburst, for example, a *World* editorial made clear that the Democrats were painfully aware of the parallels between Republican national policy toward the individual Southern states and Republican state policy toward the Democratic cities. "This Republican crusade against local self-government," it growled in response to a Republican proposal to create a capital police district in the Albany area modeled on the metropolitan police district in the New York City area, "is to be rushed through to its completion. The door was opened by the Republican crusade against state rights. It will not be closed until the people put down Republicanism."[43] The *World* may have been correct, for in a very real sense the Democrats did serve as surrogate Southerners for the New York State Radicals, who were in effect arguing that the Democratic machine in New York City, like the traditional leadership of the prewar South, should no longer be permitted to handle its own problems.

Although the Republican press feigned a righteous indignation over the outburst by Fields, the Radicals must have been

[42] Feb. 9, p. 5; 10, 1865, p. 5; the latter has a transcript of Fields' interjections. Fields later fled the country when the Tweed machine was broken in 1870 and died in exile (White, *Autobiography*, I, 104).

[43] Feb. 28, 1865, p. 4.

secretly delighted. The incident provided one more bit of evidence that the old political leaders were no longer competent to rule. Indeed, if Fields was any example, they could no longer represent even themselves coherently, much less the public interest. Seizing the full opportunity of the situation, the Committee on Cities and Villages went before the full senate the next day and had itself—minus Fields—declared a select committee. Senator Saxton Smith was added to round out the new select committee, and the senate voted to transfer Laimbeer's bill out of the Committee on Cities and Villages and into the new select committee.[44] This eliminated Fields from subsequent hearings. Under these new auspices, the committee on the fire department bill continued to take testimony for another day's session, but neither side made any significant additions to its position. Decker had the last word, claiming that the firemen were neither rioters nor political criminals, but decent, loyal, conscientious citizens performing an invaluable service to the city of New York.

On February 15, a majority of the select committee, as expected, reported in favor of the passage of "an act to create a Metropolitan fire district, and establish a paid fire department therein." The report argued that public safety, departmental efficiency, and city expenditures would all be favorably affected by the proposed legislation. Significantly, the main substantiation for these arguments was lifted intact from the data presented before the committee by Norwood, Lawrence, and Eaton. The city council proposal to let the volunteer system reform itself was dismissed with the kind of institutional argument that Lawrence had suggested: "While the new code is at present administered with commendable rigor, there is ground for apprehending that when the probability of legislative reform shall be considered to have passed by,

[44] *Senate Journal, 1865*, pp. 176–177.

the present discipline may be greatly relaxed."[45] The institutional structure itself needed alteration, not simply the spirit in which it was temporarily administered. This committee report was signed by all five of the Republicans but neither of the two Democrats.

A two-thirds vote of the senate made the fire department bill the special order of business for Thursday evening, March 2, 1865.[46] When that session convened, the Democrats attempted to delay the bill first by moving that it be committed to the Committee on Municipal Affairs and then by moving that the provision for a paid department be struck from the bill. The Committee on Municipal Affairs, officially the "Senate Committee on the Internal Affairs of Towns and Counties," had been set up as a watchdog for the protection of local prerogatives, and its limited membership might have given the Democrats a better chance to influence the outcome than they had enjoyed in the larger Committee on Cities and Villages.[47] But the motion to give that committee jurisdiction over the fire department bill was defeated on the first of several important procedural votes. The Democrats resorted next to something of a quasi-filibuster as Senator Luke F. Cozans slowly read into the record a proposed substitute of some seventeen pages and 103 sections which would have transformed Laimbeer's bill into the one adopted by the New York City Council. This amendment was likewise defeated in a straight party vote, and Laimbeer's original proposal was ordered engrossed for its third and final reading.[48]

Next morning, when the bill was called up for its final

---

[45] *Senate Documents, 1865,* II, No. 47, p. 2.

[46] *Senate Journal, 1865,* p. 251.

[47] *Senate Documents, 1865,* I, No. 21, p. 1.

[48] *Senate Journal, 1865,* pp. 302–320; Albany *Evening Journal,* March 3, 1865, pp. 2–3.

reading, the Democrats once again offered a series of amendments. These were aimed less at delaying the inevitable than at getting in a few last insults. Fields, for example, offered an amendment which would require the insurance companies to foot the entire cost of setting up a paid fire department.[49] Five similar amendments were rejected before the bill could be read for the final time in the senate. The last vote of the evening stood 21 to 6 in favor of senate passage. Every Republican voted with the majority; none of the Democrats present did so. The clerk of the state senate was ordered to "deliver said bill to the Assembly, and request their concurrence therein."[50]

v

The course of the metropolitan fire department bill through the state assembly turned out to be even more eventful than the one it had just run through the state senate. Although the same witnesses testified at the assembly committee hearings on the bill, the political personnel had changed, and this change had important consequences. The assembly was much more openly rough and tumble than the senate, party discipline was harder to maintain there, and the press of the state was in general agreement that a vote in the assembly could be "influenced" more easily than a vote in the senate. On January 20, Assemblyman Thomas E. Stewart announced his intention to introduce an assembly version of Laimbeer's senate bill, and Thomas Van Buren, a Radical who announced previously, deferred to his fellow Manhattanite.[51] Within

[49] *World*, Feb. 7, 1865, p. 8.

[50] *Senate Journal, 1865*, pp. 326–328; Albany *Evening Journal*, March 8, 1865, p. 1.

[51] Van Buren was another former Democrat turned Radical Republican. See *The Evening Journal Almanac, 1865* (Albany, 1865), p. 74, and *California Blue Book* (Sacramento, Calif., 1967), p. 105.

three days Stewart's bill had been read twice and referred to the standing Committee on the Affairs of Cities. By March 4, when the senate bill arrived for assembly approval, both sides had braced themselves for the second phase of this political battle.[52]

The assembly hearings on the fire department bill generated at least as much popular excitement as the senate hearings had. "There is a great crowd here," reported the *World*. "The lobby is fully represented, and the rush and excitement are tremendous."[53] Lawrence, Eaton, Acton, Decker, and the others each repeated for the records of the assembly his respective points. Twenty-three banks, one hundred nine insurance companies, and thirteen thousand citizens submitted petitions on behalf of the proposed measure.[54] Among them was one from the General Society of Mechanics and Tradesmen, an old, established organization interested in cultural and material advancement of workingmen.[55] This response must have fed Radical hopes that a reform program could win them support among previously Democratic segments of the population.

By this time, however, the volunteer firemen of New York City were themselves seriously upset. At a mass rally they listened to speeches opposing the Laimbeer bill and adopted a set of resolutions, drawn up by the mayor, that decried the proposal as a rebuke to the thousands of brave, loyal citizens who risked their lives on behalf of their city.[56] The firemen also sent a public letter to various city officials and to each of

[52] *Journal of the Assembly of the State of New York at Their Eighty-eighth Session, 1865* (Albany, 1865), pp. 117, 130.

[53] March 8, 1865, p. 4.

[54] *Tribune*, March 10, p. 5; 11, 1865, p. 8.

[55] *Assembly Journal, 1865*, p. 609; Thomas Earle and T. Congdon, eds., *Annals of the General Society of Mechanics and Tradesmen of the City of New York, from 1785 to 1880* (New York, 1882).

[56] *Times*, March 11, 1865, p. 8.

the Democrats in the assembly at Albany. This circular reminded those officeholders in remarkably unveiled terms that they owed their election to the activity of the fire companies in their various districts and wards; the firemen had come through for them, and now they had better come through to protect the firemen.[57] The *Tribune* began to fear that enough assemblymen might be bought off to defeat the bill if the legislature dragged the battle out much longer or if the firemen increased their pressure.[58]

On March 15, the assembly Committee on the Affairs of Cities reported the fire department bill favorably, but the abstention of one of the Republicans on the committee revealed some confusion within the party ranks.[59] This uncertainty was confirmed when the whole assembly voted to table the favorable report, twenty-five Republicans agreeing to the delay. This procedural vote revealed that the Fenton wing of the Republican Party could not yet command either instant or complete discipline in the assembly. Roughly one-third of the Republican assemblymen wanted at least to delay their commitment until the subject could be hammered out in a party caucus, which had already been called for that night.

The Republican caucus confirmed that several members of the assembly had serious doubts about the wisdom of the Radicals' new departure. It is always difficult to ascertain exactly what went on inside any party caucus, since the historian is usually forced to rely on hearsay collected by the popular press. Such reliance is especially vulnerable since the Repub-

[57] *Tribune*, March 18, 1865, p. 4; and *Times*, March 23, 1865, p. 2, both reprinted the circular with appropriate denunciations.
[58] March 23, 1865, p. 2.
[59] *Assembly Journal, 1865*, p. 660; *World*, March 16, 1865, p. 5. Assemblyman Angel of Cattaraugus, soon to be a thorn in the sides of Fenton's allies, abstained, which made the vote 4 (all Republicans) in favor to 2 (both Democrats) opposed, and 1 abstention.

lican press generally wished to present its caucuses as meetings of a smoothly functioning, highly principled organization, while the Democratic press sought to present them as venal, bickering, and badly divided bodies. In the case of the caucus on the fire department bill, however, there is strong evidence even from the Republican press that serious division arose. Though the fire department bill was finally made a party measure, enough Republican assemblymen withdrew from the caucus to keep the bill's fate in doubt.

While the Democratic *World* praised the bolters and delighted over the Republican squabbles, the Radical press struggled to maintain party discipline.[60] The *Tribune* suggested that any man who broke with his party on this measure would be strengthening the hold of the Democratic Party on New York City and betraying all those citizens who were willing to turn to a party of genuine reform.[61] "To rescue New-York [City] from the evil effects of such an organization [as the volunteer fire department or the Democratic Party which backs it] the people were compelled to make a counter appeal to the Union Party. And now, though there is no question in the mind of Union men as to the propriety of the change, it is found that some unaccountable influence has debauched a portion of the Union party." Only bribery could account for the action of the Republican bolters.[62] Even the cautious Albany *Evening Journal* tried to rally support for the Fentonite decision on the fire department bill, calling the issue neither economically nor morally local and a legitimate subject for state action.[63]

In the wake of the controversial caucus, a two-thirds vote

[60] *World*, March 18, 1865, p. 4.
[61] March 20, 1865, pp. 4, 5.
[62] *Tribune*, March 23, 1865, p. 4.
[63] April 1, 1865, p. 2.

of the assembly made the fire department proposal the special order of business for Thursday evening, March 23.[64] It was now quite clear, as the *Tribune* pointed out, that the bill had become "the most obstinately contested of the [1865] session not only because of the important reform which it aim[ed] to effect, but because it ha[d] come to be regarded as a test of party strength and discipline."[65] This test involved not only the Republicans against the Democrats, but the power of the Radical alliance within the Republican Party. Consequently, Fenton's allies selected their most able parliamentarian, John L. Parker, to direct their forces on the assembly floor.[66]

During the day session of March 23, the Democratic members of the Committee on the Affairs of Cities submitted a formal minority report opposing assembly passage of the fire department bill.[67] The Democrats also packed the galleries with opponents of the measure in anticipation of the special evening session. When the bill itself finally came up, the Democrats put into action a plan to block assembly progress on the proposal altogether. Though this plan failed in the end, it did force a series of key procedural votes which revealed the dimensions of the factionalism of New York State's Republican Party during the spring of 1865.

[64] *Assembly Journal, 1865*, p. 738.

[65] March 25, 1865, p. 1.

[66] Parker, a thirty-nine-year-old lawyer from Cayuga County, was the paradigm of a Fenton Radical. Like the Governor he had been a Free Soil Democrat until 1856, when he joined the Republican Party. He now worked for fire and health reform in New York City and for regulation of the state's railroad corporations. During debates on the Thirteenth Amendment, Parker had taken an unambiguously Radical stance (Harlow and Boone, *Life Sketches of the State Officers*, p. 319; Albany *Evening Journal*, Feb. 4, 1865, p. 2).

[67] *Assembly Journal, 1865*, p. 816; *Documents of the Assembly of the State of New York at Their Eighty-eighth Session, 1865* (Albany, 1865), VIII, No. 168.

The closest vote of the series, 40 for and 48 against, came on a motion to strike Brooklyn out of the proposed metropolitan district. The Republicans seemed uneasy about forcing Brooklyn to swallow New York's medicine undiluted; Democrat William Veeder labeled the whole business a Radical conspiracy to subvert all local rights city by city.[68] Only Van Buren's timely reminder that the inclusion of Brooklyn was necessary to the constitutionality of the measure saved the bill intact.[69] The next two votes involved whether to grant the bill a third reading. They both passed, the first 52 to 48, and the second 52 to 47. All of the Democrats voted together on these questions, while seven Republicans crossed over to join them and several others chose not to vote at all. The seriousness of crossing over was emphasized when the Republican majority denied the request of two of the most prominent crossovers, William P. Angel and Horace Bemis, to strike their votes from the record.[70] The fact that some 24 of the 76 Republicans in the state assembly either did not vote, though they surely were aware of the intensity of the struggle and the date of the bill's special session, or actually voted against their fellow party members on these procedural questions indicates that approximately one-third of the Republicans in the assembly were not yet prepared to accept the party's new direction. Conversely, however, and more significantly, two-thirds of New York State's Republican assemblymen had apparently decided to back the Radicals' domestic reform programs and to follow the leadership of Governor Fenton and his allies.

Final action on the fire department bill was taken March 30, 1865. A 70 to 46 vote brought the bill before the assem-

[68] Albany *Evening Journal,* March 24, 1865, p. 1.
[69] *World,* March 24, 1865, p. 1.
[70] *Assembly Journal, 1865,* pp. 828–829.

bly, and a vote of 81 to 39 finally passed it. Surprisingly, 12 of the 81 ayes were cast by Democrats, while all but one of those Republicans who had voted their factional apprehensions during the procedural struggles acquiesced in the majority decision on the last ballot.[71] Consequently, the final vote was misleading on both of the counts which made the fire department bill so politically significant: the contest between the Republicans and the Democrats on the one hand and the contest within the Republican Party between the new Radical leaders and the old party managers on the other.[72]

The Democrats made no bones about the final vote being unrepresentative of their strength, for they were livid over the fact that some of their members actually crossed back in the other direction on the final vote to support the now virtually united Republican Party. Indeed, the roll call was an uproarious spectacle. After several bolting Democrats had cast their ballots, others in their party began to charge bribery. At one point twenty members claimed the floor simultaneously and tried to shout each other down; Assemblyman Samuel Carpenter volunteered to step outdoors with anyone the Democrats cared to choose and settle the matter on the steps; the galleries were seething with angrily shouting firemen.[73] But the final result was a clear victory for the Fenton

[71] *Ibid.*, pp. 963–964. The one Republican was Horace Bemis, a Whiggish Republican known for his anti-Radical views and his connections with the New York Central Railroad (*Times*, March 31, 1865, p. 1).

[72] Cf. David Donald's observation (*Reconstruction*, p. 61) that this frequently tends to be the case with final votes, which are often public displays of party loyalty.

[73] *Times*, March 31, 1865, p. 1; *Tribune*, March 31, 1865, p. 1; *World*, March 31, 1865, p. 1; Albany *Evening Journal*, March 31, 1865, pp. 1, 2. The bribery charges were later perfunctorily investigated by a select committee drawn up primarily to whitewash the fiasco of the final vote melee.

Republicans and for their new departure. Not only had the doubters within their own party supported them in the end on this crucial piece of legislation, but nearly a quarter of the Democrats voting actually crossed in support of this urban reform, thereby severely disrupting the unity of the opposition. The Radicals had scored their first major triumph.

VI

Fenton signed the metropolitan fire department bill less than ten minutes after its riotous passage by the assembly—the time it took a running clerk to reach the Governor's office—because the volunteers were said to be seeking an injunction to prohibit him from signing the measure.[74] Though such an injunction might seem ridiculous, the judicial system of the state during the 1860's was so corrupt and so farcical that the possibility of a ruling like this was not out of the question. The Republicans decided to avoid the necessity of a superseding injunction of their own.[75] The volunteers, from whom some had feared a violent reaction, voted to stay on the job until the law was either declared unconstitutional or put into effect and thereby allayed the most immediate dangers.[76]

The race for the political power inherent in the bill commenced with the selection of the four fire commissioners called for in the measure. "Petitions for candidates are freely circulated for signatures," reported the press, "and the governor's office is literally besieged. All but this matter seems forgotten." The Democrats, too, were interested, for they confidently assumed Fenton would appoint at least one and prob-

[74] *World,* April 1, 1865, pp. 1, 8.
[75] The Adams brothers are justifiably harsh on the incredibly corrupt judges who customarily traded overlapping injunctions with one another depending upon whose ox was being gored at the time. See *Chapters of Erie, passim.*
[76] *World,* April 3, 1865, p. 4; *Times,* April 1, p. 8; 6, 1865, p. 8.

ably two Democrats to give balance to the new board. Yet when the nominations were announced by the Governor's office, the Democratic press could only respond with a block-letter headline: "ASTONISHMENT AND INDIGNA-TION." Three of the proposed commissioners were Radical Republicans and the fourth was a War Democrat who had supported Lincoln's Union ticket in 1864. Even Greeley had been understood to favor at least a token Tammany man on the new board, and the *World* was beside itself with out-rage.[77]

In the senate a new rift was opened in the Republican ranks by the baldly political cast of the Governor's nominees, and for the first time during the session the senators rebuked Fen-ton by turning down his proposed commissioners in executive session. The vote was 15 in favor and 17 opposed to the confirmation, with all 10 Democrats voting to oppose. This meant, however, that seven Republican senators, Cheney Ames, George Andrews, James A. Bell, Ezra Cornell, Palmer E. Havens, Albert Hobbs, and Andrew White, had also voted to reject Fenton's candidates for fire commissioners.[78]

These seven senators personified the difficulties of holding together the Radical coalition. Andrews and Cornell were the most conservative, least enthusiastic Radicals in the senate. They were both retired patricians who prided themselves on remaining "above politics," and they distrusted the aggressive former Democratic chief executive. Inherent caution and la-tent loyalty to the party's old Whiggish leaders compelled

[77] *World*, April 5, p. 5; 6, 1865, p. 8; *Times*, April 6, 1865, p. 4. Charles C. Pinckney, backed by the Union League, Martin B. Brown, a Republican printer, and James W. Booth, a former fireman turned insurance man, were all Republicans of the Fenton stripe. Samuel Sloan was the lone War Democrat-Unionist.

[78] *World*, April 15, 1865, p. 5; *Tribune*, April 21, 1865, p. 4.

them to reject Fenton's flagrantly partisan nominees.[79] In contrast, the other five were among the most idealistic, reform-oriented Radicals. Havens and Ames, like White, were young reform politicians whom White sketched in glowing terms.[80] Hobbs, representing one of the strongest of the old Barnburner districts, was a young lawyer interested in prison reform and Indian affairs.[81] Bell, who had already made a courageous record in opposition to the railroad lobby during two previous terms in the senate, was remembered by Fenton's own private secretary as "one of the most clear-headed, clean-handed, safe and useful men ever commissioned as lawmaker."[82] These senators objected to the blatant politicization of a measure which they had supported as a genuine reform. Publicly, Andrews spoke for all of the bolters when he claimed: "It was never contemplated . . . to make the paid department a party machine. It was inaugurated as a measure of municipal reform, and it would certainly operate to discourage the efforts making to accomplish such reforms, if the gentlemen who had contributed so freely of their time and means to initiate reformatory measures should find that things were simply to be turned over from one set of politicians to another."[83]

Solidly in support of the Governor's selections were the former Democratic Radicals, anxious not to lose the political rewards afforded them at last by the rise of the Fentonites to party control. These senators included Wilkes Angel, Charles J. Folger, Frederick Hastings, Stephen Hayt, Henry Low, Demas Strong, and Stephen Williams. Also in support of Fen-

[79] *World*, Feb. 16, 1866, p. 8.
[80] White, *Autobiography*, I, 102–104.
[81] *Evening Journal Almanac, 1865*, p. 67.
[82] Brockway, *Fifty Years*, pp. 247–252.
[83] *World*, April 15, 1865, p. 5.

ton's nominees were a number of political veterans who knew
well what constituted a shrewd move in the game of partisan
politics. Alexander Bailey, an assemblyman in 1849, Dan H.
Cole, a Seward appointee during the 1840's, James M.
Cook, elected New York State Treasurer in 1851, Frederick Jul-
liand, a Harrison appointee, and George Munger, a Monroe
County judge in 1855, constituted this politically seasoned
group of senators willing to use political power for party purposes. Fenton's final two defenders were John Dutcher and
William Laimbeer. They represented extremely close districts
and, after Strong, had won the next two closest races of 1863.
They needed all of the immediate partisan advantage they
could muster.[84]

The major significance of this senatorial rift was that it lay
within the Radical coalition and was not simply a case of
Radical Republicans opposing non-Radical Republicans. Just
the previous afternoon the Radicals in the senate had all voted
together in reaffirmation of their position on national questions
by excluding General Ulysses S. Grant from resolutions hail-
ing the victory at Appomattox; they considered his terms of
surrender far too lenient for defeated rebels.[85] The alliance of
reforming idealism and political expediency that still united
them on national questions, however, had broken down temporarily at the state level over the administration of the Fire
Department Act. Although the point of disagreement was
relatively minor, and although the Radical coalition quickly
pulled itself back together, the implications of this momentary
rift boded ill for their alliance should reforming idealism on

[84] *Evening Journal Almanac, 1865*, pp. 65–69; *The Evening Journal
Almanac, 1867* (Albany, 1867), p. 76; Albany *Evening Journal*, Feb.
3, 1865, p. 2; *Times*, Nov. 4, 1851, p. 1; *History of Sacramento
County* (Oakland, Calif., 1880), p. 291.
[85] *Senate Journal, 1865*, pp. 802–804.

the one hand and political expediency on the other ever come into more serious conflict in the future.

The executive session which failed to confirm the fire commissioners took place April 14, 1865, and was one of the last pieces of business conducted by the legislature for over a week. That night Abraham Lincoln was shot. Not until April 22 did the question of confirmation arise once again. This time the senate approved the Governor's nominees without alteration. Perhaps the assassination had created a new sense of unity in the party and a fresh sense of political urgency even among those whose motives were usually less partisan; perhaps a deal of some sort had been proposed; perhaps the idealists and independents felt that they had registered sufficient opposition at the previous session and were now persuaded that their reform coalition had too much positive potential to risk destroying it over this issue. At any rate, the newly confirmed commissioners were faced with the unenviable task of gradually disassembling the old volunteer structure and erecting a new professional one.

The difficulty of this task was further increased by a legal action that the old firemen brought against the new legislation. By the beginning of May political judges were trading injunctions with one another over the right of the new commissioners to impound the equipment of the old department.[86] A lawsuit charging that the Metropolitan Fire Department Act was unconstitutional had been brought by the Democrats in New York City, and pending the settlement of this matter the new commissioners and the old department each pro-

---

[86] The long battle of injunctions can be followed in *Times,* May 5, p. 1; 6, p. 4; 7, p. 8; 11, p. 8; 12, p. 3; 13, p. 2; 19, p. 2; and 26, 1865, p. 2; or *World,* May 4, p. 8; 5, p. 5; 6, p. 8; 10, p. 5; and 11, 1865, p. 4. The *Tribune* does not follow it as closely but offers summaries on May 8, p. 7; and 11, 1865, p. 8.

ceeded as if its side had already won the court battle. Needless to say, the dominant note was one of confusion. Not until
the firemen's case reached the State Court of Appeals, the
highest bench in New York, could the legality of the Laimbeer bill be ascertained. On June 15 the case began before
this court, with Norman M. Allen, the young Radical senator
who represented Fenton's home district, and Waldo Hutchins,
the Governor's chief lieutenant, representing the new commissioners. On June 21, 1865, the high court upheld the metropolitan fire department on the grounds mentioned months
earlier in the legislature by Assemblyman Van Buren: that the
metropolitan district was a new governmental jurisdiction and
consequently that the state legislature was not encroaching
upon any local rights because none previously existed for this
geographical division as a separate entity.[87]

Even with its position legally established the new metropolitan fire department could proceed only very slowly to reform
the city's system of fire protection. The political considerations which had made the Laimbeer bill so hotly contested
were not erased by its passage, and the new commissioners
spent years in winning over enough of the best trained old
firemen to man a full-time, paid department. Especially during their first summer of operation the new metropolitan units
were harassed, beaten, and occasionally had their equipment
broken by members of the old volunteer departments.[88]

Some credit should go to Chief Engineer Decker who had
so vehemently opposed the bill during the committee hearings
in Albany. He accepted the final verdict of the Court of Appeals and was generally considered responsible for persuading
the old firemen not to resign en masse and leave the city without protection during those first difficult months of transi-

[87] *Times,* June 16, p. 1; 22, p. 5; 24, 1865, p. 2.
[88] Limpus, *New York Fire Department,* pp. 250–255.

tion.[89] By late summer, two of the original comissioners had resigned: the lone Democrat because of political pressure and one of the Radicals because he did not feel that "the general transaction of business [was] up to his ideas of progress."[90]

Within a year the Democrats were charging the Republicans with exactly what the Republicans had accused the Democrats of prior to 1865: making the fire department into a political cadre. There were also frequent complaints that the new paid department was not doing any better job than the old volunteers had done. Nor did insurance rates ever fall as the insurance companies had led many of the legislators to believe they might. But the new board had begun to install more efficient hydrants by the autumn of 1865, and more modern equipment was being purchased. Even when it was most discouraged with the new metropolitan fire department, the *Times* still maintained: "We cannot go back to the old state of things; though we must see that the present system is not ruined by inefficient administration."[91]

Civil War veterans General Alexander Shaler and Colonel Theodorus B. Myers, appointed to the Metropolitan Fire Board by Fenton in 1867 after the Democrats forced an investigation of the original commissioners, eventually brought efficient administration to the city fire department. The discipline and sense of professionalism instilled by Shaler and Myers proved strong enough to resist a renewed effort by the Democrats to make the fire department once again into a political auxiliary after passage of the so-called "Tweed Charter"

[89] *Ibid.*, pp. 224–226, 236. During the draft riots of 1863 he is presumed to have barely escaped being hanged by a mob when he went to the defense of New York City's Colored Orphans' Asylum. Certainly his actions in bringing about the very close vote to stay on the job also reflect well upon him.

[90] *Times*, Aug. 27, 1865, p. 8.

[91] April 19, 1866, p. 4.

of 1870 eliminated the state's control over the firemen in New York City.[92] Thus, though supported for flagrantly partisan purposes by one bloc of Radicals in Albany, the New York City fire department bill of 1865 led to a genuine reform, just as the other bloc of Radicals hoped it might. The Fenton Republicans had also forced the city of New York to accept an institutional change which allowed it to deal more effectively with a serious urban problem. In a small but politically significant way the "reconstruction at home" was under way in New York State.

[92] Limpus, *New York Fire Department*, pp. 256–262.

3

The Politics of Public Health

On January 23, 1865, three weeks after he introduced the fire department bill, Senator William Laimbeer, one of the Radicals most committed to his party's "new departure" in the state legislature, proposed a second major reform bill of great political significance.[1] Entitled "an act to establish a Metropolitan sanitary district and board of health, to preserve the public health in said district and to prevent the spread of disease thereform," the proposal precipitated a legislative battle which raged for two full sessions.[2] The protracted fight for public health reform revealed more about the nature of the Radical coalition in New York, and also produced one of the most substantively important statutes enacted during the course of the Radicals' reconstruction of their own state.

I

New York City in 1865 was reputed to be the filthiest city in the western world. The waste material produced by the city's thirty thousand horses was packed tightly into the crevices of the cobblestone streets. Slaughterhouses shared blocks with tenement houses in several sections of the city; the blood

[1] *Evening Journal Almanac, 1865*, pp. 65–66; White, *Autobiography*, I, 103.

[2] *Senate Journal, 1865*, p. 83.

from the former establishments ran freely down open sewers through the city's streets. The carcasses of small animals and the decomposing remains of larger ones simply lay in the streets, where they were kicked about by foraging hogs which roamed the city and by cattle being driven to the slaughter pens. Tanning yards with green hides drying in the sun added to the appalling stench associated with parts of the metropolis. In some of the poorer sections of the city, where the outhouses spewed their contents into the yards and alleys, the streets had never been cleaned by the city authorities. Even in those streets where the refuse contractors fulfilled their bargain, garbage was hauled away only once a week. Mounds of organic waste gave off wretched odors in warm, humid weather and were blown about the city as dust in drier times. What citizens of the day referred to as their "sanitary condition" was both figuratively and literally nauseating.[3]

Part of the reason for the deplorable state of the city's streets lay in the contract system which was supposed to provide for their cleaning. As in the case of the old fire department, concern for public welfare had gradually become lost

[3] The appalling state of New York City's sanitation is well documented in any of the following sources: Citizens' Association of New York, *Report by the Council of Hygiene and Public Health of the Citizens' Association of New York upon the Sanitary Conditions of the City* (New York, 1865); New York State Metropolitan Board of Health, *Annual Report, 1866* (New York, 1867); Stephen Smith, *The City That Was* (New York, 1911), which tells the story through the eyes of one of the city's leading physicians involved in the fight; Gordon Atkins, *Health, Housing and Poverty in New York City, 1865–1898* (lithograph of a Columbia University Ph.D. dissertation, Ann Arbor, 1947), pp. 1–66; Charles E. Rosenberg, *The Cholera Years* (Chicago, 1962), pp. 175–191; and John Duffy, *A History of Public Health in New York City, 1625–1866* (New York, 1968), pp. 540–571.

in a welter of political considerations. The existing New York City Board of Health, controlled by the mayor and the city council, let street-cleaning contracts as political rewards and graft opportunities rather than as genuine business arrangements for which the contractors would be held responsible. The budget for street cleaning, like that for fire protection, had long been considered a party slush fund; kickbacks were required on the contracts, and party regulars were given salaried sinecures in the sanitation department. The result was chronic filth, which had become a fact of life in New York City.[4]

Whenever anyone tried to launch a new campaign to remove the refuse of the metropolis, as various individuals had occasionally done, he would become the object of jokes for a while before finally running up against a barrier of apathy on the part of the city's inhabitants. So often had this been the case that the Democrats eventually discovered that the contract system and the political arrangement which had arisen under it could not easily be altered even by themselves. In the summer of 1865, after the metropolitan health bill had been debated for a full session at Albany and while the pressure was clearly mounting on Tammany to beat the legislators to the punch by straightening out the situation by themselves, the city council let a new series of contracts. They expected these to be fulfilled for a change, and the workers were told either to be on the job or to resign from the force. In reaction, the old street cleaners staged a violent strike during July 1865, beating the men who signed on under the new contractor, wrecking his equipment, and killing his horses. The mayor

[4] The street department had a budget of $1,575,945.24 in 1864 (*Times*, Jan. 22, 1865, p. 8; Mandelbaum, *Boss Tweed's New York*, pp. 46–58).

had no choice but to negate the new contracts and revert to the old system.[5]

The repulsive condition of the city's streets, however, was only the visible manifestation of the serious lack of health and sanitary facilities in the city. The effect can only be estimated in the appalling death and disease rates of New York. Testifying before the legislature, Dr. Stephen Smith, one of the leaders in the drive to revise the city's health laws, compared the death rates of London and Philadelphia with that of New York. Using the Democratic city inspector's own figures, he mustered statistical data to demonstrate that the death rate in New York City was substantially above that in either of the two other large urban centers. While London's death rate hovered at 22 per thousand, never going above 24 or below 20, and Philadelphia averaged 20 deaths per thousand with variations from 18 to 23, New York City's death rate averaged 33 per thousand and varied from 28 to 41.[6] In a city of one million people this meant that some thirteen thousand citizens died annually from diseases and conditions which were probably avoidable. Nor was this the entire story, since it was also estimated that there were approximately twenty-eight cases of disease for each death. At that rate an enormous amount of preventable sickness was occurring in the city, and with it came not only a corresponding loss of work hours but also chronic apathy and depression. Dr. Smith, citing the findings of a team of city physicians, estimated that a 50, a 60, or

[5] *Times*, July 19, 1865, p. 8.

[6] Smith, *City That Was*, pp. 121–122; *Times*, March 13, 1865. Smith's figures were calculated for the previous eleven years, excluding 1854 when the death rate was unnaturally high due to a small cholera outbreak. The *Tribune*, May 31, 1865, p. 4, defended the validity of these statistics against the City Registrar's *Annual Report*, which used figures intended to refute them.

even a 70 percent sickness rate was not uncommon in the tenement-house districts of New York. This data was especially shocking in light of the fact that Manhattan's good natural drainage, strong tides, and sea breezes qualified it as an excellent site for maintaining sanitary conditions, even with a large population. As the *Times* declared when these statistics were published during the summer of 1865, the health conditions of New York constituted "a civic, if not a national, sin."[7]

Probably the worst conditions in the city existed among the so-called "cellar dwellers." These people were living, although barely so, under circumstances which are almost inconceivable to many modern readers. Their disease rate ran 50 percent above even that of the tenement dwellers. Dr. Ezra R. Pulling, a veteran of the Civil War Sanitary Commission and of other city inspections, noted that about fourteen hundred people occupied basements and cellars in the fourth ward alone. Pulling, a man not given to exaggeration, described their flats:

They are all damp, those in the least elevated localities, of course, being most so. In very many cases the vaults of privies are situated on the same or a higher level, and their contents frequently ooze through walls into the occupied apartments beside them. Fully one-fourth of these subterranean domiciles are pervaded by a most offensive odor from this source, and rendered exceedingly unwholesome as human habitations.[8]

To describe this scene as "exceedingly unwholesome" hardly does it justice. The health and sanitary conditions of the city, of which these cellar apartments were only the most dramatic examples, clearly cried out for reformation. Even the Democratic press on occasion heard the cry. Upset about a rise in

[7] July 7, 1865, p. 8.
[8] Citizens' Association, *Sanitary Report*, p. 55.

the number of smallpox cases reported in the city, the Democratic *World*, for example, observed in remarkably nonpartisan terms:

It cannot be denied that our health laws and health organizations are a mass of contradictions and incongruities. We have a Board of Health, but it is only in name, for the Mayor—who alone can convene it—steadily refuses to summon its members together. Then we have the Commissioners of Health, a body declared by the corporation counsel to have equal power and jurisdiction with the Board of Health. Then there is the city inspector, an executive officer, with all the machinery for sanitary inspection, &c., without the power to accomplish this purpose.

It cannot be denied that all these departments of public health have fallen into the most deplorable state of inefficiency. There is scarcely a medical man in the entire list of officials; certainly not one who is in a position to exert any decided professional influence upon the sanitary condition of this city.[9]

Not merely the quality of life, but life itself for many citizens was endangered by the failure of the Democratic political organization in New York City to react to the problems of modern urban existence. It was a fine opportunity for the Radicals in Albany, and they reached out to seize it.

As was the case with fire department reform, the Republicans were not creating a new issue, but providing the previously missing weight in an already wavering balance. Their party had a great deal to gain and very little to lose by reconstructing New York City's health administration. They might gain additional popular support in the politically hostile metropolitan area and at the same time deprive the Democrats there of yet another source of public money and influence. And just as the Radical coalition received support from pressure groups whose interests in the fire department had antici-

[9] Feb. 16, 1865, p. 4.

pated their own, they now received the aid of important organizations which had already been working toward health reform for some time. Of these groups the Citizens' Association, their ally in the fire department fight, played the most important supporting role.

Among the physicians of New York City was a group that included Drs. John H. Griscom, Joseph M. Smith, Stephen Smith, and Elisha Harris, all of whom had long been interested in public health. Prior to the Civil War they had formed an informal "sanitary association" in the city, which annually introduced a health reform bill into the legislature at Albany. With equal regularity, however, these bills had been defeated by a combination of vehement Democratic opposition and polite Republican indifference. During the war all of the members of New York's sanitary association served with the national Sanitary Commission, where they witnessed what could be accomplished by public health organizations when well administered and relatively removed from overriding political considerations. As the war drew to a close this small band of New York physicians was greatly strengthened by the formation of the Citizens' Association, whose secretary, Nathaniel Sands, had been a member of the sanitary association. Sands succeeded in interesting the newer, larger, and far more powerful organization in the cause of health reform.[10]

In 1864 the Citizens' Association made a serious effort to win from the legislature a health reform bill for the New York City area, but owing to a number of reasons their proposal had once again failed. Chief among these reasons was the fact that the Republicans had not yet embarked upon their program of civil and institutional reform; the war itself still provided sufficient political capital. Consequently, the

[10] Smith, *City That Was*, pp. 165–166; Atkins, *Health, Housing and Poverty*, p. 25.

party machinery was not consciously geared to overcome
the determined efforts of the Democrats, who were far more
forceful in opposition to the reform than were the Republicans in support of it. Furthermore, Horatio Seymour still occupied the governor's chair and would no doubt have vetoed
any such measure even had the Republicans united behind it.
The Citizens' Association, nevertheless, was convinced that
the bill had been defeated not in the give and take of political
power, but because the legislators did not fully comprehend
how appalling the City's health and sanitary situation had become. To rectify this weakness in their case, as well as to in-
form the public, the association determined to make a systematic survey of existing conditions in the city, which could
be used as evidence in future fights for a health bill.

The document produced by the association, though cum-
bersomely titled *Report of the Council of Hygiene and Public Health of the Citizens' Association of New York upon the
Sanitary Condition of the City*, proved to be a landmark in
the compilation of reliable data upon which to base legislation. Condensed from over twenty volumes of detailed investigation results to just over five hundred pages, the *Sanitary
Report* was superior to anything like it produced during the
nineteenth century and would compare favorably with any
of the various commission reports produced during the Progressive era. The city's official records looked ludicrous beside
the information amassed by the Citizens' Association. The
investigating committee had divided Manhattan Island into
twenty-nine separate districts and assigned each to a fully
qualified doctor. These twenty-nine doctors and their assistants were required to make a thorough house-to-house and
tenement-to-tenement survey of the health and sanitary conditions in their particular areas. Each inspector was given a detailed routine to follow at each address and a questionnaire to

be filled out concerning past case histories and health backgrounds on every family contacted. A few of the physicians even hired artists to accompany them and illustrate with charts and drawings the conditions they described in their reports.[11] Although the final *Sanitary Report* cost the Citizens' Association roughly $20,000 to print, the true value of the work defied estimation.

The Citizens' Association's survey had been undertaken during the winter and spring of 1864, and by that autumn the results were in.[12] At a rally in December, after the Republican triumph but prior to the convening of the new legislature, the leaders of the Citizens' Association announced that they were prepared to go once again to Albany on behalf of a health reform bill; this time they would be fully armed with their statistical evidence.[13] They neglected to mention that this time they would also have an even more valuable advantage: the Radical coalition within the Republican Party had begun to experiment with a program of civil and institutional reform as a possible means of consolidating and enlarging their political strength.

II

One of the first acts of the new Republican legislature which convened in January 1865 was the appointment of a special senatorial committee to investigate charges of mismanagement in New York City government. Governor Fenton openly encouraged this move, and he also made tentative threats to bring legal action against some of the city's officials.

[11] See report of James Ross, Inspector for 15th District (11th Ward), in Citizens' Association, *Sanitary Report*, pp. 175–176.

[12] The full *Sanitary Report* was not published, however, until the following June. See *Times*, June 19, p. 2, and July 7, 1865, p. 5.

[13] *Tribune*, Dec. 2, 1864, p. 8.

These moves were designed primarily to embarrass and harass the Democrats, while at the same time fulfilling campaign promises to investigate the flagrant corruption and inefficiency in New York City.[14]

At the suggestion of Andrew D. White, one of its members, the investigating committee decided to concentrate its probe against a single weak point in the city's political defenses in order to substantiate the usually vague accusations with specific examples and precise charges.[15] Despite the constant urging of Horace Greeley to expand the scope of their investigation,[16] the senators accepted White's idea and brought their entire pressure to bear upon what they considered the most vulnerable of the city's departments: the health department, then under the direction of City Inspector F. I. A. Boole. A month of inquiry sustained this decision. "No Health Dept. at present," scrawled White in his private committee notes. "Merely an engine of faction."[17]

When Laimbeer introduced the metropolitan health bill later in the month, the New York City Health Department was already under heavy fire. Not only was the Citizens' Association waiting in the wings for a chance to present the results of its sanitary survey, but the senate committee was taking enough testimony, as White later put it, "to condemn the whole existing system twenty times over."[18] Furthermore, the Republican press was outspoken in its belief that the health problems of New York and Brooklyn should be placed "in

[14] White, *Autobiography*, I, 108; *Times*, Jan. 5, 1865, p. 1.

[15] Albany *Evening Journal*, Jan. 12, 1865, p. 3; *Tribune*, Jan. 13, 1865, p. 5.

[16] *Tribune*, Jan. 31, p. 4; Feb. 2, p. 4; April 7, 1865, p. 4.

[17] "Investigating Committee Notes," last entry for Feb. 1865, Andrew Dickson White Papers, Cornell University Libraries, Ithaca, N.Y., microfilm.

[18] *Autobiography*, I, 126.

the hands of a competent board or commission, appointed either by the Governor or the Legislature."[19]

Throughout January and February the rapid progress of the health bill appeared to be duplicating exactly the progress of the fire department bill. In the senate both bills were referred to the same Committee on Cities and Villages, and some of the same people testified at both public hearings. Foremost among them was Dorman B. Eaton, who campaigned even more aggressively for the health bill than he had for the fire department bill. Eaton himself, as chairman of the Citizens' Association's legal committee, had actually drafted the health proposal.[20]

The committee hearings on health reform, like those on fire department reform, were characterized by the presentation of statistical data by proponents of the measure and ineffective rebuttals from defenders of the existing city department. In addition to Eaton, Robert B. Roosevelt, Charles P. Kirkland, and Charles Tracy each helped present the case for reform, at least as New York's socially conscious elite saw it. Representing the Medical Association of New York City were Drs. Willard Parker, James R. Wood, and Stephen Smith. A clergyman from the Five Points mission also spoke on behalf of the bill; the notorious "Five Points," reputed to have the highest incidence of crime in New York City, had a death rate from disease almost three times the city's average. Those opposed to the health bill were all members of the existing city health department: Inspector Boole, Dr. Lewis Sayre, and Dr. Cyrus Ramsay. Certainly the most impressive single testimony on behalf of the measure was offered by Dr. Smith before a joint committee of the senate and the assem-

[19] *Times*, Jan. 16, 1865, p. 4.
[20] *Senate Journal, 1865*, pp. 83, 205, 276, 287–288; Smith, *City That Was*, pp. 163–181; *World*, Feb. 2, p. 4; March 6, 1865, p. 4.

bly, when he prepared from the data of the *Sanitary Report* a damning oration against the laxity of the health authorities in the city. Typical of the Democratic response was Dr. Ramsay's attempt to ridicule Smith's notion that cleanliness was in any way related to the prevention of disease.[21]

Only after the health bill had been reported to the full senate did difficulties arise.[22] Eaton, influenced strongly by English public health legislation, had drafted his proposal to include the city police commissioners in its operation. He reasoned that health authorities, to be really effective, had to possess extraordinary powers and to have some means of enforcing any edicts that they might issue. By giving the police commissioners a prominent place on the board of health, Eaton hoped to achieve these ends. He worded the health law in a deliberately confusing manner in an attempt to mask the exceptional degree of independence and authority he wished to allocate to the new board of health.[23] Yet Eaton's efforts to camouflage the full power of the proposed board eventually backfired, and the metropolitan health bill began to falter over the make-up of this body.

Despite Democratic objections the Republicans had united to make the health bill a special order of business for March 1, when it was debated by the whole senate.[24] During the course of that debate, and a subsequent one held a week later, the tensions inherent in the Radical coalition came once again to the surface. Demas Strong, the lone Republican senator from Brooklyn, was not pleased with Eaton's draft of the health

[21] *Tribune*, March 3, 1865, p. 5; *World*, Feb. 17, p. 1, March 3, p. 5; 4, 1865, p. 8; Rosenberg, *Cholera Years*, p. 184; *Times*, March 16, 1865, pp. 1–2; Smith, *City That Was*, pp. 49–151.

[22] *Senate Journal, 1865*, p. 205.

[23] Smith, *City That Was*, pp. 169–170.

[24] *Senate Journal, 1865*, p. 276.

bill. Strong was a Radical constantly alert to the necessity of making reform bills also count as political strokes; he was a reformer because that position promised to be politically effective and because he needed all the advantages he could get in a usually Democratic district. As George H. Andrews made clear in the senate debate, men of Strong's outlook concluded that the proposed health bill was more than adequate as a reform, but not effective enough as a political weapon. Additionally, the Metropolitan Police Board had traditionally been aligned with the old Whiggish forces in the Republican Party; Thomas Acton, the board's president, remained loyal to the man who appointed him, Edwin Morgan. Strong, certainly aware of this long-standing political link, probably feared that Fenton's allies might be passing a reform measure which risked strengthening their rivals within the party rather than themselves. As a former Democrat who had voted to confirm Fenton's partisan fire commisisoners, Strong did not wish to surrender inadvertently the Radicals' opportunity to direct Republican Party policy.[25]

Accordingly, while the more independent Radicals like White continued to argue that the health bill was a superb piece of reform legislation which deserved to be passed as reported, Strong offered an amendment. In lieu of a board of health dominated by professional doctors and by commissioners who were serving jointly on the police board his amendment called for a health commission of five individuals to be nominated by the governor and confirmed by the senate. No particular qualifications for these five commissioners were specified. In the vital short run this would vest the multimillion-dollar health and street-cleaning budgets in hands of Fenton's choosing, rather than Tammany's or Morgan's, while

[25] *Ibid.*, pp. 287–288, 344–345; Albany *Evening Journal*, March 9, 1865, p. 1.

still allowing for a genuine reform. On behalf of his amendment Strong argued that the police could enforce health regulations whether or not they actually sat on the board of
health, and that they already had their hands full—as Acton
himself testified during the fire department hearings—just trying to fulfill their existing commitments. There was no need
to make them double as sanitary inspectors.[26]

Trying to reach a compromise, the Republicans agreed to
send the health bill back to the Committee on Cities and Villages. After only one day's closed session a proposal emerged
which appeared to reconcile both of the two leading factions
within the Radical senate: those who usually tended to vote
their commitment to reform first and their partisan calcula-
tions second, and those who tended to be reformers only if
the measure at hand seemed also to be politically expedient.[27]
Part of the compromise involved a reduction in the number
of commissioners from five to four because some reformers
believed that any odd number would lead necessarily to partisan decisions, but the major provision of the compromise
retained Strong's gubernatorially appointed health commissioners, tempered by the requirement that at least three of
the four be fully qualified physicians.[28] Even Stephen Smith
expressed his private willingness to accept this solution, adding in a letter to White: "For my own part I must confess
there is much plausibility in the assertions that an entirely
independent Health-Board will act more efficiently than one
closely allied to the Police."[29]

Although this compromise eliminated the police commissioners from the health board, the moderate *Times* had earlier

[26] *Tribune,* March 10, 1865, p. 8.
[27] *Ibid.,* p. 5; *Senate Journal, 1865,* pp. 358–359.
[28] *Tribune,* March 11, 1865, p. 8.
[29] Smith to Andrew D. White, Jan. 20, 1865, White Papers.

professed to find such a formula acceptable; and although professional doctors might not be politically oriented, the more Radical *Tribune* had also endorsed this solution.[30] The health bill now moved rapidly through a second reporting and proper engrossing toward a vote in the full senate. Partly as a delay tactic and partly for home consumption, Senator Thomas Fields then offered a substitute bill which would reorganize the existing city health department, but still keep it firmly under local Democratic control. This proposal was quickly dispatched by the Republicans, who then passed the metropolitan health bill as amended by the compromise, 17 to 6.[31] The clerk was ordered to deliver the bill to the assembly for concurrence. It was significant, however, that six Republican senators—more than a quarter of the total—dodged the final roll call. Beneath its surface amity the party's tensions remained. As the *World* sardonically observed:

The majority [of the Republicans] have not quite concluded to allow the Citizens' Association and the Medical Society to dispense the vast political patronage of the Health Department. Something had to be done, however, to satisfy them, and they have accordingly been turned over to the tender mercies of the house—a body which will require more than the usual share of coaxing and argument necessary to pass the bill.[32]

III

The actions of the assembly on the fire department bill had demonstrated the truth of the popular assumption that party

[30] *Times*, March 11, 1865, p. 4; *Tribune*, March 9, 1865, p. 4.

[31] *Senate Journal, 1865*, pp. 368, 380, 403–409. One Democrat, Orson Allaben, crossed to vote with the Republican senators on the health bill, thus accounting for the seventeenth aye. Allaben, a physician himself, evidently placed a personal commitment to health reform above party (*Evening Journal Almanac, 1865*, p. 67).

[32] March 15, 1865, p. 1.

discipline was more difficult to maintain in the lower house than in the senate. During the course of procedural votes approximately one-third of the Republican assemblymen had manifested doubts about the Radical program of civil and institutional reform. These doubts shortly proved even more substantial in the assembly's deliberations on the proposed health bill. Moreover, since the rate of re-election to the state assembly tended to be remarkably low, many more men in that house were inclined to judge proposed reforms in terms of their political expediency.[33] Thomas Van Buren, who assumed floor leadership of the health bill, surely appreciated the mixed motives with which many of his fellows viewed the measure—he had captured a previously Democratic New York City seat only four months earlier.[34]

An assembly version of the health bill had been introduced in late January and referred to the Committee on Public Health.[35] As in the senate, the committee hearings were well attended both by friends of the bill and by its opponents. "The Metropolitan Health Bill seems to attract an unusual share of attention," reported the hostile *World*.

In the first place great interests are involved; then many physicians—some from personal, and the majority from motives of public welfare—are interested; next the enemies of City Inspector Boole want to be gratified; and finally, the latter gentleman himself has no desire to be unceremoniously thrust out of office. All these causes combined to bring considerable of a throng [*sic*]

[33] In the 1864 assembly there had been only 22 incumbents from the 1863 session (see *Times*, Nov. 6, 1863, p. 4). In the 1865 assembly there were still only 38 incumbents among the 128 members, 13 Democrats and 25 Republicans. Even more remarkable is the fact that only four assemblymen in the 1865 session, one of whom was a Democrat, were serving their third consecutive one-year terms.

[34] *Evening Journal Almanac, 1865*, p. 74.

[35] *Assembly Journal, 1865*, pp. 126, 130–131.

together at the meeting of the House Committee on Public Health.[36]

For the most part the senate's witnesses reappeared before the assembly's committee, where they raised and refuted the same points once again.[37] Consequently, by the time the senate bill arrived in the assembly for concurrence the latter house was already prepared to debate the measure.[38]

The results of preliminary skirmishing in the assembly boded ill for the health bill. On April 5 an attempt to make the measure a special order of business failed to receive the necessary two-thirds vote; a large number of Republicans preferred to await further developments within the party.[39] A month earlier a Republican caucus had been unable to agree upon a unified stand regarding the health bill, and subsequent meetings had not clarified the official party position.[40] The caucus which had made the fire department bill a party measure also endorsed the health bill, but only after the dissidents had retired from the meeting. Consequently, those who left claimed that the vote was not binding on them.[41]

Of the assemblymen who opposed the health bill some objected to increasing the power of the Radical coalition within the party and felt that the provision allowing the governor to appoint the health commissioners conceded him too much additional influence. As the *World* mused, "the several proposed 'commissions' for New York city were concentrating a great deal of power in Governor Fenton's hands. If it is thought that he will use that for the benefit of a late formed

---

[36] March 3, 1865, p. 5.
[37] *World*, March 4, 1865, p. 8.
[38] *Assembly Journal, 1865*, pp. 578, 653, 798, 825.
[39] *Ibid.*, pp. 1080, 1089; the vote was 48 aye to 44 no.
[40] *World*, March 2, 1865, p. 1.
[41] *Ibid.*, March 18, 1865, p. 4; *Tribune*, March 20, 1865, p. 4; Albany *Evening Journal*, April 1, 1865, p. 2.

section of the Republican Party [the Radical coalition] . . . , the progress of this commission business may be stayed. The old power that organized the Republicans, and has been its life vigor [the Seward, Weed, Morgan men], will not patiently abide a revolution."[42] These Whiggish assemblymen, who also favored an increase in the rates of the New York Central Railroad against the resolute opposition of Governor Fenton and the entire Radical coalition, now voted with the Democrats against the progress of the health bill.[43]

Other Republican assemblymen who opposed the health bill did so for almost exactly opposite reasons: they were not convinced that the compromise version was as politically effective as it might be. Preferring to hold out for something more akin to Strong's senate proposal, these politically oriented Radicals, who had voted with their fellows on the crucial roll calls over the fire department bill, now chose to absent themselves from a vote on the health bill. The *Evening Journal* claimed that sixteen Republicans were known to be in Albany but not in their seats for this vote.[44]

The parliamentary maneuvering grew complicated when a central body of Radicals still attempted to salvage the health reform as it had passed the senate. On April 12, Republicans of all shades united to waive the assembly's rule number twenty-five, which stated that a bill could not be called out of order unless a two-thirds vote requested the call.[45] Two

[42] Feb. 15, 1865, p. 1.

[43] *Tribune*, March 21, p. 4; 23, pp. 4 and 8; 24, 1865, p. 4; *World*, March 11, 1865, p. 5; Albany *Evening Journal*, April 12, p. 1; 27, p. 2; 28, 1865, p. 1. Parker, Brandreth, Van Buren, and Pitts, probably the four most prominent Fenton Radicals in the assembly, were leading the fight against the New York Central Railroad rate bill.

[44] April 14, 1865, p. 2.

[45] *Assembly Journal, 1865*, p. 1251. Rule 25 is written out formally in chap. vii of the "Rules and Orders of the Assembly of the State of New York," *Assembly Documents, 1865*, III, No. 48, p. 6.

more procedural votes, these much closer, moved the bill toward a third reading on the next day.[46] At that session several Democrats combined with the Republicans to call for a vote on the metropolitan health bill. All sides welcomed a showdown. The main body of Radicals hoped to pass the bill; the non-Radical Republicans and the most vigorously partisan Radicals—for different reasons—both wished to defeat the measure; the Democrats delighted in the disruption of the opposition.

When the roll was called it became evident that the main body of Radicals could command a majority of those assemblymen present, but that a number of Republicans were still choosing either to vote with the Democrats or not to vote at all. Because the state constitution required a majority of those elected to the assembly, not a majority of those present, in order to pass a measure, the number of dissident Republicans proved sufficient to block final passage of the bill, even though the vote in its favor was 58 to 52. Van Buren, who saw by the time his name was called that the health bill would not carry, voted against the measure in order to have the opportunity of moving a reconsideration, which he immediately did in an effort to keep the bill alive. The motion to reconsider was barely carried by a vote of 56 to 54, and the Republicans hastily moved and carried an adjournment of the assembly until the next day.[47]

When the assembly reconvened, the opponents of the health bill moved a reconsideration of the previous day's vote; they obviously realized that the bill's defenders had not been able during the night to win the half dozen decisive votes they lacked the previous day. In what was considered another bril-

[46] *Assembly Journal, 1865,* pp. 1260–1261; the votes were 60 in favor to 52 opposed, and 60 in favor to 49 opposed.
[47] *Ibid.,* pp. 1284–1286, 1301.

liant ploy, Van Buren moved and carried an adjournment until later that evening.[48] This adjournment was not carried without the violent objection of the Democrats, however, for they knew that they had the health bill beaten and thought that Speaker George G. Hoskins ruled unfairly in favor of Van Buren's motion to adjourn.[49] An irate Democrat stood up on his desk and waved $1,000 in cash which he offered to bet on the proposition that the Speaker had ruled in error.[50] But the adjournment stood. Unfortunately for most of the Radicals, however, it had gained the health bill only a few hours, and that was not long enough.

During the evening session, as the parliamentary fencing continued, the main body of Radicals began to run out of parries. After six procedural votes the health bill was finally brought to a reconsideration.[51] In the last tally of the evening, the metropolitan health bill mustered 52 votes in favor against 60 opposed and was declared dead for the 1865 session of the legislature, which was due to end very shortly.[52] The clerk

[48] *Ibid.*, pp. 1309–1310. Both votes, the one to reconsider and the other to adjourn, were identical: 53 in favor to 51 opposed.

[49] Hoskins' election as Speaker had originally been a compromise between the Weed faction of the party and the Fenton faction. When the legislature was organized, the Radicals had not yet developed a coherent bloc and were satisfied with the compromise (Albany *Evening Journal*, Jan. 5, 1865, p. 2; *World*, Jan. 3, 1865, p. 1). Although the Speaker grew increasingly friendly toward the Radicals as they increased their power and initiated their reform program, he was not retained by them as Speaker in 1866, despite his re-election to the assembly.

[50] *Tribune*, April 15, 1865, p. 5; *Times*, April 15, 1865, p. 5.

[51] *Assembly Journal, 1865*, pp. 1311–1314; the best showing made by Van Buren and his allies was a 59 to 57 vote against adjourning once again.

[52] The 1865 session of the legislature was already one of the longest in the state's history. Since the members were only paid for one hundred days, the sessions usually ended in early April.

of the assembly was ordered to return the metropolitan health bill to the senate "with a message of non-concurrence in the passage of same"; Boole and his city health department had been granted a year's reprieve.[53]

The Republican press seemed confused about the outcome in the assembly. The Albany *Evening Journal,* treading a fine line between the growing power of the Radicals and the waning hopes of the old Whiggish conservatives, exploded with anger over the defeat of this compromise bill which might have strengthened the Republican middle ground and hurled invectives at the partisan Radicals who had absented themselves from the assembly chamber.[54] The Radical *Tribune,* which had earlier warned against logrolling on the health bill by making deals involving railroad legislation, likewise appeared upset, even though the Fentonites had clearly chosen to go down with the health bill rather than make any such deals.[55] The Governor had vetoed a proposal to increase the rates of the New York Central Railroad, and the Radical alliance in the senate had sustained his action against Democratic and Whiggish Republican support for the increase. In the assembly, where only a handful of votes would have made the difference, the Radical coalition had decided against compromising their position through deals with Republican crossovers like William P. Angel or Horace Bemis, both of whom were commonly considered to be tools of the state's largest railroad corporations.[56]

[53] *Assembly Journal, 1865,* pp. 1314–1315.
[54] April 14, p. 2; 15, 1865, p. 2.
[55] March 25, 1865, p. 4.
[56] Fenton not only vetoed another attempt to raise the New York Central's rates, but also vetoed a large number of schemes for municipal railroad franchises in New York City. The Governor's veto messages were remarkable statements of reform rhetoric. He argued that the public transportation corporations in New York State had re-

Even the Democratic press begrudgingly recognized the Radicals' aloofness from the kind of Republican with whom they had been accustomed to dealing before the war. Sketching the character of the Republican legislators early in February, shortly after the fire and health bills had been introduced, the *World* distinguished between the attitudes of the incumbent "veteran" Republicans and the "newer, younger" Republicans who entered the senate after the elections of 1863 and the assembly after the elections of 1864. In their attitude toward New York City, the latter, the new Republicans, were "the advocates of municipal reform, who hope for the wiping out of your City departments, or to make them subordinate to commissioners." Although these young men were confident of success during the coming session, they "lack[ed] the experience of their [older Whiggish] brethren" whose main interest in the city was to "secure fortunes through the laying of rails on Broadway and the cross-town streets of New-York."[57]

Still the *Tribune* could not understand how the Radicals had failed to carry the health bill, and its Albany correspondent began to allege bribery.[58] This sent Greeley off on a

---

ceived more than enough aid and encouragement from the state government and that they already made a handsome profit on their investments. Any additional revenue from authorized rate increases, therefore, should be returned to the people who had made the initial investments in the railroads and underwritten the necessary loans: the taxpayers. "*The public treasury should be benefitted by the gains accruing from these gifts*" (his italics). See *Tribune*, April 19, p. 4; 25, 1865, p. 4; *World*, April 26, p. 1; 29, 1865, p. 5; Albany *Evening Journal*, April 14, 1865, p. 2. For clear evidence of the link between the New York Central Railroad forces and the anti-Fenton elements of the Republican Party, see Alonzo B. Cornell to Andrew D. White, Aug. 23, 1866, White Papers.

[57] *World*, Feb. 7, 1865, p. 8.

[58] *Tribune*, April 14, p. 8; 15, 1865, p. 5. The rumor was that each

wild series of righteous editorials about the venality of the
New York State legislature in 1865, the kind of editorials
invariably cited by historians who have helped to perpetuate
the characterization of this postwar period as remarkable primarily for its graft.[59] Even conceding that some of the votes
on this measure were swayed less by party or principle than
by payoff, there was obviously more to the defeat of the
health bill in 1865 than the "$10,000" claimed by the *Tribune*.

The 1865 session of the legislature had seen an increase in
the strength of the Radical coalition and its first tentative
steps toward a program of civil and institutional reform in
New York State. Neither the coalition nor the program, however, was yet solidified. The tensions inherent in the Radical
alliance were still too strong to be overcome on the issue of
the metropolitan health bill, at least when coupled with the
political jealousies of the assembly. Four of the Republicans
who helped carry the fire department bill had refused to vote
on the health bill. Even more damaging was the fact that nine
other assemblymen who had either supported the fire department bill or remained neutral toward it actually voted against
the less partisan health bill. It should also be noted that the
assembly failed to pass the health bill on the same day that
the senate rejected Fenton's partisan nominees as fire commissioners. Thus, while both the Radical coalition and its postwar program of reform were taking shape by the spring of
1865, neither was yet firmly defined.

Even so, the advent of the Radical strategy of urban reform had begun to threaten the confidence of the New York
City Democrats. "It is the standing wonder of everyday
among all sensible people at the capital," observed the *World*

---

member of the city health department had been assessed one month's
pay in order to finance the fight against the health bill in Albany.

[59] *Ibid.*, April 1, p. 5; 2, p. 4; 3, 1865, p. 4.

in March, "what infatuation is in the air of the great city of New-York that its representatives, of City Hall and of Capitol, in whatever else they disagree, do not concur in upholding the power of the city to regulate its local affairs for itself."[60] The Democrats appeared seriously worried about the possibility of defections among the rank and file of their bureaucrats and lower party workers, who would have to get along with the Radicals if they expected to retain their jobs once the new commissions created in Albany assumed authority in the metropolitan area. Claiming that the Republicans were looking forward with trepidation to the forthcoming reapportionment of the state legislature because the populous Democratic districts would be granted more seats, the *World* offered its view of the Radical strategy:

Like men who see power slipping from their hands, they propose the most desperate remedies to retain it in their grasp, . . . and the remedy agreed upon is legislation. The state committee [now dominated by Governor Fenton's men] are laboring to this end, and they expect to live by increasing their patronage in the anti-Republican localities, so that the Democratic majorities may be reduced, and the party itself divided in its strongholds. The committee, therefore, urge the passage of the following bills:

Metropolitan Health bill
Metropolitan Fire Department bill.

"A prominent Republican" had confirmed that this was indeed the Radical strategy in Albany; it was no longer secret. The Democrats might be fortunate enough to delay one of these first two major bills, but they had better "preserve a united front," exhorted the editorial, or risk even more disastrous consequences "in the next Legislature."[61]

The drive to reform the health and sanitary conditions of

[60] March 10, 1865, p. 4.
[61] March 11, 1865, p. 5.

New York City did, as the *World* feared, carry over into the next legislative session. This time, however, the Radicals were much more secure in their control of the Republican Party, and they were much more definite in their support of reform measures aimed at further reducing Democratic strength in the metropolitan area. The pressure which the Democrats had begun to feel in the spring of 1865 grew more intense by the time the 1866 legislature convened in Albany. Not only had a state election intervened, but so had a wholly nonpolitical development: the threat of a cholera epidemic. The continuing battle for health reform was fought out against the background of this threat.

4

Metropolitan Health Reform

I

Today Americans know cholera simply as another of those remote and unlikely Asiatic diseases against which travelers and servicemen are inoculated, but in the late 1860's it was a dreaded plague against which there seemed to be no defense. Twice prior to the Civil War the nation faced serious cholera epidemics. During the 1830's, when the disease killed thousands across the country, people debated whether President Andrew Jackson might abate the scourge with a declaration of prayer and fasting.[1] When cholera struck again in 1849, thousands more died as the fast-spreading disease settled into the water supply of New York City and traveled west to California with the gold rush.[2] In neither of these major outbreaks had public authorities succeeded in combating the epidemic. Indeed, many communities had barely managed to bury the victims. The medical profession, not yet aware of bacteria, could offer no scientific antidote to the disease, nor were there any governmental agencies equipped to undertake

[1] Rosenberg, *Cholera Years*, pp. 40–54.

[2] *House Executive Documents*, 43d Cong., 2d sess., XIII, No. 95, *Cholera Epidemic of 1873 in the United States* (Washington, D.C., 1875), Part B: Ely McClellan and John C. Peters, *A History of the Travels of Asiatic Cholera in North America, passim;* J[ohn] S[harpe] Chambers, *The Conquest of Cholera* (New York, 1938), pp. 193–259.

even the most rudimentary precautions in the public interest.[3] Under these circumstances it is not difficult to understand the horror with which Americans in general and New Yorkers in particular contemplated another in the seemingly cyclical recurrences of cholera.

Ominous reports of the disease in Europe began to reach the United States days after the defeat of the metropolitan health bill in April 1865.[4] Always in the past these reports had been precursors of the appearance of cholera in the United States several months or perhaps a year later. Throughout the spring and summer the press kept the people of New York State informed of the inexorable advance of the epidemic westward from European Russia and northward from the Near East, until it reached England and France by the late summer of 1865. Citizens could not help but recognize that "in New-York, particularly, our population has not only swelled far beyond its numbers of twenty years ago [when cholera last struck], but is on the whole worse lodged than it then was, and exists under conditions more favorable to the spread of such a disease." Far from improving since the last outbreak of cholera, conditions had deteriorated by 1865: "The tenement-house which, twenty years ago, played an insignificant part in the city's panorama, now hives a world of human beings, so huddled and crowded together as to make them the natural prey of disease."[5] By autumn, news of approaching cholera daily shared headlines with news of the

[3] Rosenberg, *Cholera Years, passim.*

[4] On April 19, 1865, p. 4, the *World* reported an outbreak of the plague in European Russia. On April 21, 1865, the same paper ran a front-page spread on the disease as it moved into central Europe and asked in its headline, "Is New-York Prepared?"

[5] *Ibid.,* April 24, 1865, p. 4. The approach of cholera is followed in the *World,* since that paper had no interest in discrediting its own Democratic health department with scare stories about the crisis. The

state's elections. Finally, almost on the eve of the 1865 canvass, the plague reached New York's lower harbor on board the mail steamer *Atalanta*, which had picked up cholera in Havre, France.[6] Although four more ships with cholera aboard subsequently arrived in New York City prior to the New Year, New Yorkers were granted a temporary stay from the full onslaught of an epidemic by an exceptionally cold winter, which probably retarded the spread of the cholera bacilli. It was during this hiatus that the new legislature convened at Albany.

The fall elections of 1865 had resulted in another Republican triumph. Benefiting especially from Union victory in the war, the Republicans had captured additional seats in both the senate and the assembly. The new senate was comprised of 27 Republicans and only 5 Democrats, or a net gain of 6 seats for the Republican Party. In the assembly there were 89 Republican representatives and only 39 Democrats, or a net gain of 13 seats in that house.[7] Furthermore, the Republican gains represented an increase in the ranks of the Radical coalition. Although the Republicans wished to stress their unity in victory rather than their dissension over postwar settlements, most of the Republican candidates for the New York legislature were distinctly wary of the recently proposed Reconstruction policies of their party's new titular chief, President Andrew Johnson. The Democrats, in fact, all but openly endorsed the Johnsonian approach to Reconstruction, and their

---

Republican press, of course, also followed the spread of cholera very closely.

   [6] McClellan and Peters, *Travels of Cholera*, p. 660; *World*, Nov. 4, 1865, p. 5.

   [7] *Times*, Nov. 9, 1865, p. 1; *Journal of the Senate of the State of New York at Their Eighty-ninth Session, 1866* (Albany, 1866); *Journal of the Assembly of the State of New York at Their Eighty-ninth Session, 1866* (Albany, 1866).

overwhelming defeat was interpreted by newspapers around the state as a rebuke to the moderate position in both major parties.[8] The really dramatic divisions over national issues still lay some months in the future, but the organization of the new legislature indicated that the Radical alliance was the leading political beneficiary of the Union victory. Lyman Tremain, an avowed Radical who had the open support of Governor Fenton, was chosen Speaker of the new assembly despite the re-election of the former Speaker, George Hoskins.[9]

On the first day of the new session Fenton gave prominent attention in his annual message to the health crisis and raised again the possibility of a metropolitan board of health. Significantly, he placed the proposal in the context of the continued reform program initiated with the Fire Department Law of 1865: "It will be for you to determine what reformatory legislation is required," he told the senators and the assemblymen after outlining the weaknesses of the existing health programs in New York City. But, he continued:

[8] Stebbins, *Political History*, pp. 77–78. The *World* argued, Nov. 6, 1865, p. 4: "Every vote cast for our admirable state ticket will be a vote to sustain the reconstruction policy of President Johnson, to honor the noble soldiers who periled their lives for the Union, and to encourage the South in the cordial willingness it has manifested to resume the duties of allegience. The temper of the Republican Party is one of bitter hostility to the South." Here is an example of the confusing, shifting state of various political elements in the postwar era: the Democratic Party on the *state* level endorsed the titular head of the Republican Party on the *national* level during the course of a wholly local off-year campaign. After the election, the *World*'s "chief regret" was "not that a local election ha[d] been lost, but that Mr. Johnson's political measures for the early restoration of the Southern States" had been dealt a setback (*World*, Nov. 8, 1865, p. 4).

[9] *Assembly Journal, 1866*, p. 6; *Tribune*, Jan. 3, 1866, p. 6; Albany *Evening Journal*, Jan. 2, p. 1; 13, 1866, p. 2.

The success of the Metropolitan Police Law, and the law creating the paid Fire Department in New York City, as far as it could be tested with the limited opportunities and experience since the organization of the board under it, furnish a strong argument in favor of some similar provision for protecting the public health of the same populous territory. The subject will, I doubt not, receive from you such attention as its importance demands.[10]

With Senator George Andrews' subsequent reintroduction of the metropolitan health bill, attention was focused once again upon the problem of health reform.[11] But despite the intense pressure exerted by the threatening cholera epidemic, the political implications of health reform were by no means put aside. Indeed, the battle which resumed over the metropolitan health bill provided an outstanding example of the extremely political character of much of America's most far-reaching reform legislation.

II

Andrews introduced the same version of the health bill into the 1866 session that the senate had passed during the 1865 session, and as chairman of the Committee on Cities and Villages, he reported the measure favorably once again. On January 24 the first of two heated debates on the metropolitan health bill took place in the senate, and on January 30 the senate spent the better part of the day and night in a continuation of that discussion. These debates were prolonged by precisely the same difficulty that prevented passage of the bill during the previous year: the method of selecting health commissioners. Once again this question separated the Republican senators. The more idealistic Radicals advocated a nonpar-

[10] "Annual Message to the Legislature," Jan. 3, 1866, in *Senate Journal, 1866*, p. 17.
[11] *Senate Journal, 1866*, pp. 26, 30.

tisan reform in the public interest, and they were backed by the remaining members of the old Whiggish element, more uneasy than ever about the increased strength of the Governor and his allies. The more politically oriented Radicals, however, who were tied closely to Fenton and included most of those senators who had just unseated Democrats in normally Democratic districts, were reformers primarily because reform seemed to be a potent political tactic. In the eyes of this latter group, if a reform did not promise to be politically effective, it would not be worth the political risk of passing it. The Democrats, of course, though opposed to any health bill at all, prepared to work for the least partisan board they could get from the hostile majority.[12]

Senators Andrews and White, both of whom had first voted to pass the fire department bill and then to reject Fenton's nominees for the office of fire commissioner, took the lead in defending the less partisan version of the metropolitan health bill. They opposed an amendment by Senator Low that called for a gubernatorially appointed board in lieu of the physicians and police commissioners specified in the Eaton version of the bill. Even the *Tribune*, which favored the Low amendment, conceded its opponents their idealistic motives.[13] Andrews attempted to discredit the idea of a partisan commission on the grounds that a genuine reform would be politically effective by itself. There was no need to transfer the power from one set of politicians to another, he said, for "our friends in New York know what is needed and they will support us for bringing about a real reform."[14] He also asserted that Fenton had promised him a nonpartisan commission even

[12] *Ibid.*, pp. 59, 74, 80, 103–104; Albany *Evening Journal*, Jan. 24, p. 2; 26, 1866, p. 2; *World*, Jan. 31, 1866, p. 8.

[13] Jan. 23, p. 4; 31, 1866, p. 4.

[14] *Tribune*, Jan. 31, 1866, p. 5.

if granted appointive powers. White took the floor and presented a good portion of the data which his investigating committee had gathered during the course of its previous year's inquiry into the workings of the city health department. He declared that the proposed bill was an ideal antidote to the chaotic and corrupted system then existing, and the bill needed no amendments. In his opinion, "all the party patronage the Republican party ever acquired in New-York [City] was a curse to it rather than a benefit."[15]

Low responded with a frank, partisan statement. Where does all of this celebration of a nonpartisan health commission originate, he asked rhetorically; "it does not come from the Democrats, for they oppose the bill upon principle, and repudiate all connection with it." The Radicals, in Low's view, should not "sugar-coat this pill at all by dividing [the health commissioners] between the two parties. We should either submit all questions of this kind to the people, and let the majority rule," he argued, "or if we repudiate that principle, we should have the courage to make it a commission to represent the dominant party. You will be better ruled if the party that has the majority takes the responsibility."[16] John O'Donnell, who believed that any nonpartisan commission was necessarily weak, and Stephen Hayt, who wanted practical political men supervising the medical experts on the job, concurred, and the debate continued.[17]

On January 30 the senate voted on Low's amendment to strike the provisions for a nonpartisan board of health and to substitute gubernatorial appointees. Ten senators, all partisan Radicals, favored it, and sixteen, a combination of idealis-

[15] Albany *Evening Journal*, Jan. 30, 1866, p. 2; White, *Autobiography*, I, 125–126; *Tribune*, Jan. 31, 1866, p. 5.
[16] Albany *Evening Journal*, Jan. 30, 1866, p. 2.
[17] *Ibid.*, Jan. 31, 1866, pp. 1, 2.

tic Radicals, more Whiggish Republicans, and all of the Democrats, opposed it, thereby preserving the nonpartisan character of the proposal.[18] On February 2, in something of an anticlimax, the senate gave final approval to the original health bill with only three dissenting votes, all Democratic.[19] Consequently, the focus of attention shifted over to the assembly, where the health bill was already being debated.

Paradoxically, the increase in Republican strength in the assembly had not made the individual Republican members any more secure in their political positions; in fact, because so many of the new assemblymen had won close elections in swing districts, they were more than ever attuned to the political overtones of any reform which they might choose to undertake. Consequently, the relatively nonpartisan version of the metropolitan health bill passed by the senate had tough going in the assembly from the outset, especially since Fenton's politically conscious close allies clearly controlled the lower house of the legislature.

Thomas E. Stewart, a Republican so Whiggish that he would shortly bolt the party, had introduced the Eaton version of the health bill early in January.[20] Since that time the assembly had listened to various witnesses on the subject and generally marked time pending senate decision on the bill. Thomas J. Creamer, on behalf of the Democrats, introduced

[18] *World*, Feb. 2, 1866, p. 1, and Albany *Evening Journal*, Jan. 30, 1866, p. 2, concurred in the 10 to 16 vote; both *Times*, Jan. 31, 1866, pp. 4–5, and *Tribune*, Jan. 31, 1866, p. 5, called it 8 to 16.

[19] *Senate Journal, 1866*, p. 118.

[20] *Assembly Journal, 1866*, pp. 32, 38; Stewart, a Weed ally, attended the Albany "Conservative Union" convention in September 1866, which attempted to institutionalize the National Union movement in New York State. Stewart eventually supported Democrat John T. Hoffman against Fenton in 1866 and was placed on the Conservative Union central committee (Stebbins *Political History*, pp. 97–114).

a substitute measure similar to the one introduced by the members of that party in 1865, but a straight party vote summarily dismissed his alternative. Consequently, the Democrats retreated to a policy of exacerbating Republican rifts.[21]

When the senate bill was delivered to the assembly, the lower house referred it to the Committee on Public Health where it was debated for only a few days.[22] On February 6 the Republican members of the assembly held a caucus on the health bill in an attempt to reach some agreement among themselves concerning the difficult question of membership on the proposed board of health. "Politicians of all shades—Radicals, Conservatives, and Democrats—gathered in the cloak-room, anxiously waiting for news," reported the press. "The representatives of the Citizens' Association were likewise deeply interested. Messengers were running to the hotels from time to time, with intelligence of the progress of events, and, altogether, the scene was quite animating."[23] Something of a showdown was taking place within the Republican Party.

Those few Whiggish Republicans who still remained in the assembly, like their fellows in the senate, cast their lots in favor of the nonpartisan version of the bill. This was understandable; they hoped to magnify the tensions already inherent in the alliance of idealism and political efficacy which had supplanted them as Republican policy makers at the state level. Perhaps the Whiggish Republicans could dissuade the more idealistic and independent members of the Radical coalition from their current commitment to the former Democrats of the party. "It might be possible to select more devoted partisans—men of greater adroitness in manipulating caucuses

[21] *World*, Jan. 6, p. 6; 20, p. 5; Feb. 9, 1866, p. 8.
[22] *Assembly Journal, 1866*, p. 266.
[23] *World*, Feb. 7, 1866, p. 5.

and more to be relied upon for delegations to State conventions," sneered the *Evening Journal,* but the assembly should surely rise above such considerations in the face of a cholera crisis.[24] In any event the Whiggish assemblymen considered the health issue the best one upon which to make their stand, and they spread the claim that a victory for the less partisan version of the bill, even with the threat of an epidemic hanging over the proceedings, would be a defeat for Fenton.[25]

As a consequence of this challenge, the Governor and his allies risked losing control over the character of their own program of civil and institutional reform. With so much at stake the politically conscious Radicals worked hard to shore up the foundations of their ascendant position within the party. Led by Speaker Tremain, John L. Parker, Clark Cochrane, Mark Wilber, Edmund Pitts, Charles Jenkins, and George Brandreth and backed by executive patronage, the Fenton Republicans carried the party's assembly caucus by a surprisingly large vote of 63 to 11 in favor of having the board of health comprised of gubernatorial appointees.[26] "In years there has been no gathering of Assemblymen around which centered so much interest," reported the *World,* "for the struggle was known to be directly between the contending factions headed by Weed on one side and Fenton on the other. The former had achieved a marked triumph in the Senate through the consumate generalship of Andrews; the latter felt that to raise his reputation and chances for re-election as Governor, or election as Senator, he must secure an overwhelming victory in the Assembly, and his success

---

[24] Albany *Evening Journal,* Feb. 6, 1866, p. 2.

[25] *Ibid.,* Feb. 1, 1866, p. 2.

[26] *Ibid.,* Feb. 7, 1866, p. 2; *Tribune,* Feb. 7, p. 5; 8, 1866, p. 4; *Times,* Feb. 9, 1866, p. 4; *World,* Feb. 7, p. 5; 8, 1866, p. 8.

is the political event of the season." Its ramifications made the caucus "a contest long to be remembered in the political history of the State."[27]

This assessment by the Democratic press, while perhaps oversimplifying the situation, was probably a more objective view of the caucus decision than the leading Republican organs of the state were able to present. The many overlapping and crisscrossing political divisions involved in the health bill—Republican against Democrat, traditional Whiggish leadership against the new Radical coalition within the Republican Party, political considerations against rationalistic idealism within the Radical coalition, and the senate against the assembly—had touched off a vindictive editorial battle in the Republican press. Led on the one hand by the *Tribune* and on the other by the *Times* and the *Evening Journal,* this battle burst into the open by early February. The cooperation and unity which had characterized the attitude of the Republican press toward the compromise health bill in 1865 disappeared completely.

Early in the session the *Times* had announced that it intended to give the health bill "the utmost publicity, so that no member can dodge voting on it, or oppose it, or take out its essential benefits, without every one of his constituents knowing all about his action. We intend to bring the full blaze of the press on every step of its progress through both Houses."[28] Fuel was added to this blaze by the *Tribune,* which on February 1 ran a vicious attack against the opponents of the Low amendment that would give Governor Fenton the power of appointing health commissioners. If the health bill were passed as the Citizens' Association had written it, claimed the *Tribune,* then the bulk of the political in-

[27] Feb. 8, 1866, p. 8.
[28] Jan. 12, 1866, p. 4.

fluence derived from it would go to the police commissioners. This in turn would strengthen the Weed-Morgan wing of the party, which now survived largely on the patronage of the increasingly unpopular Andrew Johnson. Thus, according to the Radical *Tribune*, Eaton's draft of the bill was not really nonpartisan; it would add muscle to the otherwise slipping grasp of "that little band of wireworkers who are distinctly '*Conservative Republicans*.' "[29] The next day the *Times*, whose Henry Raymond would be among President Johnson's last Republican supporters in Congress, retaliated in kind. Charging that the "Radicals" were the real patronage-mongers in the Republican Party, the *Times* accused Fenton's allies of "endeavoring to 'manipulate' the Health Bill, as they did the Fire Bill, into a party machine."[30] When the assembly caucus finally made the Radical version of the bill a party measure, the *Tribune* gloated. On the other hand, the Albany *Evening Journal*, referring to the Radicals as "scorpions in the bosom" of the party, joined the *Times* in advocating a bolt of the caucus in favor of the senate bill.[31]

This, then, was the situation when the assembly's Public Health Committee brought the metropolitan health bill before the full house. Chairman Lyman Congdon reported the bill, including the Radical amendments concerning gubernatorial appointments. Assemblyman Wilson Berryman wanted to offer the senate version of the bill without amendments as

[29] Feb. 1, 1866, p. 4 (their italics).

[30] Feb. 2, 1866, p. 4.

[31] Albany *Evening Journal*, Feb. 7, 1866, p. 2. For this complete series of editorial blows and counterblows see *Tribune*, Feb. 1, p. 4; 3, p. 4; 6, p. 4; 8, p. 4; 10, p. 6; 13, p. 4; 14, p. 4; 17, p. 6; 21, 1866, p. 4; *Times*, Feb. 2, p. 4; 5, p. 4; 7, p. 4; 9, p. 4; 12, p. 4; 13, p. 4; 14, p. 4; 16, p. 4; March 29, 1866, p. 4; Albany *Evening Journal*, Jan. 18, p. 2; 24, p. 2; Feb. 1, p. 2; 6, p. 2; 7, p. 2; 8, p. 2; 9, p. 2; 10, p. 2; 12, p. 2; 13, p. 2; 14, p. 2; 15, p. 2; 16, p. 2; 17, p. 2; 19, 1866, p. 2.

a minority report. On the motion of DeWitt C. Littlejohn both of these reports were accepted, and the assembly staged a long, vitriolic debate on the two proposals.[32]

Berryman made most of the objective arguments in favor of the senate proposal: the cholera danger made prompt action imperative, the letters of his constituents all favored a nonpartisan health commission, both the Republican General Committee of New York City and the Union League of New York City had endorsed the senate version of the bill. Only Fentonite pressure, claimed Berryman, an Irish immigrant who had been a lieutenant of colored troops during the war, had restrained him from breaking with the caucus decision much earlier. The Whiggish Stewart sided with the more idealistic Berryman, attacked the *Tribune,* and proclaimed: "I am as strong a partizan [*sic*] as any, but God forbid that I should allow my party to come between life and health." Congdon, himself a physician and, as chairman of the Public Health Committee, a key figure in the debate, resented an earlier intimation that rural delegates like himself were "ignoramuses" on the question of urban public health. For him the deciding factor was the willingness of the prosenate men to kill the bill rather than alter it. "This began to open his eyes" to the fact that the supposedly nonpartisan senate version was just as political in its implications as any other bill and that its backers had "more confidence in F. I. A. Boole & Co. administering the Health laws of the city of New York than they have in the Governor and the Senate." He concluded by assailing Stewart simply as a blind "anti-Greeley man." George Curtis, one of the few Democrats to enter the fray, blasted the Republicans for their feuding, their partisan motives, and their commission schemes generally. He also

[32] *Assembly Journal, 1866,* pp. 335–336.

took a shot at the Citizens' Association by suggesting that the same men who "preach sanitary regulations" owned "the cellars which [were] reeking with filth. Why do they not remedy the tenement houses?" he challenged. In 1867 the Radicals would meet that challenge, too, but for the moment they still faced a fierce political fight over the health bill.[33]

The heaviest blows were landed by Governor Fenton's most dependable allies in the assembly, Brandreth, Pitts, and Parker. Because New York City was the heart of the state and of the nation, argued Brandreth, the legislators at Albany had a perfect right to keep it healthy, especially in the face of a cholera epidemic. Furthermore, "a health bill was wanted for smallpox, scarlet fever and other things as well as cholera. The cholera bell had been rung very loud by the friends of the Senate bill." The real question in his mind was not the desirability of public health legislation, but whether the metropolitan area would "have a non-partizan [*sic*] commission, or whether the Republican Party was to take the responsibility." He left no doubt about his own position: "We must give the Union Governor the power to appoint, and thus take the whole responsibility, which we are competent to discharge. . . . We can confide in Governor Fenton." He noted that 10 Republican senators and 75 Republican assemblymen agreed with the Radical position and that only 27 Republicans were holding out. "Bolters know their fate," he warned, and he reminded his colleagues that Fenton had not been afraid to purge party members in the past. In a remarkable bit of Radical rhetoric, Brandreth stated: "We, who were born into the Union party in 1861, believed the Union party was almost omnipotent. And if it could crush traitors and copperheads, if they [sic] had the power[,] they would crush out the

[33] These and the following references to the assembly debate are from transcripts in Albany *Evening Journal*, Feb. 13, p. 2; 14, 1866, p. 1.

cholera too. Give us the Assembly health bill, and we will clean the streets and make them fit to live in."

Pitts and Parker addressed the factionalism within their own party. Were not "the men at the bottom of this [Senate] Health bill . . . the persons who defeated the patriot Wadsworth?" asked Pitts. By giving power to Seymour, "they had done enough to injure the party, and they must now be ignored." Parker picked up the same theme and argued that Weed's real motives stemmed from the opposition of the reform governor to "the King of the Lobby['s]" attempts to raise the rates of the New York Central Railroad.

I want it understood by his [Weed's] dirty mouthpieces the *Evening Journal,* the New York *Times* and kindred prints, that so far as I am concerned, I ask no favors and care never a bit for their calumniations or their denunciations, and I am willing that my constituents should know that I stand up here in my place on this floor and defend Governor Fenton from the wiles and the attacks of the man, and of all who follow in his wake, who contributed so much to cheat this State out of the services of Wadsworth in the Executive Chair, and gave to us in the most trying time in our country's history, a Seymour in his place.

Speaker Tremain concluded the Radical case. He dismissed an endorsement of the senate bill by the New York City Chamber of Commerce by pointing out that only eleven of the Chamber's nine hundred members had been present at the special meeting that considered it. He identified those members of the New York City Republican Committee who were leading the fight for a nonpartisan bill as federal officeholders under Andrew Johnson. And Tremain concluded by re-emphasizing the police board's loyalty to the old Whiggish Republicans and its adamant refusal to recognize the ascendancy of Radicalism within the party.

The assembly debate ended after midnight when the question of substituting the senate's health bill for the assembly's was finally called.[34] The motion to substitute was defeated by a vote of 46 in favor to 72 opposed.[35] Although the eleven assemblymen who backed the senate bill in caucus crossed over to vote with the Democrats, the vote revealed quite clearly that the Radicals could now command not only a majority of the Republican members of the state assembly, but also a majority of the whole membership of that house. Even the *Evening Journal,* though certainly among the losers on this ballot, recognized it as "a test vote," indicative of Radical strength in the assembly.[36] The final vote, once again less telling than the earlier one, was an overwhelming 84 to 34 in favor of the amended, or assembly, health bill. All of the eleven bolters returned to vote with the Republican majority, and all of the Democrats present voted against the measure.[37] If, as the *World* reported, Thurlow Weed himself had come over to the assembly to coordinate the Whiggish efforts, the victory must have been particularly satisfying for Fenton's Radical allies.[38]

The assembly decision threw the health bill back once again into the state senate, and the Democrats began to scream more loudly than ever before that the Republicans were making the weal of New York City "the football of partisan scuffles."[39] Nicholas La Bau, acutely aware of the political exigencies in his home district of Richmond County, urged senate acceptance of the assembly's bill. Members of the lower house, he argued, were "more intimate with the wishes of

[34] *Tribune,* Feb. 14, 1866, p. 5.
[35] *Assembly Journal, 1866,* pp. 375–376.
[36] Feb. 14, 1866, p. 2.
[37] *Assembly Journal, 1866,* pp. 377–378.
[38] Feb. 12, 1866, pp. 4, 5.
[39] *World,* Feb. 15, 1866, p. 4.

their constitutents" than were the men who wore the "elephant's hide" of a senatorial toga. John O'Donnell, from an old Barnburner district, also supported Fenton's right to make his own appointments, and he was backed by Low, who reiterated his belief in frankly partisan legislation. Abel Godard, the youngest member of the senate and also from an old Barnburner stronghold, cast his lot with the Governor, too, reversing the plea for speed by pointing out that the quickest passage now would be concurrence in the assembly version. Adam Kline agreed. Perhaps Stephen Hayt, yet another of the former Democratic Radicals, was most straightforward: "When the Democratic majority from the city of New York rolled up to 40,000, the Legislature deemed it a duty to interfere." He found "an important reason for voting in favor of the Assembly amendment, in the fact that it is desired by the constituency which did not send him to Albany to legislate Democrats into office."[40]

On the other side Abraham Lent, Charles Folger, and George Andrews all urged their senatorial colleagues to stand fast. Andrew White claimed that "the [nonpartisan] Health bill had [formerly] been demanded by every organ of every wing of the party, . . . It was not until it had passed the Senate, and a faction within a faction of the party discovered that it would not promote their interests, that the principles of the measure were attacked." He urged his fellow Radicals not to let the "poison" of partisan considerations burst the idealistic "chalice" of the Republican Party. White's "faction within a faction" was an exceptionally apt phrase, for the dispute lay once again within the Radical coalition itself. As had been the case with Fenton's fire commissioners, the two most

[40] The senate debates are from Albany *Evening Journal*, Feb. 15, 1866, p. 2.

important elements in the Radical alliance—reforming idealism and political efficacy—seemed to be once again at odds.

On February 15 the assembly's amendments were reread in
the senate and a vote was taken on a motion to "non-concur"
in them. This motion carried with 19 votes in favor of retaining the senate version to 11 votes opposed, thereby creating an impasse between the senate and the assembly. The
Republican members of the senate split 15 in favor of their
own version, or nonconcurrence, against 11 in favor of the
assembly's amendments. Their lines of cleavage were famil-
iar: defenders of the senate draft once again included not
only those senators who supported a nonpartisan reform on
principle, but also those who were feeling increasingly uncomfortable under the ever-lengthening shadow of the Governor and his allies. The eleven holdouts for the assembly
measure were pleased with Fenton's blend of politics and reform and were willing to see his position within the party
strengthened in 1866.[41]

Although the Republicans appeared seriously deadlocked in
the wake of the senate's action, additional considerations increased their already substantial incentives to secure a health
reform for New York City. Not the least of these added pressures came from their own upstate constituencies. The Democrats had actually accused the Republican assemblymen from
upstate districts of not really caring whether New York City
escaped the plague because "cholera [would] cancel a large

[41] *Senate Journal, 1866*, pp. 188–190. Republicans in favor: Andrews,
Campbell, Collins, Cornell, Crowley, Folger, Humphrey, Lent, Murphy, Pierson, Platt, Stanford, White, Wilbor, and Wolcott. Republicans opposed: Barnett, Bennett, Gibson, Godard, Hayt, Kline, La Bau,
Low, O'Donnell, Sessions, and Williams. Parsons did not vote, although *Tribune*, Feb. 16, 1866, p. 5, claimed that he favored the
assembly bill.

percentage of the Democratic vote" in the metropolitan area.[42] But this was decidedly not the case since the growing towns and cities in western New York, many of which would be major population centers in any state that did not contain gargantuan New York City, saw in the case of public health, as they had in the case of fire protection, the direct relationship between themselves and New York City. Each time cholera struck New York City in the past, places like Syracuse, Rochester, and Buffalo, lying on the trade and transportation routes to the Midwest, had suffered an attack of the disease shortly thereafter.[43] Andrews, for example, pointed out in the senate that his own home district had once suffered "a fearful epidemic . . . imported by a merchant who had spent a night in New York city," and the *Evening Journal,* aware of the capital's past fate, concluded that "cholera at New York, is cholera threatening Albany, and every other city and town along the railways and water-courses, which the scourge always traverses in its desolating march."[44] Even during the 1865 session of the legislature, when the threat of cholera was not yet so intense, a majority of the petitions submitted to the assembly in favor of the metropolitan health bill had originated in upstate urban centers. These towns realized that their first line of health defense lay in New York City, and they looked to state action to bolster that line of defense.

The Medical Society of the State of New York, meeting in Albany, brought still more pressure upon the Republicans to settle their differences and pass a health bill.[45] In a resolution transmitted to Speaker Tremain the doctors were un-

[42] *World,* Feb. 15, 1866, p. 4.
[43] McClellan and Peters, *Travels of Cholera, passim.*
[44] Jan. 24, 1866, p. 2.
[45] Albany *Evening Journal,* Feb. 7, p. 1; 8, p. 1; 9, 1866, p. 1.

equivocal in their support of the proposed reform, while remaining tactful about the political roadblock preventing its enactment:

Resolved, That the Medical Society of the State of New York, now in session in this city, do hereby earnestly urge the Assembly to pass at the earliest day, a health bill which shall retain the general sanitary provisions and regulations contained in the bill which recently passed the Senate. As to the mode or manner of appointing the comissioners to execute said law, the society offers no suggestions, leaving this wholly to the wisdom of the Legislature.[46]

In its wisdom, the legislature decided to organize a joint conference committee to resolve the question of selecting health commisisoners. Accordingly, both the senate and the assembly designated members to sit on the conference committee, though not without some difficulty. In the senate, Radical James Barnett, another former Democrat and Liberty Party member from Gerrit Smith's bailiwick, growled at Andrews about the "spirit of faction" which the latter was helping to enflame by insisting on men pledged not to concede a thing to the assembly's position. Before the membership could be selected O'Donnell had joined Barnett in a vicious shouting match with Andrews.[47]

As finally chosen, the assembly members of the conference were firmly committed to gubernatorial appointment and the senate members equally adamant in their advocacy of the original version of the bill. Under mounting pressure, however, the committee managed to reach a compromise position. As reported back to the two houses of the legislature, the new version of the metropolitan health bill retained the central features of both the senate plan and the assembly plan. The four

[46] *Assembly Journal, 1866,* p. 324; *Times,* Feb. 9, 1866, p. 4.
[47] *Assembly Journal, 1866,* pp. 406–407, 436; *Senate Journal, 1866,* pp. 203–204; Albany *Evening Journal,* Feb. 16, 1866, p. 2.

police commissioners would serve jointly on the health board, as in the senate's version, but they were now to be balanced by four gubernatorially appointed commissioners, as called for by the assembly. Probably to placate the Citizens' Association and the medical profession, these gubernatorial appointees were required to be fully accredited physicians and at least one of them had to come from the city of Brooklyn. The health officer of the Port of New York was also included on the newly styled "Metropolitan Board of Health."[48] On the same day the compromise was reported to the two houses of the legislature, it was also passed by them both, though again the scenes were hardly amicable. Speaker Tremain traded old accusations and Weed editorials from the past with DeWitt Littlejohn, who read aloud to Tremain from speeches the Radical leader had made while still a Democrat.[49] In the senate the final vote was 22 for and 2 against; in the assembly, 74 for and 28 against.[50] When the Governor signed the measure, one of the most significant pieces of legislation enacted during the Reconstruction in New York State officially took effect.[51]

III

While the metropolitan health bill still hung in limbo between the two houses of the state legislature, the *Times* had

[48] *Assembly Journal, 1866*, pp. 470–475; *Senate Journal, 1866*, pp. 224–229; Albany *Evening Journal*, Feb. 17, 1866, p. 2; *Times*, Feb. 18, 1866, p. 4.

[49] Albany *Evening Journal*, Feb. 22, 1866, p. 1.

[50] *Assembly Journal, 1866*, p. 476; *Senate Journal, 1866*, pp. 229–230; Albany *Evening Journal*, Feb. 19, 1866, p. 2; *Tribune*, Feb. 19, 1866, p. 4; *Times*, Feb. 21, 1866, p. 4.

[51] *Senate Journal, 1866*, p. 1055. Fenton did not sign the metropolitan health bill until February 26, 1866, because he was in Washington conferring with other Radical leaders. He was there when President Johnson vetoed the Freedmen's Bureau bill, which opened further the rifts in the Republican Party (see *Tribune*, Feb. 22, 1866, p. 1).

finally "wash[ed its] hands of responsibility" for the measure. If the Radicals "preferred a party-machine to a health board," they would have to live with the result.[52] Likewise, the *World*, after the health bill passed the legislature, growled that the Radicals had put their stamp upon the measure, and "all we can do is to protest, and hold this commission to a stern accountability."[53] There was no doubt in either of these representative organs of political opinion that the metropolitan health bill as finally passed was the work of the Radical coalition. Furthermore, the Radicals claimed the measure as a part of their own program. The bill's leading advocates were the same senators and assemblymen who shortly after passing the health reform, as if to reaffirm their Radical credentials, voted to censure President Johnson's veto of the civil rights bill.[54] In February 1866, then, the more Whiggish Republicans and the New York State Democrats were more than willing to give the Radicals full credit for the health bill and thereby dump the whole impending cholera crisis in their laps. Within a few months, however, these groups may have sorely regretted their initial disclaimers of responsibility, for the Metropolitan Board of Health made some remarkable strides in a very short time.

By the end of February, Fenton had appointed commissioners to serve on the new board, and his decision to nomi-

[52] Feb. 16, 1866, p. 4.

[53] Feb. 19, 1866, p. 4.

[54] *Tribune*, Feb. 19, 1866, p. 4; April 5, 1866, pp. 4, 8; *Senate Journal, 1866,* pp. 626, 628, 677; *Assembly Journal, 1866,* pp. 1395–1396. Actions like these offer further evidence that some of the Republican senators, like Andrew White, Charles Folger, and Ezra Cornell, were in the Radical camp, yet opposed to the use of reform measures for flagrantly partisan purposes, while others, like George Andrews, Henry Pierson, and Charles Stanford, were motivated by their opposition to Radicalism.

nate the same four physicians designated in the original version of the health bill was hailed on all sides as a judicious one in light of the bitter contest just waged.[55] Within a few weeks the new Board of Health reached an agreement with the city's butchers to the effect that all slaughterhouses would immediately begin to clean themselves up and plan eventually to remove their operations north of Fortieth Street.[56] Both the doubting *World* and the dubious *Times* saluted this early and important breakthrough against a traditional nuisance in the city.[57]

Even more remarkable were the improvements made in the city's street-cleaning operations. The first president of the Metropolitan Board of Health was Jackson S. Schultz, another former Free Soil Democrat who had become a Republican prior to the Civil War, and he apparently had a mania for cleaning the city's streets.[58] He let new contracts and encouraged a project to remove the vast amounts of filth that had accumulated in many districts never visited by the old sanitation department. Upstate, according to the *Evening Journal*, everyone was pleased with the cleanup being effected,[59] and

[55] *World*, March 2, 1866, p. 5.

[56] This latter agreement went into full effect on January 1, 1869. Fortieth Street was then well above the concentrations of population on Manhattan Island (see Atkins, *Health, Housing and Poverty*, pp. 50–51).

[57] *World*, March 8, 1866, p. 4; *Times*, March 10, p. 4; 15, 1866, p. 4.

[58] Schultz' uncle, who remained a Democrat, was high in Tammany circles. Schultz himself had become wealthy in the leather business— in 1891 he left an estate in excess of a million dollars—and turned to civil reform during the war. His singular prepossession with the cleanliness of the city's streets continued long after he had left the Board of Health, for he went frequently before the legislature in later years demanding stronger sanitation laws and hounding lax city officials (see Atkins, *Health, Housing and Poverty*, p. 36).

[59] April 25, 1866, p. 2.

in the city itself the *Times* was amazed at the progress: "Of all the difficult things that need to be done in this municipality, everybody knows that *this* is the most difficult of accomplishment. We can specify streets, both on the east side and on the west side of the City, both up-town and down-town, that have for years been intolerable, but are now as decent as their intrinsic character will permit."[60] Far-reaching improvements in the city's water supply were made, and new standards were demanded of the milk industry in New York, but the overriding concern of the majority of citizens around the state still centered on the impending cholera epidemic.

Cholera returned to New York City with the warm spring weather just as the Board of Health and almost everyone else in the state had known it would. This time it entered the port aboard the *Virginia*, from Liverpool, on April 18, 1866.[61] Although this vessel was detained in the harbor under quarantine, there were fears that the epidemic might erupt. Consequently, on April 21, Governor Fenton declared a state of health emergency in the metropolitan area.[62] As a result of Eaton's section 16 in the health law, this proclamation of emergency clothed the new Board of Health with truly extraordinary power over the city of New York, including even the right to remove physically from his own home any per-

[60] April 28, 1866, p. 4 (their italics).

[61] McClellan and Peters, *Travels of Cholera*, p. 662. The arrival of cholera and its progress may be followed in any of New York City's major dailies, each of which gives it extensive coverage complete with hints on precautions and treatments. The hints alone are worth a chapter in the social history of the United States for they reveal many of the preconceptions of the society. Prostitutes, for example, were said to be more susceptible to cholera than other women; some stories suggested a direct causal effect between having a drink and catching the disease.

[62] *World*, April 26, 1866, p. 8.

son deemed a threat to the health of the other inhabitants of the building and to place him in a public hospital.

On the first of May the commissioners promulgated a rigid new health code for the city, which impressed even the Democratic *World*. Devoting its first two pages to a complete reprint of it, the *World* urged its readers to save that day's papers and to familiarize themselves with the code's provisions.[63] Thirty special assistants were hired by the board for the duration of the crisis in order to help with proposed house-to-house inspections and the disinfecting of establishments suspected of harboring disease. Though the dangerous summer months lay ahead, the *Times* seemed confident, notwithstanding its initial doubts about the Radical reform measure.[64]

When the first death from cholera in the city occurred May 2 in a tenement house at the corner of 93rd Street and 3rd Avenue, the board redoubled its efforts. Fenton renewed and expanded his declaration of emergency, thereby continuing the board's virtually dictatorial powers.[65] Earlier in the spring the Radicals in the legislature had amended the Metropolitan Health Law to allow the new Board of Health to enforce the city's excise laws as well as its own health regulations.[66] Since these excise laws—which were for the most part unenforced—dealt primarily with liquor licensing, the Board of Health was thus granted jurisdiction even over corner saloons. Despite Democratic bellowing, the Board of Health appears not to have made any serious effort to enforce the

[63] May 1, 1866, pp. 1, 2, 4.

[64] April 22, 1866, p. 4.

[65] *World*, May 16, 1866, p. 5.

[66] For the legislative history of these amendments, see the *Assembly* and *Senate Journals* for 1866; *Times*, March 30, 1866, p. 4; *World*, April 14, 1866, p. 8.

politically sensitive liquor laws, but instead preferred to use the threat of enforcement as a lever against particularly unclean bars.[67] With the aid of the police, whose commissioners sat on the health board, some 31,077 separate orders were served between the middle of March and the end of the crisis period, November 1, 1866. Most of them concerned cleaning and disinfecting privies, cellars, yards, and the like. Indeed, so zealous did the Board of Health become that the *World* began to complain of its "terrorism" in forcing the city to knuckle under in the face of the threat. If the commissioners kept it up, moaned that paper in apparent seriousness, the result would be self-defeating, since the board would "frighten the community into depression of nervous force and consequent disease."[68]

But this, of course, hardly proved to be the case. By isolating the cases of cholera as they broke out and by disinfecting the homes and apartments, privies, and water supplies in the area of each reported case, the new Board of Health helped keep the city's death toll under five hundred lives. This was considered a dramatic accomplishment. The Surgeon-General of the United States, for example, in an extensive report on cholera issued a few years later stated: "The tenement-houses of New York [in 1866] were probably full of cholera-infected individuals and clothing, and but for the prompt and efficient management of the Metropolitan Board of Health; but for the almost universal system of disinfection which was adopted . . . and scrupulously continued, the city of New York would, in all probability, have witnessed a most disastrous explosion of the disease." Inland cities like Cincinnati, where some 1,200 deaths occurred, or St. Louis, which

[67] *Times*, April 28, 1866, p. 4.
[68] May 18, 1866, p. 4.

lost over 3,500 of its citizens, suffered far more serious losses in 1866 than did much more populous New York City.[69]

There is no reason to overdramatize the achievements of the Board of Health established in 1866. When it published its first *Annual Report* in January 1867, there were still some swine sharing back alleys with residents and pedestrians, and there was still indescribable wretchedness in housing and health among the tenement dwellers.[70] Difficulties even arose with the New York State Medical Society over the board's partial recognition of homeopathic medicine.[71] Nevertheless, the Metropolitan Health Law was both a legislative and a public health breakthrough. Charles E. Rosenberg, in his excellent study of nineteenth-century America's reaction to cholera, put it this way:

The organization and achievements of the Metropolitan Board exerted a lasting influence; in the history of public health in the United States, there is no date more important than 1866, no event more significant than the organization of the Metropolitan Board of Health. For the first time, an American community had successfully organized itself to conquer an epidemic. The tools and concepts of an urban industrial society were beginning to be used in solving this new society's problems.[72]

The Radicals' health law set a precedent for legislation passed during the later Progressive era, and the metropolitan bill itself was widely copied in other states.[73]

Perhaps because it was such a significant reform, the highly

[69] McClellan and Peters, *Travels of Cholera*, pp. 663, 670, 671.

[70] See *World*, Jan. 3, 1867, pp. 4 and 5, for a critical response to the board's first year.

[71] *Assembly Journal, 1866*, p. 244; *Times*, Jan. 30, 1866, p. 4; *World*, Feb. 15, 1867, p. 4.

[72] *Cholera Years*, pp. 192–193.

[73] Smith, *City That Was*, pp. 158–159, 177–178; Rosenberg, *Cholera Years*, pp. 210–212.

political origins of the Metropolitan Health Law are often blurred. American medical historians, for example, when discussing the bill's passage, tend to emphasize the threat of cholera and to lay heavy stress on the role of individual physicians and farsighted public health reformers.[74] In this interpretation, the metropolitan board represents the culmination of heroic efforts by dedicated men and women, as many of whom as possible are identified and praised, in the face of a grave crisis. At its worst this approach leads to a morality drama in which noble medical men finally drive into the thick skulls of venal politicians the obvious necessity for health reform. Although there is no need to underplay the role of private individuals, there is also no reason to overplay it; nor had any of the equally virulent epidemics of the past moved previous legislatures to action.

More important than crusading doctors or a threat of cholera was the political shift that took place in New York State at the end of the Civil War. Without the rise of the Radical coalition to power the pressure of private individuals would probably have remained no more effective than it had been for the previous fifteen years.[75] Furthermore, there is some

[74] Howard C. Kramer, "Early Municipal and State Boards of Health," *Bulletin of the History of Medicine*, XXIV (1950), 503–517; Wilson G. Smillie, *Public Health: Its Promise for the Future, A Chronicle of the Development of Public Health in the United States, 1607–1914* (New York, 1955), pp. 293–294; Gert H. Brieger, "Sanitary Reform in New York City: Stephen Smith and the Passage of the Metropolitan Health Bill," *Bulletin of the History of Medicine*, L (1966), 407–429; Duffy, *History of Public Health*, pp. 564–571.

[75] Dorman B. Eaton, perhaps the most prominent of the private individuals fighting for the health bill, never did grasp this essential point. Congratulating White, he linked the measure to "the best people of this city," deplored the "partisan—*low*—mercenary" influences which "that great Christian measure of reform has encountered," and believed that the whole metropolitan health episode demonstrated that

evidence from leading public health pioneers that class bias and professional self-interest dampened the zeal of many doctors for large-scale public health programs and that the Radicals, in their willingness to use the state legislature to effect this reform, may actually have been in advance of most medical men.[76]

In this chapter passage of the Metropolitan Health Law has been placed in the context of the politics of New York Radicalism. Although their legislative actions revealed that a large number of the Governor's allies were interested in the measure primarily for political reasons, the long-term significance of what they passed is not diminished; the law remains a landmark in the history of American public health legislation. And if Radical votes delayed the health bill a year, it was the Radicals' postwar program and political philosophies, as well as their presence in the state legislature, that made health reform a realistic possibility to begin with. Regardless of their mixed motives, the Fenton Republicans deserve credit for this substantively important act in New York State's reconstruction at home.

"a disinterested devotion to the public good is a surer guarante[e] of success than the greatest skill in mere polit[ic]al craft" (Eaton to White, Feb. 2, 1866, White Papers).

[76] Henry I. Bowditch, *Public Hygiene in America: Being the Centennial Discourse Delivered before the International Medical Congress, Philadelphia, September, 1876* (Boston, 1877); Hermann M. Biggs, "An Address: Sanitary Science, the Medical Profession, and the Public," *Medical News*, LXXII (1898), 44–50.

5

Labor and Housing

During the summer of 1866, the most Whiggish Republicans voluntarily removed themselves from the party in New York State by trying unsuccessfully to ally with the Democracy in support of President Johnson's Reconstruction policies. Thurlow Weed called a state gathering to elect delegates to the abortive National Union convention in Philadelphia, and most of Weed's closest allies joined him in endorsing Tammany's John T. Hoffman for governor against Fenton. Consequently, the Radicals, who had broken completely with the President over the issues of national Reconstruction, found themselves in unchallenged control of the Republican convention at Syracuse. Fenton was renominated by acclamation; more Radicals were included on the state ticket below the Governor; and the tenets of congressional reconstruction, including the proposed Fourteenth Amendment, became the party's platform.[1]

[1] Albany *Evening Journal*, July 14, p. 2; Sept. 5, p. 2; 6, p. 1, 2, 3; Oct. 16, 1866, p. 1; Van Deusen, *Weed*, pp. 308, 312, 321–324; Alexander, *New York*, III, 136–149; Stebbins, *Political History*, pp. 91–143. Cox and Cox, *Politics, Principle, and Prejudice*, especially chaps. ii and iv, offer evidence that President Johnson was actively encouraging the formation of a new moderate party under his Reconstruc-

The collapse of the National Union alliance and President Johnson's disastrous "swing around the circle" combined to produce a Republican victory at the November election. Reuben Fenton was re-elected governor, and the Radical coalition of the Republican Party gained the largest majority it ever attained in New York State's legislature.[2] In the senate the Republican advantage of 27 to 5 carried over into the new session, since the senators had not been required to stand for re-election in 1866.[3] Although some of these Republican senators had balked at accepting the version of the metropolitan health bill favored by the Governor, the Radicals clearly held the upper hand. The new assembly contained 83 Republicans and only 45 Democrats. Furthermore, since the Republicans were virtually all Radicals, they were ready for far more cohesive organization than in past sessions. Even the *World*, which sought eagerly to uncover and to exploit any rifts in the ranks of the opposition, could find none of the divisiveness that had marked, in varying degrees, the two previous Republican legislatures.[4] The organization of the new assembly went so smoothly, in fact, that the only question remaining in the minds of most observers involved the possible uses to which Fenton's allies would put their overwhelming strength.

---

tion programs and that Seward considered the New York State situation crucial to this strategy. Greeley was not far off when he labeled the alliance the "Demijohnson Party" (Glyndon G. Van Deusen, *Horace Greeley: Nineteenth Century Crusader* [New York, 1953, 1964], p. 346).

[2] This refers specifically to the Radical coalition; although the number of Radical Republicans rose considerably in the assembly, the Republicans as a party suffered a net loss of five seats.

[3] The only change was the election of John J. Wicks to fill a vacancy created by the resignation of Stephen T. Hayt, who was elected state canal commissioner.

[4] Jan. 2, 1867, p. 4.

For the Radicals themselves, however, there were sobering aspects to their apparently one-sided triumph. Although Fenton's margin of victory had increased substantially over his majority in 1864, he still received only 13,789 more votes than his Democratic-National Union opponent, John T. Hoffman. In a total canvass of 719,195 votes this was far from overwhelming. Furthermore, although 1866 was a "Republican year" all across the North, the party's chronic weakness in the New York City area was as evident as ever. In New York County (Manhattan Island), Fenton actually ran farther behind Hoffman in 1866 than he had run behind Seymour in 1864, and only a tremendous showing in upstate counties, where the Radicals campaigned exclusively on national issues, saved him the governor's office.[5] Ironically, therefore, even though the elections of 1866 marked the highest point yet reached by the Radicals in New York State, the result threw into focus more sharply than ever before the vulnerability of the Radicals at the state level: they were forced to rely upon national issues growing out of the sectional conflict, and they were faced with an ever more ominous electoral handicap in and around New York City.

During the two previous sessions of the legislature, the Fenton Radicals had begun a program of civil and institutional reform as a possible solution to their political dilemmas. So far, however, as the returns unmistakably indicated, their anticipated electoral gains in New York City were either not forthcoming or were being counterbalanced by the Democrats. Nonetheless, the Radicals continued to believe that their best political opportunities lay in the direction of addi-

[5] *Times*, Nov. 8, 1866, p. 1; Alexander, *New York*, III, 163–164; Stebbins, *Political History*, p. 133; *Tribune*, Nov. 6, 1866, p. 4; Republican Union State Committee, "Issues of the Day," Pamphlet 2, Campaign Pamphlets, 1866, New-York Historical Society, New York.

tional similar reforms. Shifts in party allegiance were difficult to make and required patient encouragement; many of the ex-Democratic Radicals realized this from their own experiences during the 1850's. Besides, measures like the 1865 Fire Department Law and the 1866 Metropolitan Health Law had proved completely successful in other, nonelectoral ways.

The reform bills had provided the Radicals with badly needed state issues and with some local patronage at a time when they had been cut off from the federal rewards of the Johnson administration. More important, the reforms of 1865 and 1866 had provided a vehicle that permitted the Radicals to supersede the Whiggish elements within their own party. The idealists and independents of the party had abandoned the Republican leaders of an earlier day, even though their new coalition with the more politically oriented Radicals was occasionally uneasy. The reform program had also paid a wholly unexpected dividend when it became a stumbling block in the way of full cooperation between the Democrats and the Whiggish Republicans whom it helped to drive from the party. The Tammany majority at the New York State National Union convention, incensed at losing control over the fire and health departments, had insisted on passage of an anticommission resolution, which apparently helped persuade Henry Raymond of the *Times*, though he had sacrificed his political career on the altar of the National Union concept, finally to support the Fentonites in the state race.[6]

The Radical program of urban reform, then, seemed to be succeeding in all ways except one: the important business of converting Tammany Democrats into Radical Republican

[6] *Times*, Sept. 13, 1866, p. 1; Francis Brown, *Raymond of the Times* (New York, 1951), pp. 295–310; Van Deusen, *Weed*, p. 323; Alexander, *New York*, III, 136–149.

voters. In fact, an attempt to give excise powers to the Board of Health, coupled with another bill that created an even stronger excise board to regulate liquor sales in the metropolitan district, had probably cost the Republicans votes in 1866.[7] As Andrew White observed shortly after passage of the health bill, the man on the street, who customarily accounted for the Democratic majorities in New York City, was more likely to remember that he had difficulty getting a drink on Sunday than he was to consider the relatively intangible fact that he might have died of cholera had the new health board not insisted on disinfecting the privy in his tenement.[8]

The Radicals, therefore, needed measures that might speak more positively to some of the constituencies long monopolized by the Democrats in New York City. Two of the most prominent of these traditionally Democratic constituencies were the workingmen and the tenement dwellers. Both groups received attention from the Radical legislature during the 1867 session. With the vote of the workingmen in mind, an eight-hour-day law was enacted; with the vote of the tenement residents in mind, the Radicals forced through the legislature an act to regulate living conditions in the metropolitan district. Surprisingly, however, these two bills form an intriguing pair not because of their similaries but because of their political differences. In the first instance the Radicals

[7] *Assembly Journal, 1866*, and *Senate Journal, 1866*. A crisis over the constitutionality of the excise law forced Fenton to call a special session of the State Supreme Court during the summer of 1866. Although the law was upheld in the case of "Metropolitan Board of Excise *v.* John Harris, *et al.*," 34 New York, 657, the case helped the Democrats to keep the odious law in full public view as the fall elections approached (Stebbins, *Political History*, pp. 123–124; Alexander, *New York*, III, 165; and James Grant Wilson, ed., *The Memorial History of the City of New York* [New York, 1892–1893], III, 531).

[8] *Autobiography*, I, 126.

themselves were divided and uncertain; the political implications of the proposed legislation were unclear. The result was one of the least effective pieces of legislation in the Radicals' continuing program of civil and institutional reform. In the second instance the cutting edge of partisan politics came back into play. The result was another substantively important measure in New York State's reconstruction at home.

II

What labor movement there was in the United States during the early and mid-nineteenth century had long been centered in New York City. Since Jacksonian days labor organizations in the city had been politically aware and politically active to a degree not common elsewhere in the country.[9] These workers, many of them German-speaking immigrants, were far from the bottom of the social ladder. They were not likely to be found in the subtidal basements discovered by the Citizens' Association investigators. Instead, they were for the most part skilled craftsmen and laborers in specific trades: bricklayers, carpenters, millwrights, and the like. Though they traditionally voted with the Democracy, the Radical coalition had from an early date hoped to break these traditional affiliations and to win them over to the new reform alliance within the Republican Party.[10] This is not to say that the Radicals were all ideologically committed labor reformers; they were not. Their attitudes toward workingmen, however, were fairly flexible and politically optimistic because the

[9] Edward Pessen, "The Workingmen's Movement of the Jacksonian Era," *Mississippi Valley Historical Review*, XLIII (1956), 428–443; Joseph G. Rayback, *A History of American Labor* (New York, 1966), p. 104.
[10] *Times*, Nov. 4, 1866, p. 4.

laboring man was a potential Radical voter. The idea of adopting labor legislation, if it was carefully drafted to win electoral rewards, seemed perfectly sound.

When Reuben Fenton had first run for governor in the fall of 1864 against Horatio Seymour, the corresponding secretary of the New York City Workingmen's Union, John G. Woodruff, had addressed identical public letters to both candidates soliciting their views on specific labor questions. Foremost among Woodruff's queries was one asking the feasibility of enacting a limit of eight hours for a legal day's work. Seymour never answered the letter. Fenton, while avoiding a direct stand on the eight-hour issue, responded with a statement that indicated a considerable degree of compatibility between his own social philosophy and that of the workingmen.

Fenton began his response to Woodruff by contrasting the aristocratic Southern civilization, "which rest[ed] upon labor enslaved and ignorant," with the open-enterprise civilization of the North, "which glorie[d] in the freedom and enlightenment of its laborers." This contrast had been a basic tenet of Republican ideology since the party's formation.[11] He then went on to sympathize with the workingmen because the titanic struggle between the slave system and the free system had diverted public attention from the problems of Northern workingmen just when those problems were growing more acute than they had been during earlier stages in the nation's development. Fenton perceived clearly that "the wonderful virgin resources of this country," what Frederick Jackson Turner later regarded as labor's safety valve, had already become, in practical terms, inaccessible to any "excess of labor"

---

[11] Foner, *Free Soil*, chaps. i and ii.

in New York. As the nation grew older and the frontier receded, fresh opportunities became "more distant and difficult,
the elements of society indurate[d] into fixedness, and the
tyranny of capital, which is naturally selfish, [began] to be
manifested." Consequently, Fenton suggested to the workingmen, he believed that the state now had a legitimate role to
play in solving the "great problems of social economy."[12]

Workingmen at the same time offered substantial hints to
the Republicans that they could indeed be lured away from
their traditional Democratic ties. And the Republican press
in New York City gave these hints prominent coverage. During the same gubernatorial campaign, for example, the *Times*
reported happily that the woodworkers of the city had held
a mass rally to urge reform of the city government. They
not only resolved "to shake from our limbs the debasing chain
of party despotism, by which we have been bound, and arise
in the native dignity of workingmen to assert and maintain
the equal right to participate in forming and executing the
laws by which we are governed," but voted to constitute
themselves an adjunct of the Citizens' Association in order to
help work for municipal reform, if need be, from the state
level. Mr. Poer, the principal speaker at the rally, asserted
that the Citizens' Association and the Republican Party were
the workingmen's friends rather than their enemies as the
Democratic Party had so long argued. "And, my friends," he
continued, "if they don't succeed, though I think they will,
they will at least have dissipated forever the idea that wealth
and aristocracy was [*sic*] the enemy of the workingman."
Jacob Simon offered similar remarks in German, emphasizing particularly the sanitary reforms then getting under way.
Such statements surely nourished Radical hopes that a reform

---

[12] Fenton to Woodruff, published in *Times*, Oct. 8, 1864, p. 4.

program might win the support of the "honest mechanic" class.[13]

The *Tribune* was even more optimistic than the *Times* that workingmen might be brought into the Republican fold, particularly in light of the party fluidity of the postwar era. During the campaign of 1864, the *Tribune* gave prominent attention to union activities that suggested the labor vote might be drifting away from its old Democratic moorings and hinted that workingmen might now be induced to attach themselves to the party offering them the most attractive legislative program.[14] On the eve of the elections of 1864 the *Tribune* ran an "Appeal to Workingmen," urging them to enter the Republican camp immediately.[15] Although the workingmen did not seem to respond in very great numbers that year, the significant fact is that the Radicals came increasingly to believe that such a merger was more than a fleeting possibility. Especially as the rift between themselves and the old Whiggish leaders of the party grew wider during 1865 and 1866, the Radicals felt that the labor vote might be won over.

During 1865 and 1866, workingmen themselves continued to reinforce this impression. The price they seemed to demand for their support was adoption of their most prominent issue: the eight-hour day. In 1865, Ira Steward, one of the leading spokesmen for the eight-hour movement in the United States, published a pamphlet entitled *A Reduction of Hours Is an Increase of Wages.* In this popular tract Steward dreamed of an America where every man might become a capitalist in the sense that classless cooperation would replace individual exploitation.[16] Moreover, he believed that institutional reform

[13] *Times*, Sept. 2, 1864, p. 8.
[14] Sept. 19, 1864, p. 6.
[15] Nov. 4, 1864, p. 8.
[16] Ira Steward, *A Reduction of Hours Is an Increase of Wages* (Bos-

and positive legislation rather than violent class revolution would bring this about. Steward's view seemed reasonably in accord with the Radicals' own view of social development.[17] It seemed almost inevitable that these two groups would eventually drift together, the one hoping to offset a political weakness which labor support would remedy, the other trying to place upon the state law books the principle that eight hours constituted a just day's work, and both sharing complementary theories about the future of society and the role of government.

This drifting together, however, proved to be an uneven and ambiguous process. During February 1866, while the legislature was in session, the New York State Workingmen's Assembly met in Albany. Many points were discussed, but primary interest centered on a call for a state-wide general strike beginning March 10 should the legislature fail to respond to the workingmen's plea for an eight-hour law.[18] Although this motion was not carried by the full labor convention, the members of the state legislature could see with increasing clarity that the workingmen were in earnest about their desire for legislative action.

George A. Brandreth, a prominent Radical, had already introduced an eight-hour bill into the lower house. Early in the session it was referred to the Committee on Trade and Manufactures.[19] By the end of February the bill was still bottled

---

ton, 1865), reprinted in John R. Commons *et al.*, eds., *A Documentary History of American Industrial Society*, IX (Cleveland, 1911), 284–301; Joseph Dorfman, *The Economic Mind in American Civilization* (New York, 1946), II, 980.

[17] Montgomery, *Beyond Equality*, pp. 259, 305, and *passim*.

[18] *Times*, Feb. 7, 1866, p. 1; *Tribune*, Feb. 7, 1866, p. 5; Albany *Evening Journal*, Feb. 10, 1866, p. 1.

[19] *Assembly Journal, 1866*, pp. 32, 39. Brandreth, an incumbent, had voted during the 1865 session for both the fire department and the

up in that committee, so Brandreth decided to offer a resolution forcing the committee to report the measure. When he did so, however, John L. Parker, an equally prominent Radical, appended a crippling amendment, and the venture was finally scrapped by laying the original motion on the table.[20] Parker had been the floor manager of previous Radical reform bills, and his voting record on the fire and health measures corresponded exactly to Brandreth's. Perhaps nothing illustrates more pointedly the divided feelings of the Radicals on the problems of labor.

The major Republican dailies reflected the ambiguous outlook of the New York Radicals on this issue. In Albany the *Evening Journal* recognized the immense political potentiality of the eight-hour issue, but urged the workingmen to seek a nonlegislative method of securing their demands before having recourse to political action. Perhaps the laborers could persuade the factory owners that a shorter day would actually result in greater and more efficient production.[21] The *Times* believed that "statutory restrictions to the natural workings of the laws of trade always deaden the energy of those whom they favor."[22] Adam Smith could not have put it more plainly. "It is to be hoped," the *Times* editorialized, "that the intelligent men among the laboring class, who are quite capable of reasoning for themselves on this subject [i.e., they did not need unions or political demagogues], will understand the wisdom of harmonizing their interest with that of their em-

---

health bills. He had also voted earlier in the 1866 session against substituting the senate version of the health bill for the one favored by the Fenton Radicals in the assembly.

[20] *Ibid.*, p. 494. Parker's amendment would have changed the date of reporting from March 2 to May 2. The assembly customarily adjourned in mid-April.

[21] Albany *Evening Journal*, Feb. 10, 1866, p. 2.

[22] Feb. 25, 1866, p. 4.

ployers, and will fully study all the bearings and consequences of the proposed reform, before committing themselves to its support." In the finest Whig tradition, the *Times* simultaneously banged the drum of the cooperative movement as an alternative to legislation like the eight-hour day.[23]

The *Tribune* also searched for some less objectionable alternative to the specter of strikes and class legislation. It was in this connection that Greeley uttered some of his more famous remarks concerning the desirability of workingmen moving west. But as Governor Fenton himself had already pointed out, this was no answer. The *Tribune*'s other alternative was to interest workingmen in directing their political energies toward procuring a higher tariff as the best means of insuring their prosperity.[24] When a general strike, as suggested in the workingmen's convention, began to loom as a serious possibility in March 1866, the *Tribune* advised strongly against it.[25]

Throughout February and March 1866, petitions poured into the state assembly in favor of the eight-hour bill, which still hung in committee. These petitions, many of which came from workingmen in urban centers like Buffalo, Rochester, Utica, and Oswego, aptly testified once again that the problems of urban industrial life were beginning to affect the entire state. New York City and its immediate vicinity still remained the center of labor activity, however, and the largest single petition, carrying over eight thousand signatures,

[23] Feb. 8, 1866, p. 4.

[24] Van Deusen, *Greeley*, pp. 330–332, points out that the *Tribune*'s editor shared Radicalism's ambiguous attitude toward the problems of the workingman. He was a frequent and popular speaker at labor functions, and he had a genuine desire to help the workingman get ahead, but he never believed that unionization was wise and did not support the eight-hour day until he ran for President in 1872.

[25] March 31, 1866, p. 6.

came from Brooklyn.[26] With this pressure increasing, the eight-hour bill was at last reported from committee on March 9, one day prior to the strike deadline previously suggested by the more activist labor leaders. Yet on the same day Brandreth failed to muster the necessary two-thirds vote to bring the measure before the assembly. Not until late the next day, taking advantage of a sparsely attended Friday session, could Brandreth reverse this vote and carry his motion to have the bill made a special order of business.

The special order was made for Thursday evening, March 16, and at that meeting of the assembly the bill was advanced to a third reading by the unusually tiny vote of 45 to 20. After proper engrossing, the bill came up ten days later for its final passage. Brandreth availed himself of that occasion to deliver a major address on the subject of the eight-hour bill, ticking off reason after reason for supporting the measure. Over 93,000 workingmen stood behind the demand, he asserted, and some 27,000 had actually petitioned for the bill. Why had no capitalists petitioned in opposition, if it was really so bad? An eight-hour law would produce labor uniformity throughout the state, permit more efficient production, enable factory owners to utilize more labor-saving machinery, and offer the workingman more time for educational and cultural pursuits. Less working time would allow more travel time; consequently, the workers could spread out into the villages and escape the debilitation of urban crowding. The workingman had rallied to the Union in its hour of need; it was now time to rally to the cause of the workingman. "Make this bill a law," Brandreth claimed in his peroration,

[26] *Assembly Journal, 1866*, pp. 159, 220, 267, 326, 494, 495, 499, 536, 638, 686, 706, 729, 776, 877, 1151.

"and the plaudits of a grateful people, the approval of an enlightened conscience will always attend us."

Brandreth also introduced a great deal of quasi-scientific evidence which purported to demonstrate that eight hours was the perfect period of labor for the human animal and that longer periods of work shortened human life. Interestingly, his evidence persuaded him that this was only true for factory labor. There was nothing to suggest that farm labor in any amount shortened human life. As a result he was able to accept a stipulation insisted upon by John Parker which exempted agricultural workers from the provisions of the proposed law. Brandreth made one of his best points in response to a challenge from the floor. When asked whether he had tried in his own pill factory the experiment that he now urged upon the entire state, the assemblyman could answer yes and expound from personal observation the validity of each of the theoretical arguments he had just presented.[27] Notwithstanding Brandreth's efforts, however, the final vote went against the eight-hour bill: 53 assemblymen favored passage, while 64 members cast ballots in opposition.[28]

A division within the Radical ranks was evident on this vote. Although Brandreth led the fight to secure passage of the bill, and Edmund Pitts, who was later elected Speaker of the assembly by the Radical majority in 1867, moved an unsuccessful reconsideration of the vote which defeated it, a significant number of votes against the measure were cast by Republican assemblymen who had consistently favored each of the other reforms undertaken by the Radical coalition. Forty-six of the seventy-two assemblymen who had backed the Governor by voting against the senate version of the metropolitan health bill now opposed the eight-hour bill. Most

[27] Albany *Evening Journal*, March 28, 1866, p. 1.
[28] *Assembly Journal, 1866*, pp. 669, 701, 796–797, 1046–1047.

of the rest of the negative votes came from Whiggish Republicans, members who had bolted the caucus which decided to support the Radical version of the health bill. Moreover, although the leading Democratic journals opposed the measure in even stronger terms than the Republican press, a majority of the Democratic assemblymen voted in favor of the eight-hour bill, apparently due to constituent pressure in their home districts. In short, the political implications of the labor movement in New York State, at least as they pertained to the specific issue of the eight-hour day, were far from clear during the 1866 session of the state legislature. Though the *Evening Journal* was surprised that the eight-hour bill could muster 53 votes at all, a disappointed Brandreth vowed on behalf of the workingmen's association to fight the issue through again next year despite rumors that the manufacturers were organizing counterassociations of their own.[29]

The political implications of the eight-hour movement were still hazy when the new, and more decidedly Radical, session of the state legislature convened in 1867. In fact, the same story seemed to be unfolding once again. The Republicans appeared uneasy over the issue, and their popular organs begged the question. The Democrats were again under intense constituent pressure to back such a measure, even though their own newspapers still opposed it unequivocally. The only thing not in doubt was the attitude of the workingmen themselves.

The New York State Workingmen's Assembly, again holding its annual meeting in Albany, was just as anxious as ever that its pet project be enacted. When the newly elected president of the assembly suggested that continued agitation on the eight-hour question might rock the reasonably prosperous boat in which the skilled trades found themselves during the

[29] Albany *Evening Journal*, March 29, p. 2; 30, 1866, p. 2.

first months of 1867, he was threatened with instant impeachment and with a walkout by the convention's largest delegations.[30] John Parr of the Albany Printers' Union seemed more in tune with the predominant notes of the meeting when he reminded his fellows that the "house-painters and ship-caulkers had suffered a reverse in the failure of their attempt to obtain the same benefit by other than legislative action," and that the workingmen should, therefore, maintain pressure on the legislature as the best possible means of establishing eight hours as a legal day's work.[31] The convention eventually endorsed the eight-hour resolution of the National Labor Congress and even went on record in favor of forming a separate labor party.[32]

The political aspects of the eight-hour question were further muddled when the 1867 version of the eight-hour bill was introduced into the assembly, not by a Radical as in 1866, but by a Brooklyn Democrat, Patrick Keady, former president of the New York Practical Painters' Association and one of the most prominent labor politicians in the state.[33] Keady may have been trying to steal a march on the Republican majority by introducing the eight-hour bill himself, or more likely, the individual Radicals were loath to sponsor a measure which might again divide them. By allowing a Democrat to introduce the measure, those Radicals who favored the eight-hour bill could help to pass it, while avoiding the necessity of making it a party issue and therefore a bone of contention with those Radicals who did not believe it belonged in their postwar program of civil and institutional reform.

[30] *Tribune*, Feb. 7, 1867, p. 4.

[31] *Times*, Feb. 6, 1867, p. 8, April 15, 1866, p. 4.

[32] Albany *Evening Journal*, Feb. 7, 1867, p. 2.

[33] *Journal of the Assembly of the State of New York at Their Ninetieth Session, 1867* (Albany, 1867), pp. 40, 47; Montgomery, *Beyond Equality*, pp. 106, 210–211.

The press did little to straighten things out. The *Times,* delighted with the bill's defeat in 1866, continued to view the scheme as "unwise and ill-advised." It still considered the eight-hour bill "calculated to damage industry, injure the workingman, and disarrange the legitimate workings of economic laws."[34] The elimination of the most Whiggish Republicans in the wake of the 1866 elections, however, greatly reduced the influence of the *Times* in Albany, and even though a number of the Radicals surely agreed with the *Times* on this particular issue, the stance of the New York City Democracy and the Fenton press would prove politically more significant.

Ironically, the *World* and the *Tribune* found themselves similarly torn. Neither believed that the eight-hour bill was sound in principle, yet both recognized its serious political ramifications. If the labor vote could really be drawn off by the party which championed the eight-hour idea, then there was a great deal of political influence at stake, perhaps even control of the state in the foreseeable future. Nevertheless, the *World* decided to take a forthright stand against the eight-hour bill. In light of the traditionally close links between the Democracy and urban labor this was a reasonably courageous, if somewhat unexpected, position. "He is no friend of the workingman," ran a major editorial after the defeat of the bill in 1866, "who does not tell them [*sic*] plainly that in this struggle which they have sought, justice was not on their side. As for legislating eight hours to be a day's work, it is contrary to the true interest of the workingmen that government, city, state, or federal, should meddle with the matter at all." Nor did the *World* stop with these arguments. Sounding almost like those Republicans pilloried in later decades as "robber barons" and plutocrats, the most articulate voice of

[34] March 30, p. 4; April 1, p. 4; 8, 1867, p. 4.

the downstate Democracy presented all of the usual refine-
ments of laissez-faire doctrine:

Such a law would benefit only a small class of workmen . . . no
law whatever, no number of hours, can hereafter, any more than
now, be the measure of a day's work in the various industries of
different men. . . . a great war has to be paid for; we must take
less wages for the same work. . . . the banker can avoid [paying
off the war debt] not a whit better than the hod-carrier; the long-
shoreman must submit to it as well as the lawyer.[35]

This editorial stance never altered throughout 1867, but
the political situation grew more complex. Not only had most
Democratic legislators favored the bill in 1866 and a Democrat introduced the new bill in 1867, but the Democratic
Party in neighboring Connecticut also came out for the eight-
hour day in that state. Despite the increasingly uncomfortable
position in which the *World* thus found itself, it stuck to its
belief that the eight-hour idea was a chimera. It was not the
lack of an eight-hour law which hurt the workingman, but
rather "the extravagance of a Radical Congress."[36] The *Tribune*, champion of the New York State Radicals, preferred
to say nothing on the subject of the eight-hour bill throughout the early spring of 1867, thereby accepting rather than
attempting to resolve the ambiguities and the individual dilemmas within the Radical coalition.

Keady's eight-hour bill was referred to the Committee on
Trade and Manufactures, where it remained throughout the
month of February. In early March, prompted at least in part
by a renewed flood of petitions from around the state, the
bill's most active Radical proponent, Henry Cribben of Roch-

[35] May 14, 1866, p. 5.
[36] Feb. 16, 1867, p. 4. The *World* blamed the workingmen's trou-
bles on the protective tariff, the greenbacks, and the stagnation of the
Southern economy under Radical government.

ester, reported the measure to the full assembly.[37] Cribben, a thirty-two-year-old iron moulder who had immigrated from England, was a workingman himself and a Republican "representing the laboring classes" who knew from "his own experience, what [was] for the good of the working people, both in his own city and in the State at large."[38] Although the lower house denied a motion to print copies of the bill for circulation to the various lawmakers, the motion of another Radical assemblyman, John Oakey of Brooklyn, made the measure a special order for March 22, 1867.[39]

At the appointed time, the eight-hour proposal was debated for almost three hours, and the Radicals' uncertainty over the problems of labor grew obvious. Oakey defended the bill in a major speech, while John Parker, still skeptical, branded it "class legislation." Oakey responded that all legislation was in some degree class legislation, and the discussion ran on.[40] Finally, in a vote of 60 to 12, the measure was passed on for engrossment.[41]

As finally engrossed, however, the eight-hour bill contained a bundle of legal contradictions and open questions. Unlike many working-day laws, this one was not limited to governmental employees and theoretically applied to every worker in the state. Consequently, a massive problem of enforcement was built into the proposal. Furthermore, the rural legislators had insisted upon exempting farm labor from the provisions of the proposed statute. Worst of all, from the point of view

[37] *Assembly Journal, 1867*, pp. 219, 317, 378, 423, 424, 464, 466, 504, 534, 535, 580, 605, 665, 821, 872, 910, 1027.
[38] Harlow and Boone, *Life Sketches of the State Officers*, p. 233.
[39] *Assembly Journal, 1867*, pp. 566, 695.
[40] Albany *Evening Journal*, April 2, 1867, p. 1.
[41] *Assembly Journal, 1867*, p. 891. Thirty-seven Republicans and twenty-three Democrats voted aye, ten Republicans and two Democrats nay.

of the workingmen, was a guarantee of the freedom of contract. In practice this might render the law meaningless, since the worker in any industry was free to negotiate any contract that he desired or that his employer made a condition of retaining his job, and thereby ignore the eight-hour stipulation.[42] Still, an endorsement of the basic principle seemed to be at stake, and individual members of the Radical coalition continued to agonize over whether to make it. Not until March 27 did the measure come up for a final vote. Amid confusion and doubt, and with an unusual number of assemblymen asking to be excused from the roll call, the eight-hour bill passed the assembly 73 to 39.[43] Thirty-five Republicans voted for the bill while thirty-six Republicans voted against it: excellent evidence of the Radical uncertainty. Speaker Edmund Pitts, Fenton's chief lieutenant in the lower house, voted against this Keady measure though he had favored Brandreth's proposal a year before. The Democrats, despite the unbending opposition of their leading political journal, voted overwhelmingly in favor of passage, 38 to 3.

The eight-hour bill arrived in the senate on March 28, 1867. By April 1 the Committee on Manufactures had reported it to the whole senate, and on April 5 the proposal was debated at length. Senator Charles Folger offered an amendment calling for a restriction on the factory work of people under eighteen years of age, in essence a child-labor law. Adam Kline and Samuel Campbell, both in the woolen milling business, responded that such a law would kill their entire industry, and the amendment was rejected. Though Thomas Parsons, a Fenton Radical from labor-conscious Rochester, delivered a

---

[42] Montgomery, *Beyond Equality*, p. 303.
[43] *Assembly Journal, 1867*, p. 970. The vote became 75 to 39 after two assemblymen were allowed to add their ballots to the roll call (*ibid.*, pp. 972, 975).

prepared speech in favor of the eight-hour bill, Kline bluntly summarized the feelings of those Republicans in opposition. "This is a free country," he asserted in an almost classic cliché of nineteenth-century industrialism, "and everybody ought to be allowed to work just as long as he pleases. The whole matter is in the hands of the employés [*sic*] themselves."[44] Unwilling to pass the law, yet not anxious to go on record against it either, the majority voted to lay it on the table of the Committee of the Whole.[45]

While the bill remained frozen, apparently in danger of expiring, external pressure for passage increased sharply. The senators not only received the usual petitions, but also learned of a serious strike threat in the New York City area.[46] A similar threat had been made during the previous spring, and although no strike had materialized then, the unrest had convinced several building contractors to delay desperately needed housing starts in the city lest the construction trades walk out and abandon half-finished structures.[47] By the spring of 1867, labor's accumulated frustrations were one year greater, wages were tapering off, and the national economy had begun to stumble.[48] Furthermore, during the summer of 1866, the advocates of a national labor union had also picked up the

[44] Albany *Evening Journal*, April 6, pp. 1, 2; 13, 1867, p. 1.

[45] *Journal of the Senate of the State of New York at Their Nine-tieth Session, 1867* (Albany, 1867), pp. 555, 608, 705.

[46] For the petitions, see *ibid.*, pp. 654, 922. For the threat of a strike in New York City, see *World*, April 16, 1867, p. 4; *Tribune*, March 28, 1867, p. 4; *Times*, April 8, 1867, p. 4.

[47] *Times*, April 27, 1866, p. 4. This had the secondary effect of worsening the housing shortage and the tenement problem.

[48] Ralph Andreano, ed., *The Economic Impact of the American Civil War* (Cambridge, Mass., 1962, 1967), Table IV-2, pp. 220–221, reveals that the wages of the unskilled fell precipitously between January and July 1867, while the wages of the skilled only held steady after a long series of gains.

eight-hour cause and now used it as a rallying point and organizing principle.[49] In short, the prospects of a major strike
appeared very real in the spring of 1867, and New York
City's journeymen were threatening to touch it off by walking out in early April.[50] When they did so, legislative action
resumed in the senate.

On April 16, 1867, Charles Folger moved that the eight-
hour bill be granted its third reading, and the senate accorded
it a place on the docket for the very next day. The strike in
th metropolitan area was then ten days old, and the prices
of food and building materials, both of which had doubled
since the outbreak of the war, were shooting up rapidly once
again.[51] The press reported that similar strikes had begun in
various parts of Pennsylvania, in Chicago, and in New England. A period of widespread labor unrest seemed imminent.
This labor turmoil, when combined with the political pressure
already bearing on many senators, proved sufficient to bring
about a hasty concurrence by the upper house in the assembly's passage of the eight-hour bill. Though George Andrews
continued to insist that the measure was a humbug "profess-
[ing] to do something it does not do, and cannot do," in part
because, "the classes excepted from its provisions are those
from whom the most hours of labor are requireed," Folger
shot back with a defense of the principles and precedents
inherent in the bill. Radical James Gibson concurred, calling
the proposal "a step in the right direction," and he expressed
displeasure that children's and women's provisions had not
been incorporated in it.[52] The final vote, taken April 17, 1867,
was 23 in favor to 5 opposed.[53] Although Fenton delayed

---

[49] Rayback, *American Labor*, pp. 115–117, 127.

[50] *Tribune*, March 28, 1867, p. 4; *Times*, April 8, 1867, p. 4.

[51] *World*, April 16, 1867, p. 4.

[52] Albany *Evening Journal*, April 17, 1867, p. 2.

[53] *Senate Journal, 1867*, p. 929. Republicans Andrews, Barnett, Platt,

signing the bill for almost three weeks, he ultimately approved "an act to limit the hours of labor constituting a day's work in this State to eight hours."[54]

The *Tribune* admitted that the eight-hour bill had not been a strict party measure; it could hardly have argued otherwise. But even so, that paper was not hesitant in trying to claim for the Radicals whatever political benefit might be derived from the bill's passage. "This is the spirit of a Republican Legislature," asserted the *Tribune,* and "we ask our opponents in Connecticut [where a spring election was about to take place] to note."[55] Or again: "The Workingmen of Connecticut will remember that this is the act of a Republican Legislature."[56] Considering the final votes, especially the one in the assembly, these declarations must have rung hollow. A strong case could have been made by the *World,* which vied with the *Tribune* for influence in Connecticut as well as in New York, that the Democracy was the party most committed to the principle of the eight-hour bill and that the Republicans, uncertain and divided, were acting almost exclusively from motives of fear. Yet the *World* never made this argument. Instead it continued to believe that the bill was the wrong answer to a difficult question.[57] The *Tribune,* invariably less reticent in such matters, had no qualms about claiming another feather for the cap of Radical reform in New York State. In short, while the *World* had a good claim that

and Wilbor and Democrat Chambers voted no; Republicans Pierson and Williams and Democrats C. G. Cornell and Sutherland did not vote. All other senators voted yes.

[54] Fenton delayed signing until May 9, 1867, pending developments in the various strikes around the nation, particularly the large and violent one which rocked Chicago in the first week of May (Montgomery, *Beyond Equality*, p. 324; *Times*, May 13, 1867, p. 4).

[55] March 23, 1867, p. 4.

[56] *Tribune*, March 28, 1867, p. 4.

[57] *World*, March, 29, 1867, p. 8.

it did not want, the *Tribune* had a weak claim that it tried to assert for whatever political benefits the claim might be worth.

The *World* had called the eight-hour bill, passed as it was during the journeymen's strike, worthy of "Danton or Mirabeau," and agreed with George Andrews that the law was a farce.[58] Both Senator Andrews and the *World* may have been correct in their contempt for the measure, though possibly for the wrong reasons. The eight-hour bill proved one of the least substantial of the postwar reforms passed by the Radicals of New York State. The phrasing of the law had left it extremely weak, and the Albany *Evening Journal* pointed out at the time what recent research has subsequently confirmed, that all eight-hour legislation was ultimately worthless "unless some administrative agency compelled citizens to comply with the laws' provisions."[59] And as the workingmen themselves soon realized, New York State did not turn out to be one of those places where the governmental authorities worked actively to implement the reform statute.[60] Four months after the bill's passage, the New York State Workingmen's Association complained that the law was not being enforced and requested the Governor to issue a special proclamation compelling local authorities to abide by its provisions. Fenton refused to do this.[61] Where laborers wanted the eight-hour day in fact as well as in principle, they had to win it for themselves, as the New York City bricklayers did in 1868 with a well-fought strike. Otherwise the actual impact of the

[58] April, 19, 1867, p. 5.

[59] Albany *Evening Journal*, March, 28, 1867, p. 2; Montgomery, *Beyond Equality*, pp. 325–326.

[60] *Times*, June 24, 1867, p. 4.

[61] Fenton to Alexander Troup, secretary of New York State Workingmen's Association, Sept. 26, 1867, published in *Times*, Oct. 1, 1867, p. 1.

Eight-Hour Law on the conditions of labor in the state was practically negligible.

As a matter of principle, however, the Eight-Hour Law cannot be ignored entirely. It is possible to accept the futility of the measure in practice, but still recognize that it did have some symbolic importance. Regardless of the inefficacy of the statute, workingmen did want to see the measure placed on the law books. Furthermore, even after the weakness of such laws had been demonstrated, workingmen continued to lobby for more of the same.[62] The Eight-Hour Law also had some importance as a legal precedent, not only for labor's demands in later decades but for subsequent federal legislation.[63] Nevertheless, New York's Eight-Hour Law cannot be labeled one of the substantively important results of the reconstruction at home. Labor's one big demand during the postwar period had not really been met; it had been neutralized.

III

None of the confusion and ambiguity that beset the Radicals on the eight-hour bill was evident in their effort during the same session of the legislature to impose certain standards of health and safety on tenement houses in the metropolitan district. Instead, a pattern closer to the 1865 fire department battle and the 1866 health department fight emerged. The Fenton Republicans, needing local issues, votes in New York City and Brooklyn, and an ongoing program to hold them together as the issues arising from the sectional conflict receded, decided to force additional civil reform from the state level on the entrenched Democrats at the local level. In the question of tenement house standards the Radicals hit upon an-

[62] Montgomery, *Beyond Equality*, p. 326.
[63] Rayback, *American Labor*, pp. 118–119.

other particularly acute social problem desperately in need of governmental attention.

The seriousness of the problem of tenement conditions had been recognized, of course, long before the 1867 session of the legislature got under way. Lawrence Veiller, a resident New Yorker and perhaps the best-known figure in the long, slow process of housing reform, credited City Inspector Gerritt Forbes with first identifying the tenement as potentially dangerous in 1834. Very little notice was taken, however, until 1842, when another city inspector, Dr. John H. Griscom, appended to his annual report a special section stressing the hazard to public health and safety created by the increasing number of tenements in the city. Dr. Griscom seems to have been the first to suggest that legislation might be brought to bear upon the problem. After the founding of the Association for Improving the Condition of the Poor (AICP) in 1846, somewhat more heed was paid to conditions in the city's tenements, especially after the AICP published a special report on the subject in 1853. A more rigorous AICP study of housing conditions in the eleventh ward appeared in 1854, and in 1856 a legislative committee was sent to New York City to look into the housing situation. This committee reported that conditions in the city's tenement districts were just as horrible as the AICP and others had described them. But the legislature took no action; indeed, it even denied the committee public funds to extend its brief survey through the summer months. Consequently, as the Civil War broke out, housing standards in New York City remained completely free from legislative regulation.[64]

[64] Lawrence Veiller, "Tenement House Reform in New York City, 1834–1900," in Robert W. DeForest and Lawrence Veiller, eds., *The Tenement House Problem* (New York, 1903), pp. 71–92; Atkins, *Health, Housing and Poverty*, pp. 9–10.

Even before the end of the war, New York City had faced a housing shortage. When the conflict ended, discharged Union soldiers began to drift into the city and an already substantial rate of immigration rose even higher, worsening the problem. Landlords demanded and received extremely high rents for the few vacancies, and according to the press, many families were forced to contract for rentals well above what they could reasonably afford to pay for lodging. The result was to force additional people into the already cramped tenement districts of the city, where conditions had been wretched to start with. Moreover, since there was no difficulty renting any available space for a handsome rate regardless of its condition, landlords had no incentive to make improvements. In this situation, the traditional open market, with its sacred laws of supply and demand, worked not to the betterment of society but to its detriment. Government at some level would have to step in and demand of the tenement owners the health and safety standards that the market failed to exact from them.[65]

The city press had seen problems developing even as the war ground to a halt. As early as December 1864, for example, the *Tribune* ran a major editorial deploring the conditions then existing in the tenements. Comparing an article from the Manchester (England) *Examiner* describing conditions in that city with the annual reports of the local city inspector, the *Tribune* concluded that the very worst tenements Manchester had to offer would appear cheery and healthful beside their counterparts in New York. Among other factors, the editorial pointed out that only the poorest sections of the English city were characterized by "a house of four rooms to every 1½ families, averaging 3.64 persons each," whereas "in

[65] *Times*, Dec. 12, 1864, p. 4; *World*, Feb. 11, p. 4, March 16, p. 4; 25, 1865, p. 8.

the *whole* of this city the average number of families per house is three, and of persons, fifteen."[66] The *Times* had begun to call for state action directed at the housing crisis in January 1865, and it hoped that the Republican administration might pass something akin to London's 1848 Lodging-House Act, which among other things had limited the number of persons permitted to reside in a given amount of space.[67] In February 1865, the *Tribune* likened continued inaction on the tenement problem to "gambling with Satan."[68]

The data concerning health standards in the tenements brought out by the *Sanitary Report* of the Citizens' Association in 1865 combined with the threat of cholera in 1866 to focus public attention still more sharply on the deplorable conditions in New York's poorest housing complexes. Significantly, those conditions were now viewed not only as wretched for the inhabitants, but as a threat to the health of the entire city. The *World*, for instance, took time out from its election coverage during the fall of 1865 to warn New Yorkers about the deterioration of health and safety standards. Calling the average tenement "King Cholera's Five-Story Throne," the paper, albeit somewhat melodramatically, pointed out that "slowly, but surely, across the deep" the king was coming to claim his seat:

Scattered all over our city are pestilential hells, which are commonly known by the mild and insignificant title of Tenement Houses. They are nothing more nor less than repulsive plague-spots, reeking with filth and rank with poison and disease.

Truthfully it can be said, and those who are qualified to speak from experience will verify the statement, that of all the diabolical, horrid, atrocious, fiendish, and even hellish systems of money-

[66] Dec. 27, 1864, p. 4.
[67] Jan. 23, 1865, p. 4.
[68] Feb. 16, 1865, p. 4.

making ever invented by the mind of man, the tenement-house system of this city, is the most horrible, and the sum of all that is enormously repulsive, fearful and devilish.[69]

Bearing in mind that the *World* would not only cry first, but would also cry loudest and longest, for the principle of local jurisdiction over local problems, this was one of the most forthright indictments of the tenement house system to appear in the popular press.

As was the case with both the fire department and the health department, political complications had allowed the situation in the tenements to get out of the hands of local Democrats, whose working agreements with the tenement owners had become still another political liaison standing in the way of needed reform.[70] As a result, individual Democratic state legislators found themselves facing a political dilemma. On the one hand, their constituents wanted something done about living standards; on the other hand, the local Tammany Democracy refused to take any action. During the spring of 1866, tenement residents in predominantly German and overwhelmingly Democratic Tompkins Square held a rally to protest against the conditions where they and almost all other immigrants were forced to live. Democratic assemblymen from neighboring districts felt compelled to attend this meeting, though the legislature was still in session in Albany, and despite rain squalls three of them addressed the crowd. Each legislator vowed to support any bill which would, as one of the German translators phrased it, "oppose the aggression of the rich upon the working-classes." Thomas J. Creamer even risked reminding the audience that "you are the fountain of power and of law; be careful, therefore, that you send only such men to your legislative halls as will obey

[69] Nov. 2, 1865, p. 1.
[70] *Tribune*, March 12, 1867, p. 1.

your interests and do as you tell them."[71] This, of course, was exactly what the Radicals hoped voters like these would do, for the Radicals knew that the Democratic Party was not, in fact, addressing itself to the plight of the tenement dwellers.[72]

With Creamer's reasoning in mind, the Radical majority in the 1867 session of the legislature adopted the cause of tenement house regulation as a part of its program of civil and institutional reform. Although Patrick Keady, the same Democratic assemblyman who had started the eight-hour bill on its erratic course through the legislature, was the first to call for state action, the Radicals essentially commandeered his motion for an investigation of tenement house conditions in the metropolitan district. The Committee on Public Health and Medical Colleges and Societies was instructed to undertake "a thorough examination into the present condition of tenement houses in the cities of New York and Brooklyn, and report thereon to this House by bill or otherwise, suggesting such improvements as may be deemed necessary for the better protection of life and health."[73]

Under the chairmanship of Charles M. Crandall, a Fenton Republican from Allegany County, the Public Health Committee delegated to the new Metropolitan Board of Health

[71] *Ibid.*, April, 3, 1866, p. 4. The other Democratic assemblymen who spoke were Jacob Seebacker and Joseph Lyons. Former State Senator Luke F. Cozans also addressed the crowd, as did a long list of German-speaking orators.

[72] The Democrats had proposed a bill that would permit wives to testify to the terms of an orally arranged rental agreement. Many landlords were arbitrarily raising rents, even though the tenants thought that they had bargained for a specific rate for a specific period of time—an oral lease. Since the wife was often the only witness, and her testimony was not allowed against the landlord, tenants rarely won their legal grievances over arbitrary rent increases. This, however, was a minor tenement problem.

[73] *Assembly Journal, 1867*, pp. 69, 88–89.

both the jobs of preparing a report on the tenement system and of suggesting remedial legislation. This apparent abdication was actually a shrewd move for at least two reasons. First, the committee stood to receive a far better report from the Board of Health than it could possibly have prepared for itself by trooping down to New York City and poking around for a few days in the slums. Second, by referring the inquiry to the institution which they had created during the previous legislative session, any forthcoming proposals would not only bear the Radical stamp, but would also have the character of belonging to an ongoing program. In other words, the 1867 drive for tenement house regulation could now be seen as an expansion and a logical continuation of the Radical drive for municipal health reform during the 1865 and 1866 sessions.

The Metropolitan Board of Health prepared a report during the month of February and submitted it to the assembly committee in early March. The report gave Brooklyn a relatively clean bill of health. While noting that minor nuisances certainly did exist among its 2,406 tenements, the report concluded that on the whole there was really no comparison with the situation on Manhattan Island, which was much worse. In New York City itself the board counted 18,582 tenement houses and declared that 52 percent of them were "in a condition detrimental to the health and dangerous to the lives of the occupants."

The report went on to suggest two causes of improper housing conditions: unwise initial construction and subsequent overcrowding. Under the first heading were discussed factors like insufficient ventilation, absence of light, the use of basements and cellars as apartments, deficient drainage, inadequate provision for water closets or privies, and the lack of fire escapes. Under the second heading were included "accumulations of garbage, excrement and filth of every description in the yards and cellars; broken down and overflowing privies; filthy halls, stairways, water-closets and rooms; leaky rooms and broken windows"; all of these aggravated original faults of construction.[74]

This report caught the attention of the *Tribune* which thanked the Board of Health for its timely efforts. In a perceptive observation, the *Tribune* noted that the danger of epidemic was always so great in the worst of the tenement districts that "we ought to look upon this part of the tenement system as an organized epidemic and lose no time in reforming it."

We are well advised that it is possible to institute a steady, inevitable reform—as regards these catacombs above ground. By such a reform any increase of these evils can surely be prevented, and it only needs a persistent effort on the part of the Board of Health, assisted by the other authorities, to work a gradual dimuition [sic]. Owners are certainly responsible for the sanitary condition of the houses to which they condemn those who pay them for the privilege of being treated to slow poison. We trust that some time the power to call them to account, at least to insist on reform, will be made apparent.[75]

On March 1, Keady introduced "an act for the regulation of tenement and lodging-houses in the cities of New York and Brooklyn."[76] The bill, drafted to take effect July 1, 1867, spelled out a number of basic standards to be met before tenement houses could be licensed as rental spaces. Every sleeping room must have some source of direct ventilation in all new

[74] "Report of the Committee on Public Health, Medical Colleges and Societies, Relative to the Condition of Tenement Houses in the Cities of New York and Brooklyn," in *Documents of the Assembly of the State of New York at Their Ninetieth Session, 1867*, VII, No. 156 (Albany, 1867), p. 4.

[75] Feb. 15, 1867, p. 4.

[76] *Assembly Journal, 1867*, p. 467.

buildings erected after the law went into effect. Where this was impossible in older buildings, transoms would have to be installed to give the bedrooms a connection with the hallway or with other rooms that did have direct ventilation. For the first time, fire escapes would be required and would be subject to inspection by local authorities. At least one toilet for every twenty persons was required—in some of the older tenements the ratio had been closer to one for every hundred— and regulations concerning their proper drainage and their connection to sewers were established. It would henceforth be illegal to keep domestic animals in residential buildings. Basement apartments, the worst of which were the subtidal flats described in the Citizens' Association report two years earlier, were singled out in specific sections of the proposed code. Probably the most crucial clause in the bill declared the tenement landlord liable to a daily fine for each violation that he permitted to remain uncorrected after official notification of its existence. And the agency responsible for presenting these notices of violation was to be the Metropolitan Board of Health.[77]

More than any other feature of the proposed legislation, this inclusion of additional regulatory powers for the Metropolitan Board of Health made the bill a partisan issue. Even though Patrick Keady maintained his interest in the measure, the other Democrats in the assembly cooled on the tenement house bill when they realized that it was designed to increase both the influence and the public stature of what already seemed to be the most successful of the Radicals' municipal reforms. On March 8, Chairman Charles M. Crandall of the Public Health Committee submitted the tenement house report prepared by the Board of Health, and he also reported in favor of Keady's bill. On the 20th the proposal came up

[77] *Tribune*, March, 2, 1867, p. 5.

for debate by the whole assembly, and the bill was referred temporarily to a subcommittee of the whole. The subcommittee reported in favor of passage, and after proper engrossing, the tenement house bill came up for its third and final reading in the assembly on April 11, 1867. The assemblymen first defeated a motion by Patrick Burns of Brooklyn to have the proposal of his fellow Brooklyn Democrat recommitted for further delaying debate, and then ordered the measure's final reading. The vote to pass the bill was 66 to 32. The Republicans united in favor of the bill and accounted for all but 3 of the 66 ayes; all 32 noes were cast by Democrats.[78]

Any doubts about the partisan implications of the vote were dispelled publicly when Assemblyman Levi Blakeslee claimed on the floor that Democrats Michael Murphy, Henry Woltman, Patrick Russell, and Patrick Burns had formed a "ring" to "oppose any bill in which any member who voted for [the tenement house bill] was interested." Though Burns denied the allegation, Murphy avoided an investigation by owning up to the substance of the accusation. Murphy insisted, however, that the three renegade Democrats who answered aye "had committed an outrage in voting for a bill relative to New York, against the protests of nearly all the members from that city," and deserved party censure.[79]

The tenement house bill arrived in the senate on April 11, 1867, and was immediately referred to the Municipal Affairs Committee.[80] There technical changes were made in the statute to clarify some of the specific building provisions. The committee also reduced the amount of the daily fines imposed

[78] *Assembly Journal, 1867*, pp. 598, 809, 1147, 1297, 1310; *Tribune*, April 12, 1867, p. 1. That several Democrats asked to be excused from the vote indicates disagreement on this bill.

[79] Albany *Evening Journal*, April 12, 1867, p. 1.

[80] *Senate Journal, 1867*, p. 794.

by the law, but required that the name and address of the owner of every tenement be posted in some prominent place in or on the building itself.[81] The measure was reported by Chairman George Andrews on April 13 and ordered to its third reading later the same day. On April 17 the measure passed its third reading by a vote of 17 to 7.[82] When the assembly approved the senate's amendments, the Tenement House Act was sent to the Governor, whose signature made it a New York State law.[83]

The press in New York City favored the tenement house bill during its course through the legislature. The *Tribune*, which endorsed the idea from the outset, never altered its position. The *World*, although it remained silent following the Democratic decision to regard Keady's bill as a partisan measure for the opposition, had publicly supported the plan for housing regulation when the proposal was made in March.[84] The *Times* likewise endorsed the concept of tenement regulation, apparently oblivious to a contradiction in its argument on the one hand in favor of housing codes and on the other against the eight-hour bill. Referring to tenement house laws passed in Great Britain, the *Times* observed:

There were many objections urged against the granting of these exceptional powers [English landlords would ultimately be subject to forfeiture of any property which they continued to rent in violation of the housing code], the main argument being that if everyone is left to work out his own ideas of right, it will in the long run conduce to the welfare of the whole community. But to this objection there was the ready answer that this convenient theory has led to the very state of things that necessitates

[81] The changes are recorded verbatim in *Assembly Journal, 1867*, pp. 1670–1671.
[82] *Senate Journal, 1867*, pp. 834, 849–850, 933.
[83] *Assembly Journal, 1867*, p. 1671.
[84] *World*, March 13, 1867, p. 4.

legislation. Just as long as landlords can squeeze exorbitant rents out of tenants for dirty and fever-stricken cellars and garrets will they refuse to build better habitations.

The same theory of the open market, when applied to the length of the working day, had not been "convenient" and false but "natural" and true. In disease the *Times* evidently discerned a more direct threat to the larger community than it did in ten- or twelve-hour work days: "The fevers and other diseases bred in blind alleys and the dens, cellars and garrets, where the families of workingmen are packed together, [can and do] spread into more favored localities."[85] Whatever the theoretical inconsistencies, however, the *Times* was pleased with the new housing law and hailed it as a first step in the right direction, "if faithfully and energetically carried out."[86]

In later decades this foreboding provision, "if faithfully and energetically carried out," proved to be the rub. The *Times* felt certain that granting regulatory functions to the Metropolitan Board of Health would insure proper administration. And so it might have, if the board had remained a state commission in later years. Encouraging progress was being recorded in the annual reports of the AICP while the Metropolitan Board of Health continued to function as the Radicals had set it up.[87] But the Board of Health, like the other reform commissions imposed by the Radicals during the postwar era, reverted to local Democratic control following the fall of the Fenton Radicals from power and passage by the state legislature of the so-called "Tweed Charter" for New York City in 1870. Under Democratic administration the Tenement

[85] April 18, 1867, p. 4.
[86] April 19, 1867, p. 4.
[87] Veiller, "Tenement House Reform," pp. 96–97.

House Law ceased to be enforced, and the champions of housing reform were led off on the ultimately regressive tack of searching for the "model tenement." When this search turned up the notorious "dumb-bell" plan in the late 1870's, the Radical-passed Tenement House Law of 1867 had to be emasculated by amendments to make the design legal.[88]

The 1867 law did have flaws; the definition of a tenement, for example, as any "house, building or portion thereof, which is erected for, or rented to, or leased to more than three families, living independently of each other," permitted some of the worst buildings to escape its jurisdiction because only three large families lived in them.[89] Nevertheless, the Tenement House Law passed by the Fenton Republicans was the most progressive measure in the field of housing reform enacted prior to the twentieth century and the rise of the Progressives themselves.[90] For the first time a governmental authority, in this case the state of New York, had stepped in to demand

[88] Roy Lubove, *The Progressives and the Slums: Tenement House Reform in New York City, 1890–1917* (Pittsburgh, Pa., 1962), pp. 28–32.

[89] *Tribune*, March 2, 1867, p. 5; Lubove, *Progressives and Slums*, p. 26. The complete legal definition, of which this quote is only one section, may be found in Veiller, "Tenement House Reform," p. 94. Except for this three-family clause, which was eliminated twenty years later, the definition of a tenement established by the Tenement House Law of 1867 remained the legal definition well into the twentieth century.

[90] Lubove, *Progressives and Slums*, p. 27 and *passim*, sees 1901 as the next major breakthrough in housing legislation, and he considers a good deal of the legislation enacted between 1867 and 1901 as an ultimately regressive series of compromises with the forthright principles of regulation inherent in the 1867 statute. In many ways, in fact, the Progressives' greatest contribution seems to have been enforcing the basic provisions of the 1867 code, rather than devising codes of their own.

of tenement house owners certain basic standards of health, safety, and human decency which the open market was not demanding of them. It represented still another legislative achievement of the reconstruction at home undertaken by the Radicals in postwar New York State.

6

Educational Progress

I

When pressed to identify an enduring positive legacy of the Reconstruction era, most historians cite advances in the field of public education.[1] Frequently, however, they refer exclusively to the former Confederate states. Few historians note that far-reaching educational reforms were enacted by Radical state governments in the North at the same time. In New York the Fenton Republicans took significant action regarding both higher education and the common schools.

The politics of public education differed considerably from the politics of urban reform during the years following the Civil War. They were less obviously partisan than issues like the fire department, the Metropolitan Board of Health, or the Tenement House Law, since neither major party opposed the basic principle of better education. Lines of dispute over school bills were less likely to reflect party affiliations than

[1] Examples would include William A. Dunning, *Reconstruction, Political and Economic, 1865–1877* (New York, 1907, 1962), p. 206; W. E. Burghardt DuBois, "Reconstruction and Its Benefits," *American Historical Review*, XV (1910), 781–799; John Hope Franklin, *Reconstruction after the Civil War* (Chicago, 1961, 1967), pp. 107–110, 140–141; Kenneth M. Stampp, *The Era of Reconstruction, 1865–1877* (New York, 1965, 1967), p. 172; and Rembert W. Patrick, *The Reconstruction of the Nation* (New York, 1967), pp. 234–239.

financial considerations, local pride and jealousies, or religious divisions. The politics of public education also shifted the focus of the Fentonite reform program away from problems felt most acutely in New York City to problems felt more widely throughout the state.

To state that the politics of educational reform were not bitterly partisan in the same way that the fire, health, or tenement issues had been, however, is not to imply that they were above the political struggles of the day. They certainly were not. Deals were made, votes were bought or traded, and public opinion was mobilized just as effectively as it was for the issues of urban reform and probably on a wider scale. The popular belief in education as the prime means whereby the lowest child in society might rise on his merits to a position of higher status was just gaining strength during the period after the Civil War. Consequently, public opinion was in a state of flux; interest in the future of the state's educational structure was widespread and lively.

Nor should the observation that educational issues often tended to cut across party lines blur in any way the importance of the role played by the Radical Republicans in the drive toward significant school reform. Although many Democrats voted with Republicans in favor of various educational projects, members of the Radical coalition and political allies of Governor Fenton were the ones who not only championed the school reforms but consistently did the all-important political spadework that prepared the ground for their enactment into law. The Radical Republicans who entered the state legislature during the war and continued to build their strength during the immediate postwar years infused new life into the educational system of New York State, and in doing so revealed more about the ideological predisposition of their coalition. At the level of higher education they took two important actions. One, the founding of Cornell University, is well known, while the other, a bolstering of the state's capacity to train teachers, is frequently overlooked. At the level of elementary education they also took two important steps. The first was an extensive codification of the state's conflicting and confusing body of school law, and the second, which was among the most significant measures passed during the reconstruction in New York, abolished what was called the "rate-bill" system of school finance.

II

Although historians have placed the founding of Cornell University in different contexts, comparatively little has been done to connect the story to Radical Republican reform.[2]

[2] Devoted alumni and analytical scholars alike have told and retold the story, sometimes savoring the most minute details. Lawrence R. Veysey, *The Emergence of the American University* (Chicago, 1965), is an impressive study which places Cornell primarily in the context of an evolving sense of what the universities should teach. Merle Curti and Roderick Nash, *Philanthropy in the Shaping of American Higher Education* (New Brunswick, N.J., 1965), are concerned with the way in which Ezra Cornell's course of action became a model for others to follow during the later nineteenth century. Allan Nevins, *The State Universities and Democracy* (Urbana, Ill., 1962), integrates the story into the broad movement for a practical higher education open on an equal basis to all children in the society. Philip Dorf, in his biography of Ezra Cornell, *The Builder* (New York, 1952), naturally devotes considerable attention to the origins of the university. Waterman T. Hewett devotes a substantial portion of the first volume of his massive *Cornell University: A History*, 4 vols. (New York, 1905), to the founding, and Morris Bishop's condensed and updated *A History of Cornell* (Ithaca, 1962) naturally also discusses that event. In the first volume of his *Autobiography*, Andrew Dickson White likewise treats the circumstances surrounding the inception of the university. But probably the finest single account

Instead, most scholars have either placed it in the much larger perspective of the evolution of higher education in the United States, or they have seen it as something of a fluke, a lucky happenstance not necessarily congruent with the other events of its day.[3] Neither of these approaches takes into account the specific political circumstances that brought about the founding of the university, even though the legal chartering of Cornell was an eminently political act undertaken by the publicly elected legislators of the state of New York. Andrew Dickson White and Ezra Cornell did not come together, as Carl Becker once half-whimsically suggested, "as if by the Providence of God"; Republican voters in their home districts had sent them both to the state senate.[4] These two officeholders, one who had retired from business with close to half a million dollars more than he believed his family would need, and the other a young man fresh from a college teaching post in the Midwest who harbored the dream of a great American university in the Empire State, were thrown together in January 1864 when the legislature convened in Albany. They were not thrown together in a vacuum, but in a political arena. Moreover, they had the results of another eminently political

of the founding of Cornell University is Carl L. Becker, *Cornell University: Founders and the Founding* (Ithaca, 1943). This last was the most useful secondary source, especially since several important documents pertaining to the founding are appended, pp. 139–190. In light of the extensive research already published on this event, the present discussion is primarily concerned with placing the founding in the context of postwar reform and relies upon rather than attempts to supersede the already adequate studies just cited.

[3] The former, of course, is necessarily the perspective of studies like those of Veysey and Nevins. The latter view is implied in the studies by Bishop, Hewett, and Dorf and frankly stated in the analyses by White and Becker.

[4] Becker, *Cornell University*, p. 81.

measure to work with: the federal Morrill Land Grant College Act passed by a Republican Congress in 1862.[5]

Ezra Cornell would appear at first to be a good example of the older Whiggish sort of Republican. He acquired a fortune when his own telegraph ventures were bought out against his will in return for Western Union stock, which subsequently skyrocketed in value.[6] He was elected to the New York State senate in the fall of 1863 after two years in the assembly as a regular Republican. When the Radicals began to assume a stronger hold over the Republican Party at the state level, however, Cornell demonstrated both his political acumen and his heritage of Quaker independence by supporting the young reformers, while trying to minimize their partisan activities. In short, he became a Radical on national questions and a member of the state coalition that was enacting the Radicals' reform program, though he was not anxious to strengthen any further the position of Fenton and the former Democrats in his party.[7]

Now approaching sixty years of age, Cornell was looking for a suitable cause to which he might donate a substantial portion of his accumulated wealth. For several years he had been attracted to the idea of agricultural education at the college level, and passage of the Morrill Act intensified his interest. The most likely object for his beneficence seemed to be the struggling New York State Agricultural College located at Ovid, only twenty-five miles northwest of his beloved town of Ithaca in the heart of the Finger Lakes region of the state.[8]

[5] For the political maneuvering behind this law, see Nevins, *State Universities, passim,* and Becker, *Cornell University,* pp. 23–42.

[6] Dorf, *Builder,* pp. 192–201; Becker, *Cornell University,* pp. 43–65.

[7] Alonzo B. Cornell to White, May 5, Aug. 23, 1866, White Papers.

[8] This college, chartered in 1853, opened in 1860 as the first agricultural college in the nation. For the details of its history, see Alfred

Cornell had already begun a campaign to have at least half the funds which New York would derive from the Morrill Act reallocated to it, even though the entire proceeds had been voted by the state legislature in 1863 to the so-called People's College at Havana, New York.[9] That grant had been made conditionally, however, and it was becoming more and more obvious that the People's College, which did not physically exist, would be hard pressed to fulfill the conditions. Cornell had in mind supplementing the reallocated public funds with a donation of his own, and he believed that the combined sum might offer the institution at Ovid a reasonable chance to survive.

Cornell's reallocation bill first brought him into direct contact with Andrew White, who was on the Literature (Education) Committee of the senate. Ironically, this initial contact was a political collision because White rigidly opposed dividing up the Morrill funds. He believed that the amount likely to be realized from the whole of New York's scrip, variously estimated at up to $600,000, would be little enough as a college endowment without further parceling it out to a number of different recipients. To divide the sum, in his view, would be to reduce its potentially significant effects upon a single institution to useless drops in a number of practically empty buckets. Consequently, he fought Senator Cornell's

---

Hazen Wright, *The New York State Agricultural College* (Ithaca, 1958), No. 20 in the *Cornell Studies in History* series (Ithaca, 1937–1965).

[9] This act was passed May 14, 1863, and the allocation was in large part owing to the support given by Horace Greeley to the People's College project. Greeley was a member of the board of trustees of the college and had long been active in the revolt against classical studies. See Nevins, *State Universities*, pp. 5, 11, 16; and Alfred Hazen Wright, *The New York People's College* (Ithaca, 1958), No. 21 in the *Cornell Studies in History* series.

bill and succeeded in blocking the measure in committee. The two senators were still at loggerheads when the 1864 session of the legislature ended.[10]

No doubt intending to win over the young senator who was blocking his plan, Ezra Cornell invited White during the summer of 1864 to attend a meeting of the New York State Agricultural Society, of which Cornell was the president. The society met in Rochester, and there Cornell unveiled a new version of his plan. He told the Agricultural Society and the Board of Trustees of the Agricultural College at Ovid, as he later put it more formally in a letter to John A. King:

If you will [re]locate the College at Ithaca[,] I will give you for that object a farm of three hundred acres of first quality land desirably located, overlooking the village of Ithaca, and Cayuga Lake . . . I will also erect on the farm suitable buildings for the use of the College, and give an additional sum of money to make up an aggregate of three hundred thousand dollars, on condition that the Legislature will endow the College with thirty thousand dollars per annum [a portion of the anticipated interest on the total lump sum derived from the sale of the scrip] from the Congressional Agricultural College fund, and thus place the College upon a firm and substantial basis, which shall be a guarantee of its future prosperity and usefulness, and give to the farmers [*sic*] sons of New York an institution worthy of the Empire State.[11]

Although the trustees of the Agricultural College were delighted at the prospect of salvaging their sinking venture, White still had reservations. As he later wrote: "Much to the disgust of the meeting, I persisted in my refusal to sanction any bill dividing the fund, declared myself now more opposed

[10] White, *Autobiography*, I, 295–296; Becker, *Cornell University*, pp. 81–84.

[11] Oct. 4, 1864; reprinted in Becker, *Cornell University*, pp. 160–161.

to such a division than ever; but promised that if Mr. Cornell and his friends would ask for the *whole* grant—keeping it together, and adding his three hundred thousand dollars as proposed—I would support such a bill with all my might."[12]

White's proposal, bold as it was, eventually won over the austere Ithacan, who also decided to increase his offer from three hundred thousand dollars to half a million. Since the 1865 session of the legislature was already under way when Cornell informed White of his new position, the two hastened to draft a bill that might realize the dream they had finally agreed upon. The entire plan now hinged upon their ability to persuade the legislators that the Morrill money should be transferred away from the People's College and granted instead to their proposed institution at Ithaca; the new institution would also be authorized to incorporate within itself the relocated Agricultural College.

On February 3, 1865, White gave notice of his intention to introduce a bill to reallocate the Morrill proceeds, and by Feburary 7 he was ready to present to the senate his draft of "an act to establish the Cornell University, and to appropriate to it the income of public lands granted to this State by Congress, on the 2nd day of July, 1862." The bill was successfully referred to a joint committee of White's own Literature Committee and Ezra Cornell's Agriculture Committee.[13] But the subsequent progress of the bill was hardly smooth. As White later remembered, "the introduction of this new bill into the legislature was a signal for war," and he wrote to his friend Daniel Coit Gilman about the "desperate struggle" he had to wage on behalf of the measure during the rest of the session.[14]

[12] *Autobiography*, I, 296.
[13] *Senate Journal, 1865*, pp. 144, 155.
[14] *Autobiography*, I, 300; White to Gilman, May 6, 1865, Daniel C. Gilman Papers, Johns Hopkins University Library, Baltimore.

Each "army" in this "war" over the Cornell University bill was comprised of separate corps. Lining up in support of the bill were the New York State Agricultural Society and, incredibly enough, several members of the Board of Trustees of the People's College, the institution which stood to lose its state grant. The most valuable of these institutional turncoats was Horace Greeley, who had become disgusted with the lack of progress made by the People's College and was ready to support any new scheme with a better prospect of success.[15] Erastus Brooks, Daniel S. Dickinson, and former Governor Edwin Morgan, all of whom were also trustees of the moribund People's College, would eventually join the Radical editor in transferring their allegiances to the new project in the senate. Even Amos Brown, president of the People's College, came over to support White's and Cornell's plan to eliminate his job.[16] Brown's influence with church groups in the state proved helpful once the fighting got rough.

In the opposing army were at least three powerful corps that would have to be met in political battle. The first group, headed by former state Senator Charles Cook, was composed of the men who remained loyal to the People's College and wished to see it retain the funds awarded to it in 1863. Cook had been responsible for locating the People's College in Havana and had considered promising that institution his own large fortune.[17] He exerted his still considerable influence in

---

[15] Van Deusen, *Greeley*, p. 334.

[16] Brown to White, Aug. 15, 24, 1864, White Papers; Becker, *Cornell University*, pp. 86–89, 97n, 231; Ulysses Prentiss Hedrick, *A History of Agriculture in the State of New York* (New York, 1933, 1966), p. 422.

[17] Cook to White, Feb. 24, 1864, White Papers. Cook's actions are difficult to explain satisfactorily. He seems to have tacitly promised the People's College his fortune in return for its location in his home town, but he then seems to have backed out of his promise. Neverthe-

the legislature through Stephen T. Hayt in the senate and Lorenzo Webber in the assembly, both of whom were also from the district where the People's College was located.

Allied with Cook, and forming the second significant corps of the opposition, were nearly all of the small denominational colleges in the state of New York.[18] These institutions had at least two solid reasons to oppose the new scheme. First, Andrew White was known to desire, with Quaker Ezra Cornell's concurrence, a scrupulously nonsectarian university. This led to protests against the "godlessness" of their plan, protests that might effectively influence the upstate farmers whom Cornell and White looked to for support. Second, the denominational schools had financial axes of their own to grind, for if the People's College failed to meet its original conditions and was deprived of the Morrill proceeds, then they too would be interested in any reallocation that might take place.

The third important element lined up against the Cornell University bill was a sector of the popular press that seemed more intent upon slandering Ezra Cornell as a symbol of cor-

---

less, he still fought bitterly to keep the Morrill proceeds pledged to the institution. Daniel Dickinson never understood Cook's motives either, even though he was on the board of trustees of the college, and the confusion helped to persuade Dickinson that White's new plan offered a better hope of success. For lack of a better explanation of Cook's vacillations many fell back on an "illness" that Cook had suffered shortly before this period. Probably a stroke, the illness left him partially paralyzed and had been the reason for his retirement from the state senate. See Becker, *Cornell University*, p. 231, n. 11, and Henry S. Randall to White, Oct. 9, 1865, White Papers. During the constitutional convention debates in 1867, Thomas Alvord mentioned that "a cloud came over the mind" of Senator Cook. See *Proceedings and Debates of the Constitutional Convention of the State of New York Held in 1867 and 1868 in the City of Albany* (Albany, 1868), p. 2821 (hereafter cited as *Constitutional Debates*).

[18] There were over twenty of these, according to the annual report of the board of regents for the academic year 1863–1864.

porate wealth than opposing the actual proposal for a university. The Rochester *Democrat*, for example, apparently carried a grudge against the Western Union Company and vented its frustrations in a vicious series of editorials directed at Senator Cornell, the company's largest single stockholder. Striking up a handy alliance with tiny Rochester University, this paper posed as a defender of the people against "moneyed aristocrats" like Ezra Cornell.[19]

From the outset this tripartite force proved formidable in the legislature. The spokesmen for Havana's local interests formed a working agreement with several Whiggish Republicans who were interested above all else in securing an increase in the rates of the New York Central Railroad, and desperately needed allies of their own in order to do so.[20] Especially since Governor Fenton was known to oppose their railroad scheme, the opposition of these Whiggish Republicans gave White's bill a more Radical coloring, and several senators found themselves drawn in different directions. Of these, influential Charles J. Folger, the only member of the senate serving a third consecutive term, was in perhaps the most revealing situation. He actually helped White draft the Cornell bill, but was forced to oppose its early progress because the existing Agricultural College was located in his home district. Even before White's plan was formally introduced, citizens in the Ovid area sent Folger a remonstrance against ever removing that institution of higher learning.[21] The way White circumvented Folger's dilemma is worth sketching, for it at once gives insight into the backstage maneuverings of Andrew White, the politician, and a brief consideration of still another important postwar reform.

[19] Becker, *Cornell University*, p. 94.
[20] *Ibid.*, p. 96.
[21] *Senate Journal, 1865*, p. 85.

Just as various doctors had sought for many years to improve health standards before the rise of the Radical coalition finally gave them an opportunity to help pass the metropolitan health bill, so also had various other physicians long sought to improve the condition of the state's mentally ill. The situation of many of the mentally ill, as White described it, was "heartrending" indeed: "Throughout the State, lunatics whose families were unable to support them at the State or private asylums were huddled together in the poorhouses of the various counties. . . . They were constantly exposed to neglect, frequently to extremes of cold and hunger, and sometimes to brutality; thus mild lunacy often became raving madness." For many years, the leading champion of these miserably treated souls was Dr. Sylvester D. Willard of Albany. Each year he introduced a bill into the legislature to establish what he called "the Beck Asylum for the Chronic Insane," in honor of the leading champion of the same cause in the generation preceding his own. But session after session the bill was just as regularly rejected, "the legislature shrinking from the cost of it."[22]

In early April, as the Cornell University bill continued to founder and Folger's support was sorely needed, news reached the senate floor that Dr. Willard suddenly and dramatically, "while making one more passionate appeal for the asylum, had fallen dead in the presence of the [assembly] committee" then taking testimony on his Beck Asylum bill.[23] Andrew White did not allow whatever personal grief he may have felt to interfere with his political instincts, for he states in his *Autobiography* with surprising candor that "while the Senators were still under the influence of . . . a deep and wide-

[22] White, *Autobiography*, I, 333.
[23] *Ibid.;* Albany *Evening Journal*, April 3, p. 2; 6, 1865, pp. 1, 2,

spread feeling of compunction," he went to Folger with the
following deal:

It rests with you to remedy this cruel evil which has now cost
Dr. Willard his life, and at the same time to join us in carrying
the Cornell University Bill. Let the legislature create a new
asylum for the chronic insane of the State. Now is the time of all
times. Instead of calling it the Beck Asylum, give it the name of
Willard—the man who died in advocating it. Place it upon the
Agricultural College property on the shores of Seneca Lake in
your district. Your constituents are sure to prefer a living State
asylum to a dying Agricultural College, and will thoroughly
support you in both the proposed measures.[24]

The press considered the proposed asylum a fitting tribute
to Dr. Willard's memory, and Folger decided to accept this
dubious trade, thereby resolving his dilemma.[25] White later
felt compelled to justify his behavior by stating:

Quite likely doctrinaires will stigmatize our conduct in this
matter as "log-rolling"; the men who always criticize but never
construct may even call it a "bargain". There was no "bargain"
and no "log-rolling", but they may call it what they like; I believe that we were both of us thoroughly in the right. For our
coming together in this way gave to the State the Willard Asylum
and the Cornell University, and without our thus coming together neither of these would have been created.[26]

White was probably correct in his final assessment, even if

[24] *Autobiography*, I, 333.
[25] Albany *Evening Journal*, April 6, p. 2, May 1, 1865, p. 2.
[26] *Autobiography*, I, 334. The bill to create the Willard Asylum
for the Insane Poor passed easily and was signed by Fenton on April
8, 1865. The Governor, incidentally, was known to favor this bargain.
Willard had been Fenton's surgeon-general, and the Governor had
made specific reference to Willard's efforts on behalf of the insane
poor in his annual message less than two months earlier.

he shrank from straightforward terminology. There was a great deal of thoroughly political dealing involved in passage of the most constructive measures of the post-Civil War period. In the case of the urban reforms the most effective political pressures had been partisan. In the case of educational reform the political pressures emanated from local, religious, and financial interests, but these were no less intense and their manipulation was no less political. As many historians would have scholars see only the wirepulling of the postwar period, White would have scholars see only its positive results. One of the primary aims of this study is to see the former in the context of the latter.

More flagrant bargains than the creation of the Willard Asylum—bargains without the redeeming value of that one—were also in the works. Indeed, a few were already consummated. White had first reported the Cornell bill out of committee on February 25, but at that time the proposal was tabled on a motion by Senator Folger, who of course remained a member of the opposition until Willard's death in early April.[27] On the 28th of February the bill was removed from the table and sent back to the joint committee. Not until March 9, 1865, did White again attempt to report the bill to the whole senate. It was debated at some length during that evening and the following morning, but then recommitted for a second time to the joint committee.[28] Though White seized an opportunity during the debate to deliver a powerful speech favoring passage, a speech which he and Ezra Cornell later had published for general distribution, the bill was clearly in trouble.[29]

[27] *Senate Journal, 1865*, p. 244.

[28] *Ibid.*, pp. 275, 367, 371–372, 374–375; Albany *Evening Journal*, Feb. 27, p. 2; 28, p. 2; March 10, 1865, p. 1.

[29] White, *Autobiography*, I, 302; Albany *Evening Journal*, April 4,

With the measure bottled up in committee, White struck the first of several political bargains that determined its fate. Along with two of his allies in the senate he signed an agreement to support an amendment to his bill which had been drawn up by Cook's forces. The amendment, which tacked onto the bill's title the clause "and to restrict the operation of chapter 511 of the Laws of 1863," was actually a provision spelling out the terms under which the People's College might yet retain the Morrill proceeds. That institution was granted an additional three months in which to deposit with the state board of regents an amount of money deemed sufficient guarantee by the regents that the People's College would fulfill the conditions spelled out in the law of May 14, 1863: that is, to erect the specified number of buildings, to enroll the requisite number of students, and to meet the other obligations imposed by the legislature. This rider had the effect of giving Charles Cook three more months to decide once and for all whether or not to pledge his fortune to the bankrupt college in his home town.[30] This allowed the People's College a ray of hope, offered its advocates a chance to save face, and won for White and his friends a promise from Cook's forces to "withdraw all opposition to the [Cornell University] Bill in all its stages through the assembly [*sic*] and elsewhere." The bargain was formally witnessed, recorded by a clerk, and signed by Andrew White and two other leading defenders of

---

1865, p. 1. As Becker, *Cornell University*, p. 97, points out, not the least effective of the points made by White was that the states had a five-year period in which to meet the congressional requirements imposed by the Morrill Act or forfeit their share. Three of New York's five years had already passed, and the conditions had not yet been met.

[30] The regents set the amount at roughly $300,000; Cook's fortune was estimated at approximately $400,000.

the Cornell bill, Radicals James A. Bell and Alexander H. Bailey.[31] With this agreement reached, White reported the measure for the third time to the whole senate on March 15; on March 16 the bill was finally passed, 25 to 2, and sent over to the assembly.[32]

Opponents of the Cornell University bill in the assembly obviously did not consider the senate agreement as binding upon them as White and his allies had hoped. When the bill arrived in the lower house, it was promptly referred to a joint committee consisting of the Committee on Colleges, Academies, and Common Schools plus the Committee on Agriculture. There the proposal remained for almost a month while the session drew closer and closer to final adjournment in mid-April.[33] The bill's enemies, particularly the small denominational colleges, had gained control of a majority of the joint committee, and they planned simply to let the bill expire there without ever reporting it. Since a two-thirds vote was required to force any committee to report a bill, White's allies in the assembly, who were led by Abram B. Weaver and Henry B. Lord, had their work cut out for them. They decided to launch an attack on three fronts.[34]

The first front involved personal persuasion and public opinion. Andrew White and Ezra Cornell began a systematic campaign "to enlighten" the assemblymen, as White put it, with a series of private browbeating sessions in Albany. Next, the two senators went to New York City to enlist what edi-

[31] "Agreement in the Senate in Respect to the People's College Amendment of the Cornell University Bill, 1865," in Becker, *Cornell University*, pp. 167–168.

[32] *Senate Journal, 1865*, pp. 417, 438. Cook's man, Hayt, and a Democrat from New York City, Henry C. Murphy, cast the only votes against the bill.

[33] *Assembly Journal, 1865*, p. 696.

[34] White, *Autobiography*, I, 302.

torial support they could recruit among the larger dailies with state-wide circulations. They could already count on Greeley of the *Tribune* and Erastus Brooks of the *Express,* both of whom had been People's College trustees and had come over to the Cornell University plan. Somewhat more surprisingly, they also managed to obtain the editorial support of Manton Marble and the Democratic *World.* In fact, that paper had already come out in favor of an effective agricultural college. Though sorry about the impending demise of the experiment at Ovid, the *World* saw in Senator Cornell's plan the chance to "endow an institution which shall take rank at the head of American colleges or universities for instruction in those branches bearing upon the great farming interest in the country. We trust that the wisdom of some practical men in the Legislature will be directed to this subject," urged the *World,* "and that the present session will not close without some definite action being taken."[35]

If historians insist upon finding something "providential" in the passage of the Cornell University bill, this editorial stance by the *World* would seem to be a leading possibility. The Republican press could be expected to support the idea, and it did.[36] But the Democrats received very little political support in the rural sections of upstate New York, and the legislators who were actively spearheading the battle for the establishment of Cornell University were the very same upstate Radicals also struggling to pass the loathsome fire and health bills. Yet the *World* held to its policy even after the fighting grew heavy in the assembly. On March 28, while the bill was still sitting in the assembly committee, the *World* expressed disgust over the unaccountable delay: "In regard to real worth and usefulness, the Cornell Bill is the great measure

[35] Feb. 1, p. 4; 4, 1865, p. 5.
[36] Albany *Evening Journal,* Feb. 27, 1865, p. 2.

of the session. By it we shall possess a great school for the use of the poor as well as the rich."[37] When another week went by and still no action had been taken, the *World* asserted flatly: "If the Legislature allows the cause of education in this state to lose this offered advantage it will deserve the maledictions of all wise citizens."[38] Given the political circumstances, it would be difficult to discover better evidence of the American faith in education than this editorial policy of the *World*.

The second line of attack chosen by the friends of the Cornell University bill to force the hands of the assembly committee was a formal debate staged before the joint committee's members in the assembly chamber. For this occasion Ezra Cornell engaged a leading lawyer, and the opposition did the same. Unfortunately for the advocates of the Cornell bill, this debate went very badly for their side. While Senator Cornell's man offered a speech which was "cold, labored, perfunctory, and fell flat," the speaker against the measure "knew well the best tricks for catching the average man," and delivered a stinging blow. He denounced the Cornell bill as a "monopoly," a "wild project," a "selfish scheme," a "job," a "grab," and a plan to "rob the state."[39] His attacks upon Ezra Cornell personally drove the senator to write out a formal statement defending the morality and the motives of his project.[40] Although White thought the opposing lawyer's remarks "thin and demagogical," he was clearly upset by the mere memory of them. This phase of the attack could only be labeled a defeat.

[37] March, 28, 1865, p. 5.
[38] April 5, 1865, p. 4.
[39] White, *Autobiography*, I, 303.
[40] See "Ezra Cornell's Statement," in Becker, *Cornell University*, pp. 168–170, and draft of the assembly bargain in White's hand in the White Papers.

The third and probably the most effective of the actions taken to overcome assembly opposition involved an outright payoff of the most obstinate segment of the religious college opposition. By early April tiny Genesee College, a Methodist school thirty miles south of Rochester, had become a focal point for the denominational forces of the state. An agent of that college, Angus McDonald, introduced a bill into the legislature which would grant Genesee its "fair share" of the Morrill proceeds, a sum estimated by them to be the profit on the sale of 100,000 of New York's approximately 1,000,000 scrip acres. This bill had been successfully resisted by the Cornell University people on their old grounds that New York could not hope to create a really first-rate institution if it divided Morrill money among many small colleges. Even if it could not manage to have its own scheme passed, however, Genessee College, since it commanded the immense support of the Methodist church around the state, was still in a position to block the Cornell bill. "The situation was obviously conducive to bargaining, and a bargain was in fact arranged."[41]

Apparently first proposed by Genesee College, but readily enough acquiesced in by Senator White, the bargain called for a monetary donation to be given by Ezra Cornell to Genesee College for the purpose of establishing a department of agricultural chemistry or an endowed chair in some similar subject.[42] The figure was set at $25,000, and Senator Cornell

[41] Becker, *Cornell University*, p. 104.

[42] The details of the bargain, and who first approached whom, were later illuminated during the course of debates at the constitutional convention of 1867–1868. McDonald argued that the idea had been White's and that White had actually "bid" on the amount, starting at $15,000 and going up to $25,000 (see *Constitutional Debates*, pp. 3795–3797). Both Charles Folger and James Bell, however, substantiated the version given by White: that the proposal came first from

insisted that payment be made out in the open rather than in the lobby where the bargain had been struck; he apparently did not wish to be accused of buying votes underhandedly. Accordingly, a clause was actually written into the Cornell University bill stipulating in effect that Ezra Cornell would have to "give twenty-five thousand dollars to Genesee College, before he could be allowed to give five hundred thousand dollars to the proposed university."[43] This was barely distinguishable from legislative blackmail, and the Ithaca *Journal* suggested that the chair at Genesee College be called the "Captain Kydd Professorship."[44] Yet the bargain seemed to have positive effects, and for the first time during the session the Cornell University bill seemed to have a reasonable chance of advancing toward passage.

Still, White, Cornell, and their allies had to keep up the pressure. The former let it be known to friends of the New York Central that their rate increase measure would be blocked in the senate until they called off their Whiggish allies in the assembly, who were helping to hold the Cornell bill in committee. In a similar tactic Assemblyman Lord, an influential member of the Ways and Means Committee, told the backers of a bill to erect a new capitol that their project would not be reported until the Cornell University bill had been placed before the full assembly.[45] On April 12, immediately following the assembly's vote to suspend the two-thirds rule for the metropolitan health bill, John L. Parker, the Radical parliamentary tactician, offered a resolution instructing the joint committee to report the Cornell University bill.[46] Since this

the Methodists (see *ibid.*, pp. 2820–2822; and White, *Autobiography*, I, 300–301).

[43] White, *Autobiography*, I, 301.

[44] Quoted in Becker, *Cornell University*, p. 105.

[45] *Ibid.*, pp. 106–108.

[46] *Assembly Journal, 1865*, pp. 1251–1252.

resolution would need a two-thirds majority, the backers of the measure could not afford to have very many doubtful assemblymen, "men who feared local pressure, sectarian hostility, or the opposition of Mr. Cook to measures of their own," slip off the floor. While Andrew White and several of his close friends "stood in the cloakroom and fairly shamed the waverers back into their places," the resolution was carried by a vote of 70 to 22.[47] On the next day the committee duly reported the bill as the resolution ordered, and the measure was made a special order of business for early in the following week.[48] On April 21 the Cornell University bill was passed by the assembly, 79 to 25, and sent over to the senate for concurrence in the assembly's amendments, including the clause which required Ezra Cornell to pay Genesee College the $25,000.[49] On that same day the senate rendered its approval, and the bill to establish Cornell University was sent to Governor Fenton.[50] The act took effect immediately upon Fenton's signing it, April 27, 1865.[51]

The subsequent history of Cornell University is probably better known than the circumstances of its founding. When the People's College failed to meet the conditions imposed by the state law of 1863 and also failed to post their "bond" with the regents as stipulated by the amendment to the Cornell

[47] White, *Autobiography*, I, 304–305; *Assembly Journal, 1865*, p. 1252.

[48] *Assembly Journal, 1865*, pp. 1280, 1288.

[49] *Ibid.*, p. 1336. Ten of the twenty-five votes cast in opposition to the Cornell University bill came from Republicans who backed the health bill during the same week. Most of the rest of the nays came from disinterested Democrats. For a complete transcript of the amendments, see *Senate Journal, 1865*, pp. 856–860.

[50] *Senate Journal, 1865*, pp. 860, 899. The vote to concur was 25 to 1 with Henry Murphy the lone dissenter.

[51] *Assembly Journal, 1865*, p. 1586.

University bill, the proceeds of the Morrill land grant became legally earmarked for the new university in Ithaca. Ezra Cornell let it be known at the first meeting of the board of trustees that his choice for president of the institution would be Andrew White. Under White's guidance the academic reputation of the university rose quickly to the top rank of the nation's schools of higher education. Emphasizing the utilitarian and somewhat more practical branches of learning, pioneering in both the natural sciences and the social sciences, and helping to break the grip of the classics on American collegiate education, Cornell University became a giant among American institutions of higher education virtually within the lifetimes of the two Republican politicians who had engineered its creation.[52] Ezra Cornell's shrewd management of the university's financial affairs eventually permitted New York to rank first among the states, not only in the total amount of money realized from the Morrill Act, but also in the average price per acre which it finally received for educational purposes from its share of the scrip.[53]

Even while noting the university's subsequent success, however, it is important to keep the circumstances of Cornell's founding sharply in focus. The law which chartered it was not an aberration; it was part and parcel of the political circumstances of the postwar era. Although Andrew Dickson White is best remembered in American history as the first

[52] See Veysey, *Emergence of the American University, passim.* Harvard seemed mildly jealous of the new upstart virtually from the beginning. See John C. Gray, "Remarks on Cornell University," *Proceedings of the Massachusetts Historical Society,* XI (1869–1870), 85–92.

[53] Albany *Evening Journal,* March 31, 1866, p. 2; Paul W. Gates, *The Wisconsin Pine Lands of Cornell University: A Study in Land Policy and Absentee Ownership* (Ithaca, 1943); Nevins, *State Universities,* pp. 33–34.

president of Cornell University, it should not be forgotten
that his skill as a politician—indeed, his lack of compunction
about deals as crude as the Genesee College clause—made possible both his later career and the university itself.[54] White
wrote Gilman privately that the only reason for his decision
to stand for re-election in 1865, despite his desire to devote
full time to building the university and despite the bitter opposition of his wife, was to make certain that his new institution would have a friend in the legislature, "so that if we want
more favors, we can get them."[55] It may sound discordant to
state that a great university was the work of two Republican
politicians and their temporary allies who managed to pry, to
buy, and to logroll it into existence and afterward between
them to direct respectively its financial and educational policies. Yet this was the case. The founding of Cornell University should be placed where it belongs: in the context of the
institutional and civil reform movement launched under Radical rule in New York State.

III

Although less dramatic than the founding of Cornell University, and certainly less well known than that event, a second
important step was taken in the field of higher education by
New York during the postwar era: an expansion of the state's

[54] In 1867, perhaps from guilt, White initiated a successful effort
in the legislature to repay Ezra Cornell with public funds the $25,000
that he had paid to Genesee College. This law was passed by a con-
trite and wholly Radical-controlled legislature and signed by Governor Fenton on March 28, 1867 (see *Assembly Journal, 1867*, p.
1861). The title of the law minced no words: "An act to refund to
the Cornell University the amount paid by Ezra Cornell to the
Genesee College at Lima, pursuant to section six, of chapter 585 of
the laws of 1866." Folger praised this belated act of retribution in
Constitutional Debates, pp. 2820–2821.

[55] White to Gilman, May 15, 1865, Gilman Papers.

facilities for teacher training. While the results of this act may have been less conspicuous than the results of the Cornell University bill, the decision to create new "normal" or teachers' colleges was just as significant as the Cornell legislation, if not more so, since it represented a commitment by the state to provide the necessities of public education. Chapter 466 of the New York State laws of 1866, which established a commission to select sites and authorize the erection of four new normal schools, was the kind of commitment upon which the American theory of broad education for all members of the society ultimately rested.

Prior to the Civil War, provisions for the education of schoolteachers had been meager at best. Beginning in 1827 the state modestly subsidized selected private academies, provided those schools in turn would offer a course "in the science of common school teaching" in their curricula.[56] In 1845 the state officially assumed financial responsibility for a previously private academy in Albany and transformed it into the first full-time normal school in New York.[57] During the war the town of Oswego had founded a city normal and training school to supply teachers for its area, and when this experiment proved immensely successful and its graduates were greatly in demand, the state pledged limited financial support for this venture as well.[58] All together, however, these facili-

[56] Victor M. Rice, "Eleventh Annual Report of the Superintendent of Public Instruction," in *Assembly Documents, 1865,* IV, No. 75 (Albany, 1865), p. 32 (hereafter cited as "Superintendent's Report, 1865"). The law of 1827 had been updated in 1855.

[57] Frederick Lamson Whitney, *The Growth of Teachers in Service* (New York, 1927), pp. 6–7, Table 1. Although Massachusetts had previously established a state normal school, this was the first instance of a state taking over a formerly private academy and turning it into a teachers' training institution.

[58] George Willard Frasier and Frederick Lamson Whitney, *Teachers College Finance* (Greeley, Colo., 1930), p. 5.

ties could not supply the state with enough adequately trained teachers to maintain decent standards in the common schools. During the school year 1863–1864, when some 15,807 teachers were employed in the public schools for more than six months, there were only 301 undergraduates in the normal school at Albany and a total in the various subsidized academies of "1,643 pupils who had signed a declaration of intention to teach in the common schools of the State."[59] The inevitable result was appallingly low-quality teaching, in which "the principal qualification" demanded of many of the teachers was "an ability to thrash big boys."[60]

In his first annual message to the legislature in 1865, Governor Fenton emphasized the need to expand the number of institutions training public schoolteachers. Skipping lightly over the usual statistics, Fenton came quickly to the point:

To give full force and effect to [the Consolidated School Act of 1864], and to increase parental solicitude for the proper instruction of the young, the propriety of making more ample provision for an annual supply of thoroughly qualified teachers is suggested. Creditable provision for this purpose has already been made in the Normal School, teachers' classes in the academies, teachers' institutes [summer seminars and refresher courses begun before the war], and the Oswego Training School for primary teachers; but these, as now supported, are manifestly inadequate to supply so great a demand.[61]

The superintendent of public instruction, Victor M. Rice, who was simultaneously beginning his campaign against the rate-bill system of finance in the public schools of the state,

[59] "Superintendent's Report, 1865," p. 33 and Abstract A, Table 8, p. 75.

[60] Andrew S. Draper, *Origin and Development of the Common School System of the State of New York* (Syracuse, 1905), p. 103.

[61] "Message of the Governor," Jan. 3, 1865, in *Senate Journal, 1865*, pp. 7–24.

kept up the pressure for more normal schools in his own annual report submitted to the legislature in February 1865.
"I am firm in the belief that no State has a better school system than our own," asserted the superintendent, "except for
the preparation of teachers. . . . no cost should be counted
too great which [is] necessary to supply the schools with
enlightened teachers"; if the legislature failed to add more
normal colleges around the state, he would support a reallocation of common school funds for that purpose.[62]

Under this steady pressure the legislature, led by recently
elected upstate Radicals, agreed to assume a more generous
portion of the financial responsibility for the Oswego Training School, which Rice had visited and heartily recommended
to the lawmakers in his annual report.[63] Still, this act represented the amplification of a previous decision rather than a
new commitment to create a system of teachers' training
schools commensurate with the state's needs. Both Fenton and
Rice realized this, and both maintained their pressure.

The Governor's second annual message in 1866 included
the flat assertion that the legislature ought to establish additional normal schools in New York State and that it ought
also to increase both the student capacity and the educational
facilities available at the two colleges already in operation.[64]
Superintendent Rice was even more emphatic. After noting
that the state sorely needed something more permanent than
the academy subsidy program of teachers' training, he concluded his annual report in 1866 with the specific suggestion
"that a commisison be appointed to locate three or more Nor-

[62] "Superintendent's Report, 1865," pp. 40–42.

[63] *Ibid.*, pp. 36–40; *Senate Journal, 1865*, pp. 332, 338, 368, 445, 450,
793; *Assembly Journal, 1865*, pp. 429, 602, 605, 722, 797, 1091, 1164,
1239, 1579.

[64] "Message of the Governor," Jan. 2, 1866, in *Senate Journal, 1866*,
pp. 7–24.

mal and Training Schools for the special preparation of teachers, in such eligible places as shall offer the greatest inducements by way of building, school apparatus, etc., and that an appropriation be made for their efficient support."[65] This session of the New York State legislature, whose majority members were more closely allied with the Radical governor than in the previous year, responded to the problems of teachers' education.

The legislative response took the form of a bill introduced by that champion of higher education from the previous session, Andrew White.[66] With the Cornell University fight behind him, White was free to pursue this less personal goal in 1866, and "out of the multitude of projects presented," he remembered: "I combined what I thought the best parts of three or four in a single bill, and although at first there were loud exclamations against so lavish a use of public money, I induced the committee to report my bill, argued it in the Senate, overcame much opposition, and thus finally secured a law establishing four State normal schools."[67]

The opposition seems to have emanated primarily from Senator Hayt, whose battle with Senator White over the Cornell University bill may have left bitterness, and secondarily from a couple of New York City Democrats, who believed that the expansion of the normal schools was aimed largely at

[65] Victor M. Rice, "Twelfth Annual Report of the Superintendent of Public Instruction," in *Documents of the Assembly of the State of New York at Their Eighty-ninth Session, 1866*, V, No. 90 (Albany, 1866), pp. 37, 57 (hereafter cited as "Superintendent's Report, 1866").

[66] *Senate Journal, 1866*, p. 260.

[67] *Autobiography*, I, 107. White places this event out of chronological order, implying that his efforts on behalf of normal schools preceded his efforts on behalf of the Cornell University bill—that is, implying he turned to his more personal project only after attending to the larger problems faced by the state's public school system.

providing better teachers for upstate districts. Although New York City faced the same teacher shortage as the rest of the state, it was relatively better off because it could afford to offer substantially higher salaries as a lure to those few who were already being graduated from the Albany Normal School and the Oswego Training School.[68] Furthermore, at the suggestion of Superintendent Rice, the bill was drafted to provide for the selection of future college sites by a special commission. Given the make-up of the legislature, and, therefore, the probable make-up of the commission, the likelihood of New York City being selected as a college site was extremely slim. On the other hand, the commission device was politically astute, for it helped neutralize the local jealousies which had so hindered the Cornell University bill. Each representative could vote for the measure as proposed and attempt to influence the selection process later, which was exactly what happened.[69] After assurance that the measure set no precedent for later attacks upon the integrity of the common school

[68] Table 4, "Abstract of Statistical Reports of the School Commissioners of the State of New York, for the year ending September 20, 1866," in Victor M. Rice, "Thirteenth Annual Report of the Superintendent of Public Instruction" in *Assembly Documents, 1867*, IV, No. 79, p. 67 (hereafter cited "Superintendent's Report, 1867"). New York City trailed only Oswego and Albany in the numbers of normal school graduates in its district. Also compare Table 8, part I, "Statistical," with Table 8, part II, "Financial," in *ibid.*, pp. 81–82, which reveals that the urban districts considered as a unit spent almost exactly the same amount of money on teachers' salaries as did the rural districts considered as a unit, even though the latter employed more than three times as many teachers. See also Victor M. Rice [and A. G. Johnson], "Special Report on the Present State of Education in the United States and on Compulsory Instruction," in *Assembly Documents, 1867*, XI, No. 237, p. 49 (hereafter cited as "Special Report, 1867").

[69] A. W. Cowles to White, March 1, 1866, Jan. 28, 1867; Victor M. Rice to White, July 27, 1866; Henry Barnard to "Dear Sir," Nov. 15, 1866; B. F. Angel to Charles J. Folger, March 13, 1867; Henry Ballard

fund, the normal school bill won approval of the senate on March 21, three weeks to the day after its introduction, and was sent to the assembly.[70]

The normal school bill fairly breezed through the assembly. Unlike the Cornell University bill, which had met its most determined opposition in the lower house, the normal school bill was swept up in the rush of business which year after year marked the last weeks of the legislative session. Also unlike the Cornell University bill, when the press of the state had been mobilized by both sides, the popular news media barely mentioned the normal school measure. The bill passed the assembly on April 6, 1866, without a single dissenting vote. The very next day Reuben Fenton signed another act in New York State's reconstruction at home.[71]

The Normal School Act of 1866 had almost immediate positive effects upon the state's educational structure, as the Superintendent of Public Instruction was able to demonstrate in his subsequent annual reports. Colleges were quickly awarded to the towns of Potsdam, Cortland, Brockport, and Fredonia, all of which were in Radical Republican districts and a long way from New York City. The last town, Fredonia, was located in Fenton's and Rice's home county of Chautauqua. The two new colleges at Brockport and Fredonia were accepting students by the academic year 1867–1868.[72] Furthermore, once the decision had been made for the state to build

to White, March 14, 1867; B. F. Angel to White, March 21, 1867, White Papers.

[70] *Senate Journal, 1866,* p. 449; Albany *Evening Journal,* March 21, 1866, p. 2. The final vote was 23 to 7. Three weeks was an exceptionally short time for passage.

[71] *Assembly Journal, 1866,* p. 1339; *Senate Journal, 1866,* p. 1076.

[72] "Superintendent's Report, 1867"; and Rice, "Fourteenth Annual Report of the Superintendent of Public Instruction," in *Documents of the Assembly of the State of New York at Their Ninety-first Session, 1868,* VIII, No. 80 (Albany, 1868), pp. 43–52 (hereafter cited as "Superintendent's Report, 1868").

normal schools, it was relatively easy for the 1867 legislature, which was even more Radical than the one in 1866, to increase the number. Accordingly, the commission established during 1866 was authorized the next year to select two additional sites, thus bringing the total number of teachers' colleges to eight.[73] Although Victor M. Rice continued to encourage the legislature to increase the number even further, a significant improvement in the educational system of New York State had been effected.[74]

The relative obscurity of the Normal School Act ought not to detract from its long-range significance. The American system of public education depended upon these specific measures to implement the more general commitment. And once again, this was a case where the need for reform legislation had been long recognized, but awaited the formation of a political bloc in the state legislature which was sufficiently interested to generate action. The Fenton Radicals, desiring more professional teachers for their own districts, provided the necessary initiative. The New York State teachers' college system thus became another result of the reconstruction at home.

IV*

Underlying New York's recently bolstered facilities for higher education lay the state's vast system of common

[73] "Superintendent's Report, 1868," pp. 47–51; *Journal of the Assembly of the State of New York at Their Ninety-first Session, 1868* (Albany, 1868); *Journal of the Senate of the State of New York at Their Ninety-first Session, 1868* (Albany, 1868).

[74] "Special Report, 1867," pp. 47–52.

* An early version of this section appeared in the *New-York Historical Society Quarterly*, LIII (1969), 230–249, under the title "New York State's Free School Law of 1867: A Chapter in the Reconstruction of the North."

schools. Both the legislators and the public clearly conceived of the common schools (which in modern parlance would be termed public grade schools or elementary schools) as the fundamental unit of the state's educational structure. The reason for creating the normal colleges was to help raise standards in the common schools, which were also viewed as the base upon which Cornell University would be erected. The assembly had amended the Cornell bill, for example, to require the new institution to accept annually without tuition one undergraduate from each of the state's assembly districts. This was done to tie the new university firmly to the common school system of the state; the legislators did not wish to see Cornell become like the old elite eastern colleges, which were almost completely disassociated from the public school systems of their respective states. Victor Rice called the proposed university at Ithaca "the crown of our public school system," and he had high hopes that the scholarships to Cornell would "excite and keep up an interest in education throughout the State."[75] Likewise, one of the principal points in Andrew White's senate speech of March 10, 1865, was that "any institution for higher education in the State must form an integral part of the whole system of public instruction; that the university should not be isolated from the school system, as were the existing colleges, but that it should have a living connection with the system, should push its roots down into it and through it, drawing life from it and sending life back into it."[76]

In 1864, White had been instrumental in helping to infuse life into the public school system in a somewhat more direct fashion: by consolidating and codifying the huge, unwieldy body of school law that had gradually built up since colonial

[75] "Superintendent's Report, 1867," p. 51.
[76] *Autobiography*, I, 331.

days.[77] This produced the so-called Consolidated School Act, referred to by Governor Fenton in his annual message of 1865. Although this measure had also aimed at increasing attendance in the public schools by uniformly appropriating money to local districts on the basis of their actual attendance reports rather than on the number of school-aged children residing in the district, its results were not all that its backers had hoped.[78] The structure of public elementary education in New York State had a much more serious flaw than overlapping statutes and lax local administration: through 1867 it still retained the so-called rate-bill system of finance.

The principle of public education in the United States may be as old as the Massachusetts School Law of 1642, but its practice, even in Massachusetts, certainly is not. Contrary to the assumptions of many Americans, the nation's state-supported grade schools, completely free from tuition or fees, are a relatively recent product of the American political system. In New York State, where the over-all quality of the educational system caught up with and surpassed that of Massachusetts by mid-nineteenth century, the principle of state-supported public schools was not fully realized until 1867, when Governor Fenton signed a bill entitled, "an act to amend an act entitled, 'An act to revise and consolidate the general acts relating to public instruction,' passed May 2, 1864, and to abolish the rate bills authorized by special acts."[79] The wording of this title hardly placed it in jeopardy of becoming a ready cliché, and the act became known as the

[77] *Ibid.*, pp. 106–107. White had performed the tedious task of going through the state's school laws "section by section, paragraph by paragraph, phrase by phrase" looking for conflicts, overlaps, and revisions. White attributes the idea for a consolidation, however, to the superintendent of public instruction, Victor Rice.

[78] "Superintendent's Report, 1865," pp. 45–46.

[79] *Assembly Journal, 1867,* p. 1872.

Free School Law. In the official title of the Free School Law the last phrase was the most important, for the issue of free public education in New York had come to rest squarely on the question of abolishing the rate bills as means of helping to finance the local schools of the state.

School finances in the state of New York prior to 1867 were extremely complex, and several sources of revenue were involved. Each school district received a specified amount of state funds, which it was required to devote to its local schools. This became the basic operating figure. Except for the period 1800–1805, the state had provided this base since 1795. Until 1849, the funds which the state annually doled out were drawn primarily from a "permanent school fund" established by the legislature in 1805 and subsequently supplemented by money received under the federal Deposit Act of 1836.[80] The amount provided annually by the state, however, consistently failed to cover the total expenses incurred by the individual school districts. Even a general state-wide school tax passed in 1851 proved inadequate. Almost every district, therefore, regularly faced a deficit.

In light of this situation the function of the rate bill was fairly straightforward: it helped make up the difference between local expenditures and funds received from the state. Under New York State law the individual district was entitled to calculate how much additional revenue had been required to maintain the schools in any given year and to bill the parents of each pupil for the balance in proportion to the

[80] Sullivan *et al.*, eds., *New York*, p. 2146. New York's share of this grant was $4,000,000.00, of which $160,000.00 was added annually to the state school fund at the request of Governor William L. Marcy. For the details concerning this and other federal grants, see Fletcher Harper Swift, *Federal and State School Finance* (n.p., n.d.), or Swift, *History of Public School Funds in the United States* (New York, 1911).

number of days of school that pupil had attended. Since there were no compulsory attendance laws at this time, the size of these rate bills could vary considerably from family to family. In families too poor to afford the added expense of a rate bill, the head of the house could formally declare himself a legal pauper, in which case the state would pay any rate bills incurred by any of his children while attending school.

On the surface, then, the rate-bill system did not appear horribly unjust. It simply required those who took advantage of the public schools to help defray the extra cost of maintaining them. The school system of the state of New York had been functioning successfully under this arrangement, with local variations, since 1814. Both Horace Mann and Henry Barnard, the two leading school authorities of the time, praised New York's educational system highly.[81]

By 1867 not every district in the state continued to use rate bills. An increasing number of communities had decided to follow the lead of the state's largest urban centers and substitute general district taxation for rate billing. As early as 1842, New York City secured a special law from the state legislature granting it the power of taxation required to establish a self-contained public school system within its borders. Crowded with the children of industrial workers and impoverished immigrants, New York City had been unable to educate its young people without taxing the property of the entire district for the funds required, including the hitherto untapped sources of industrial wealth. By the end of 1848, approximately one-fourth of the school districts in the state had "free" school systems similar to that of New York City. The overwhelming majority of these were located in urban areas, and they included the school systems of the three most

[81] Draper, *Common School System*, pp. 48–49.

prominent upstate urban centers: Buffalo, Rochester, and Syracuse.[82] In 1848 these cities were models of the way in which the public school system throughout the state of New York would be financed twenty years later.

During the 1850's and early 1860's, some of the smaller population centers also began to reject the rate bills. Since special acts of the state legislature were required to grant the taxation powers which allowed these districts to raise the money previously collected by rate bills, the growth of this tendency was recorded in the annals of the state's legislative sessions. The legislature passed at least one of these special "free district" statutes per year in each of the twenty years preceding 1867, and the total number of free systems had by then reached nearly two hundred.[83]

But in spite of the growing tendency of cities and towns to abolish rate bills, this system of school finance was far from dead. As late as 1866, the last year before their elimination, the rate bills accounted for $708,003.03 or roughly one-third of the state's total educational outlay.[84] This helps to explain why the men who led the fight for the Free School Law in 1867 later remembered it as "the greatest contest concerning schools which the State has known."[85] They initiated that contest by emphasizing publicly what they considered to be

[82] Charles E. Fitch, *The Public School: History of Common School Education in New York from 1633 to 1904* (Albany, 1905), p. 36. By the end of 1848 the following population centers had "free" schools: New York City, Brooklyn, Buffalo, Rochester, Syracuse, Poughkeepsie, Flushing, Newton, Williamsburg, and Lansingburg. The districts in Albany, Utica, and Troy were substantially, though not yet entirely, "free" by that date as well.

[83] Albany *Evening Journal*, April 27, 1867, p. 2; Thomas E. Finegan, *Free Schools: A Documentary History of the Free School Movement in New York State* (Albany, 1921), p. 525.

[84] "Superintendent's Report, 1867," pp. 14–15.

[85] Draper, *Common School System*, p. 80.

the two most unfortunate consequences of the rate-bill system: poor teachers and low attendance.

Although the state had been contributing toward the payment of teachers' salaries since 1815, the amount apportioned annually to each district for this purpose during the decade and a half prior to the Free School Law of 1867 amounted only to about twenty dollars per teacher.[86] Thus the largest percentage of money raised by local districts through rate billing went toward supplementing teachers' wages. Those concerned with the quality of the state's educational program argued that this arrangement was extremely detrimental to the securing of qualified teachers. Since those administering the rate bills naturally sought to keep them at the lowest possible level, teachers' salaries were frequently very low. In 1867 the Superintendent of Public Instruction reported that the average annual salary of a teacher in a rural district was only $203.76.[87] Typical of the assaults against the rate-bill system on this front was one launched by the commissioner of the Montgomery County school district: "Trustees employ second-rate teachers at low wages to make a cheap school; perhaps keep them just long enough to use up the appropriation from the State; thus, year after year, this programme is gone through with, to save a few paltry dollars, at the expense of the education of the children."[88]

By far the most damaging indictment brought against the rate-bill system, however, was that it kept a large proportion of the state's young people out of school. The necessity of paying a rate bill offered a convenient excuse for the withdrawal of one's children from the public schools, especially in rural districts where an extra hand could be put to more

[86] Sullivan *et al.*, eds., *New York*, p. 2149.
[87] "Superintendent's Report, 1867," p. 17.
[88] *Ibid.*, section G, p. 195.

profitable use in the fields.[89] For families on marginal or sub-
sistence incomes the rate bill posed an additional financial burden which the head of the house understandably hesitated to
assume. The alternatives of becoming either a legal ward of
the state or a temporary district debtor were rarely chosen;
almost invariably a man's pride dictated that he withdraw his
children from the public schools rather than submit to either
of these humiliations.[90] Indeed, this was the reason that so
many urban centers had already found the rate-bill system
intolerable. The majority of their young people, because they
came from poor families, simply were not being sent to school.

By 1864 a majority of the state's district commissioners had
come out against the rate bills. Surprisingly, however, since
the commisisoners unanimously agreed that the rural districts
were affected most adversely by the rate bills, the rural commissioners themselves were the ones least opposed to their
continuation. Commissioner Bartholomew Becker of rural
Schoharie County, for example, stated flatly, "the people are
in favor of the present rate bill system and pleased with the
present school system." Commissioner E. H. Brown of Steu-
ben County agreed with this opinion, even while including

[89] *Ibid.*, Table 4, pp. 66–71, indicates that the average pupil in an
urban district (where roughly 5/13 of the school-aged children in the
state resided) attended school for 92.2 days per year. In the rural
districts (where roughly 8/13 of the children lived) the average pupil
attended school only 73.6 days per year. This does not include the
fact that nearly a quarter of a million of the 844,219 children between
five and twenty-one years of age residing in rural districts did not go
to school at all. Although the distinction between rural and urban
districts by no means corresponds exactly to the distinction between
rate-bill and nonrate-bill districts, the vast majority of the districts
where rate bills remained were in rural areas and the vast majority of
the urban districts had abolished them by 1866, the year for which
these figures were amassed.

[90] "Special Report, 1867," pp. 57–58.

a serious reservation. "I think the public sentiment generally is in favor of the rate bills," he reported in 1864, "yet in many small schools they tend to lessen the already small attendance."[91]

Had abolition of the rate bills actually meant "free" schools, no author, editor, or politician would have defended them. But the proposal of the Free School Law meant that the necessary revenue for schools would be provided in full by the state of New York rather than by each local district making up an annual deficit either through continued rate billing or special district taxation. In other words, the annual base provided by the state would be raised in each district to a level capable of sustaining a full year's school expenses. This system would obviously help the man whose children attended a school where rate billing had been necessary, but would have little tangible economic appeal either to the man who paid no rate bills or to the taxpayer who had no school-aged children. For the majority of taxpayers and voters, then, "free" schools meant that they would pay additional New York State taxes. Free schools would be schools free of the old rate-bill system, not schools without cost. As Governor Myron Clark had pointed out as early as 1855, abolition of the rate bills meant institution of "a system based upon the principle that the State is even more deeply and permanently interested in the education of its children than their parents, and that the expense of providing it should be borne by the aggregate of the property within its limits."[92]

[91] Rice, "Tenth Annual Report of the Superintendent of Public Instruction of the State of New York," in *Documents of the Assembly of the State of New York at Their Eighty-seventh Session, 1864,* VI, No. 90 (Albany, 1864), Section G, pp. 113ff.

[92] "The Governor's Message in Senate," January 2, 1855, in *Documents of the Senate of the State of New York at Their Seventy-eighth Session, 1855,* No. 3 (Albany, 1855), p. 13.

Only in this light does the substantial rural opposition to a state-supported school system make any sense. Many small independent farmers were apathetic toward the idea of increased education, especially if that meant more state taxes. Under the rate-bill system a man had only to pay his three-quarters mill state tax toward the education of his children. When his local district school used up the state apportionment provided by this tax, he pulled his children out of the public school and put them to work in the fields, where in his eyes their true education took place anyway. A conservative folk belief prevailed in many rural districts, as remembered by one contemporary, to the effect "that there never was such a school as the one in the little red school-house near their country home, with its slab benches [and] text books handed down through many generations."[93] The yeoman had in this way learned all that was necessary to be a good farmer, and probably in his opinion, a good deal that was unnecessary as well. There was little reason for him to waste additional money improving a school system for his children which he already regarded as mildly superfluous.

From the immediate point of view, then, any proposal to substitute a state-supported school system for the existing rate-bill system promised an increase in the farmer's New York State taxes, something that he regarded with aversion. In the longer run, however, additional economic considerations would soften this added expense. Certainly the most attractive of these softening considerations was the fact that the rural districts would receive a larger proportion of the school tax fund than they paid into it, because the distribution of that fund was such that the largest urban centers were already paying a disproportionate amount. This helps to explain why

[93] Draper, *Common School System*, p. 103.

New York City was not in the forefront of agitation for the Free School Law, even though it had been the first district to abolish rate bills. Under existing law, the city was able to spend all of its local school taxes on its own schools; it was a self-contained system. Under the Free School Law the city would be able to utilize only part of the school taxes collected in its district.

This same consideration helps to explain why the upstate urban centers, the vast majority of which were Radical bastions, led the movement for the Free School Law of 1867. These communities were far less wealthy than New York City, and yet they supported considerable populations, especially by national standards. A growing number of union free school districts and special taxation bills testified that these communities had already decided to abandon the rate-bill system and to tax themselves for support of the public schools. Consequently, the upstate municipal centers favored anything which would ease the financial burdens of their commitment to the social importance of mass education. By tapping the immense wealth of New York City, a free school law would do just this. New York City itself remained begrudgingly neutral in this process, realizing on the one hand that the rate-bill system was indeed intolerable, but fearing on the other hand the financial drain which it would suffer in any state-wide and state-supported school system.[94]

Foremost among the Radical spokesmen on this issue was

[94] The Schenectady, N.Y., *Republican* spelled this out in detail in an editorial published April 13, 1867, while the free school bill was pending in the legislature: "The entire valuation of the state is $1,659,552,615; of New York [City] $736,088,908; Kings [Brooklyn], $143,817,295, so that of the State tax these two counties pay more than half" (quoted in Finegan, *Free Schools*, p. 562). See also speech of Andrew D. White, Albany *Evening Journal*, April 9, 1867, p. 2.

New York State's active superintendent of public instruction, Victor M. Rice of Buffalo. No stranger either to political manipulation or to the methods of public persuasion, Rice had studied law and edited the Buffalo *Cataract* before moving up through the administrative positions of the Buffalo school system. This background stood him in good stead during his years as superintendent, for he was able to keep the most odious aspects of the rate-bill system constantly before the state legislature by means of the annual reports he was required to submit. Furthermore, Rice was no naive crusader who somehow stumbled into a den of wily politicians. During the early 1860's he had served in the state legislature, and he was an old friend of Reuben Fenton from their earlier political days in western New York. Many considered him to rank among the Governor's most trusted advisers. He had already scored successes in the Consolidated School Act of 1864 and the normal school legislation of 1866; the Free School Law would be the crowning achievement in his campaign to reconstruct public education in New York.[95]

The drive for a free school law gained momentum rapidly under Rice's guidance. Though a majority of the district commissioners opposed the rate-bill system in 1864, there still remained a considerable difference of opinion. During the 1866 session of the legislature David Aldrich, a Radical from rural Warren County, delivered a strong appeal for a state-wide free school system, and an extended debate between enthusiastic Radicals and skeptical Democrats over a free system for the capital city itself helped prepare the ground for larger plantings.[96] When the 1867 superintendent's report appeared,

[95] Harlow and Boone, *Life Sketches of the State Officers,* pp. 55–58; C. W. Bardeen, *Dictionary of Educational Biography* (Syracuse, n.d.), pp. 183, 207; *Tribune,* May 22, 1865, p. 8.

[96] Albany *Evening Journal,* April 4, 1866, pp. 1, 2.

opposition to the rate bills approached unanimity. Several of
the district commissioners were recent converts to the cause
of state-supported schools, evidence of efforts of Rice and
others behind the scenes.[97]

In 1867, Rice adopted a characteristic Radical tactic which
had proved effective during the battles for municipal reform.
He began to offer systematic statistical evidence about the existing structure of New York State's common school system.
This was the first time in the state's history that comparable
information had been collected, and Rice's statistics, which
were given a prominent place in Fenton's annual message to
the legislature, allowed the Governor to buttress his previous
arguments for free schools with much more impressive data.[98]
"At an early day," the Governor asserted, education was
"deemed essential to the security, progress, and power of the
people." He then sketched the history of common schools in
the state in order to suggest to the current legislators that they
were in a position to culminate over seventy years of educational progress. He also argued that the people had long manifested a willingness to pay state taxes in support of their
schools, a questionable point. But the meat of Fenton's remarks followed his brief historical discourse.

Rice's report, the Governor stated, revealed "that the number of children and youth in daily attendance at the public
schools [was] 30.02 percent of the entire number between
five and twenty-one years of age." Even allowing for private
and parochial schools, both of which were viewed with some
suspicion by many of the state's citizens, this was a strikingly

[97] "Superintendent's Report, 1867," Section G, pp. 107, 172, 180,
185–186.

[98] *Ibid.*; "Special Report, 1867," pp. 3–4; Fitch, *The Public School,*
p. 53.

low figure. Governor Fenton apparently felt the shock himself, and while putting the best face on the matter, he called for prompt action:

Although this average attendance upon the public schools is the largest ever reported, it is, nevertheless, believed that by judicious legislation it may be essentially increased. . . . With the conviction that universal education is a necessity of the State, I recommend that all impediments in the way of its free acquisition be removed, whether in the form of rate bills, poor and incommodious school houses, or the want of teachers specially trained to their vocation.[99]

Concerning the last of the Governor's references, the necessity of having more trained teachers, the legislative machinery designed to increase the number of normal colleges from two to six was, of course, already in motion. The central issue left to the legislators was clearly the rate-bill system.

The legislators reacted quickly to the Governor's recommendation. Assemblyman Joshua Smith, a Radical whose constituents sent him to the state legislature as a slap against Andrew Johnson after the President removed him as local postmaster, gave notice on Tuesday, January 8, "that he would at an early date ask leave to introduce a bill to establish a system of free schools in the State of New York."[100] On Wednesday, January 30, Smith M. Weed of Plattsburg, another small urban center, made a similar announcement. His bill would "make the common schools of the State of New York free to all," by eliminating rate bills, "and provide for

[99] "Annual Message of the Governor," January 2, 1867, in *Documents of the Senate of the State of New York at Their Ninetieth Session, 1867*, No. 2 (Albany, 1867), pp. 27–29.

[100] Harlow and Boone, *Life Sketches of the State Officers*, pp. 363–364; *Assembly Journal, 1867*, p. 56.

the government and maintenance of said schools," by establishing a state-wide system.[101] Though Weed was a Democrat, the Radicals deferred to his bill. This not only lent the proposal a nonpartisan aura, but also offered an opportunity to boost the prestige of the only Democrat in the New York State legislature willing openly to entertain the possibility of Negro suffrage in the United States.[102] Not surprisingly, however, it was Victor M. Rice who actually drafted Weed's proposal.[103]

The bill made rapid progress through the assembly and on the motion of former abolitionist Ornon Archer, from the Committee on Colleges, Academies, and Common Schools, Speaker Edmund L. Pitts, another of Fenton's lieutenants, made it a priority measure. On Friday, March 22, the bill was read for the required third time and passed unanimously. The Speaker ordered "that the Clerk deliver said bill to the Senate, and request their concurrence therein."[104]

The senate acted promptly on the assembly bill. White explained and praised the measure to his colleagues and tried to persuade the metropolitan senators that any disadvantages to New York and Kings counties were slight when compared with the benefits to the whole state.[105] The senators clarified the wording of one clause and then passed the bill in a lopsided vote.[106] The assembly concurred in the senate's amendment and repassed the bill without debate on Saturday, April 13. Once again the vote was unanimous. Governor Fenton

[101] *Assembly Journal, 1867*, pp. 223, 265, 320, 755, 873.

[102] Albany *Evening Journal*, Feb. 19, 1867, pp. 1, 2.

[103] Weed to an unnamed correspondent, Oct. 29, 1918, in Finegan, *Free Schools*, p. 546.

[104] *Assembly Journal, 1867*, pp. 320, 755, 873.

[105] Albany *Evening Journal*, April 9, 1867, p. 2.

[106] *Senate Journal, 1867*, p. 550.

signed the act immediately after receiving it on Tuesday, April 16, 1867.[107]

V

The unanimity of support for the Free School Law should not be allowed to blur the role of the Radical Republicans in bringing about this educational reform. Though the free school question had been a prominent issue in New York State since the 1840's, and though the drawbacks of rate billing had been frequently pointed out before the war, no previous group of legislators had cared to invest the considerable political energy necessary to authorize a major taxation measure in support of the public schools. It was indicative of the Radicals' general philosophies that they did.

In their school legislation the Radicals clearly confirmed their tendencies to centralize, to rationalize, and to exercise the full powers of the state, tendencies previously evident in the municipal reforms. Where local authorities seemed either unable or unwilling to take what the Radicals regarded as essential steps in the public interest, those steps were taken in Albany. Their biases in favor of systematic statistical evidence on the one hand and professionalism and expertise on the other likewise became more pronounced, especially in the reports of Superintendent Rice and in the legislative support afforded the normal school bill.

With their educational undertakings the Fenton Radicals also tied themselves more firmly to a larger tradition of nineteenth-century reform. Recent historians of ante-bellum reform have identified a trend initiated by middle- and upper-class Americans who were simultaneously benefiting from and frightened about the social dislocations that accompanied industrialism and urbanization. Among the prominent institu-

[107] *Assembly Journal, 1867*, pp. 1434, 1872.

tional expressions of this trend were the standardized and bureaucratized public school systems associated with the generation of Horace Mann and Henry Barnard. Such reformers believed the public school would not only provide opportunity for all, but socialization and Americanization, as they defined those terms, for everyone as well. And it is not difficult to place the Radicals' school reforms in this broad tradition.[108]

The Fentonites certainly worked closely with and helped significantly to bolster the educational bureaucracy established in New York State during the 1840's. Rice himself had been president of the New York State Teachers' Association before becoming superintendent of public instruction, and his department used state funds to subsidize the association's organ, *The New York Teacher*, as well as to underwrite an extensive program of teachers' institutes.[109] Rice also worked with members of the Radical coalition to increase both the powers and the salaries of state school commissioners.[110] The legislature could not have been ignorant of the fact that normal schools would institutionalize the professionalism so favored by the educational bureaucrats or of the fact that the Free School Law would not only create more teaching jobs but also raise the pay of the average teacher in the state.

Moreover, the rhetoric of the Radical school reformers was at times strikingly similar to that of their ante-bellum prede-

[108] Michael B. Katz, "From Voluntarism to Bureaucracy in American Education," *Sociology of Education*, XLIV (1971), 297–332, and *The Irony of Early School Reform: Educational Innovation in Mid-Nineteenth Century Massachusetts* (Cambridge, Mass., 1968), especially pp. 115–160.

[109] Fitch, *The Public School*, p. 114; "Superintendent's Report, 1865," pp. 33–36, 42–43; "Superintendent's Report, 1866," pp. 37–40; "Superintendent's Report, 1867," pp. 47–50.

[110] Benjamin S. Gregory to White, Jan. 21, 1865, White Papers; "Superintendent's Report, 1866," pp. 54–57.

cessors. Rice, for example, sounded defensive and uneasy when he feared for the next generation's "proper appreciation of the principles of social ethics," when he suggested the establishment of state reform schools "by which the idle, poor, and truant children in the cities may be provided for," and when he broached the possibility "that the time may come when the State will be obliged, for her own safety, to make attendance obligatory."[111] Fenton sounded very much like the member of a ruling social elite when he noted that the "intelligent and philanthropic citizens" were the ones who "evince[d] a deep interest in the promotion of regular and general attendance at our schools," though obviously that class could have provided easily for the education of its own children.[112] Nor should it be forgotten in this context that many of the small upstate urban centers which favored the Free School Law were experiencing for the first time during the postwar years the upsetting social dislocations of industrialization and urbanization on a really substantial scale.[113] Their sense of urgency during the postwar 1860's was no doubt similar to that felt by schoolmen of the state's larger cities a generation earlier.[114]

To some extent, then, the Radicals, at least in their educational legislation, did hark back to a reform tradition which had begun to break out into the open, at least at various local

[111] "Superintendent's Report, 1866," p. 22; "Superintendent's Report, 1867," p. 53; "Special Report, 1867," pp. 28–29.

[112] "Annual Message," 1866, in *Senate Journal, 1866*, p. 14.

[113] Fenton, "Annual Message," 1867, noted that a comparison of the 1860 federal census and the 1865 state census made obvious the fact that "large villages and cities" were growing rapidly while the agricultural population remained "nearly stationary."

[114] The urban context is a key point in the Katz analysis. See, for example, "The Emergence of Bureaucracy in Urban Education: The Boston Case, 1850–1884," *History of Education Quarterly*, VIII (1968), 155–188, 319–357.

levels, during the ante-bellum period. And insofar as the so-called Progressive period represents a re-emergence of similar phenomena at the national level, the Radicals form a link between these two reform eras and reform groups. Caution should be exercised in stretching this link too far, however, especially too far backward, even in the area of educational reform. The Radicals, for example, were neither as monolithically middle and upper class nor as solidly racist as the ante-bellum schoolmen appear to have been.[115] Moreover, the Radicals were explicitly aware of the potentially undemocratic aspects of state-imposed education and stopped short of supporting compulsory attendance laws. They maintained that maximal attendance was important to the nation's future, but their program was designed to make the schools so attractive that parents would voluntarily want to send every child, which was the situation that Rice believed to prevail already in certain northern European countries. As he phrased it in his "Special Report on the Present State of Education in the United States and Other Countries, and on Compulsory Instruction," compulsory attendance laws should never be resorted to "until the persuasive power of *good teachers, commodious and comfortable school-houses,* and *free schools,* shall have been tried."[116] And such laws were not enacted in New York State until the middle of the 1870's, when the general character of the Republican Party had shifted dramatically.[117]

Finally, there is the great ambiguity of who was imposing what upon whom in the school legislation of the postwar years. The Radicals were not forcing standardized education

[115] Katz, "From Voluntarism to Bureaucracy," pp. 318–320.

[116] "Special Report, 1867," pp. 44–45 (italics in original).

[117] New York's first compulsory attendance law was passed in 1874 and took effect January 1, 1875 (Fitch, *The Public School,* p. 96).

upon the urban proletariat nor seeking to Americanize immigrant populations with their Free School Law. They were not trying to establish a cadre of state-trained party-line teachers with their Normal School Act. Instead, the Radicals were attempting to gain what they believed to be economic and educational advantages for their own districts: state money and better teachers. And the school structures most dramatically altered by the Radicals' Free School Law would not be in urban areas, but in rural areas. The Fentonites may be accused of trying to wrench a portion of their own constituents into the world of industrialism and urbanization, the same world, ironically, that they tried to deal with in their municipal reforms, but it is difficult to attribute their activities solely, or even primarily, to class or to race. Those leitmotivs were certainly present in the Radical ideology, as their previous debates over labor law and their subsequent involvement with black suffrage both attest. But so were other crucial factors including financial self-interest, an established propensity to rationalize and to centralize, a desire for viable political issues at the state level, and a genuine idealism, whether misplaced or not. It was the blend of them all that made educational progress one of the enduring legacies of New York's reconstruction at home.

7

The Drive for Negro Suffrage

In 1867 the Radical coalition under Governor Reuben Fenton undertook what might have been the crowning achievement of their postwar reconstruction at home: the revision of New York State's constitution. The existing constitution demanded a $250 property qualification of every "man of color" in order to vote, thereby effectively disfranchising all but a handful of New York's Negro citizens. No such requirement was imposed upon white voters. The Fenton Radicals hoped to eliminate this discriminatory provision from the constitution of New York State, and the drama of their attempt forms a political tragedy in the classical pattern of five distinct acts.

The first act sets the political scene and suggests the reasons which led the Radicals to champion the cause of franchise reform in New York State. In the second act the Fentonites in the state legislature pass a bill to initiate the process of constitutional revision. The constitutional convention of 1867 provides the focus of attention in the third act. There the Radicals win the summer's most crucial political struggle when the delegates vote to include a nondiscriminatory suffrage article in the proposed constitution. Consequently, Fentonite fortunes have never seemed brighter than at intermission. The spotlight returns to the political arena in the fourth act, where the turning point is reached. This act deals with electoral pressures and political doubts, and before it ends the Fenton Republicans abandon the cause of suffrage reform in the face of impending defeat. There is a denouement, but as dramatically it should, it merely confirms the demise of franchise reform in New York State. What was designed as the supreme achievement of the Radicals' reconstruction at home proved instead to be the coalition's undoing.

I

When the Fenton Radicals won their greatest victory at the polls in the fall of 1866, there had been a proposition on the ballot asking the people of New York whether they wished to call a state constitutional convention.[1] Section two, article thirteen, of the existing constitution, in effect since 1846, required that such a proposition be submitted to the voters at least once every twenty years. In 1866 this worked to the advantage of the Radicals, who for three years had been considering a convention call. Horace Greeley, for example, probably the most outspoken advocate of constitutional reform in the state, had tried to persuade the Radicals to ask for a convention a year earlier than required.[2] During the spring of 1865 the Radical majority in the assembly passed the necessary legislation, but the proposal died in the senate owing to a technicality rather than a desire to block constitutional revision.[3] During the 1866 session of the legislature,

[1] Albany *Evening Journal*, Nov. 1, 1866, p. 2.

[2] *Tribune*, April 22, p. 4; 26, 1865, p. 4; *World*, April 27, 1865, p. 4.

[3] The 1846 constitution stated that no law which created or increased any state debt could be submitted to the people "at any general election when any other law, or any bill, or any amendment to the Constitution shall be submitted, to be voted for or against." Since the so-called bounty bill (which would allow the state to assume the debts incurred by those districts that had been forced to bid competitively for Civil War volunteers) had priority on the ballot, the

however, since there were no conflicting technicalities and since the twenty-year period from 1846 had expired, the lawmakers had enthusiastically authorized the constitutional referendum that appeared on the November ballot.[4]

In the November 1866 election 352,854 New Yorkers voted in favor of the proposal to call a new constitutional convention, while only 256,364 voted against it.[5] Yet this result did not automatically insure a convention, for a fine legal point remained in doubt: the majority in favor of calling a convention was less than a majority of the total number of eligible voters in the state. Since the old constitution could be read in such a way as to require not only a majority of those who actually voted, but also a majority of all those who were eligible to vote, the status of the proposed constitutional convention was still unclear as the 1867 session of the legislature got under way in January.

As soon as Governor Fenton's message was read to the new legislature, however, all doubts were resolved; the Radicals were pushing ahead with constitutional reform. Choosing to interpret the vote as a mandate for constitutional revision, Fenton charged the legislators to set up a special election for convention delegates. He sketched in general terms the reasons why New York needed a revision of its organic law and singled out specifically the problem of the state debt incurred in fighting the Civil War, the need to revise antiquated taxation stipulations, and the incredibly complicated, confusing, and corrupt system of overlapping judicial jurisdictions. But

senators feared the anomaly of having the referendum on the constitutional convention declared unconstitutional (see *Tribune*, May 1, 1865, p. 5).

[4] *Assembly Journal, 1866*, pp. 216–217, 296, 367, 438, 757; *Senate Journal, 1866*, pp. 37, 77, 82, 98, 100, 103, 212, 364, 373, 375, 1061.

[5] *Assembly Documents, 1867*, II, No. 34, p. 1.

he left unstated the question of franchise reform. Never has the phrase, "conspicuous in its absence," seemed more appropriate, for every member of the legislature and every newspaper-reading citizen in the state realized that the suffrage question would be the single most dramatic issue of constitutional revision.[6]

Although the Fenton Republicans had campaigned in 1866 primarily on the basis of the proposed Fourteenth Amendment and in the interest of party harmony had omitted equal suffrage from the state platform drafted the previous summer, there were a number of clear hints that they would be willing to tackle the long-standing problem of discriminatory franchise.[7] For one thing, the effort had been made before. As early as 1857, a handful of the Radicals' predecessors had wanted to retaliate against the Dred Scott decision with a referendum to erase the state's separate voting requirements for blacks.[8] In 1860, when a constitutional amendment for impartial suffrage was actually placed on the ballot in New York, the then outnumbered proponents of nondiscriminatory franchise campaigned hard for its acceptance.[9] Although they failed in 1860 and the amendment was defeated, there was little reason to expect them to abandon their ideal now that the political tide both in the party and in the state appeared to be flowing more strongly in their direction.

The Radicals had also shown from the outset of their rise

[6] "Governor's Message," 1867, in *Senate Journal, 1867*, pp. 8–9; Albany *Evening Journal*, Feb. 9, p. 2; 15, pp. 1, 2; 28, 1867, p. 2.

[7] Van Deusen, *Greeley*, p. 346.

[8] *The Daily Union* (Washington, D.C.), April 11, 1857, p. 2.

[9] James M. McPherson, *The Struggle for Equality: Abolitionists and the Negro in the Civil War and Reconstruction* (Princeton, N.J., 1964), pp. 25–26; John L. Stanley, "Majority Tyranny in Tocqueville's America: The Failure of Negro Suffrage in 1846," *Political Science Quarterly*, LXXXIV (1969), 412–435.

to power within the state legislature an inclination to work for black equality in other areas besides voting. Andrew White, for example, who represented one of the most racially liberal districts in New York and who was a close friend of the abolitionist crusader Samuel J. May, attempted in 1864, when he helped codify the state's school laws, to remove a clause permitting local districts to maintain segregated schools if they so desired.[10] Though his efforts were unsuccessful at that time, the Radicals had been steadily gaining strength for three years, and the issue of Negro rights now dominated American national politics to a greater extent than ever before.

While debating resolutions that attacked President Johnson's vetoes of the Freedmen's Bureau and civil rights bills of February 1866, a number of prominent Radical state legislators had gone on record in favor of Negro suffrage. Senators John O'Donnell, Andrew White, James Gibson, and Henry Low all endorsed the principle at that time, as did Speaker of the Assembly Tremain. Stephen Williams told his fellow senators that "I too agree with those who hold that the [13th Amendment, which] confers the right of citizenship upon the coloured people, also confers the right of suffrage as included in that citizenship." While discussing resolutions concerning the District of Columbia equal suffrage bill of 1866, Senator Wolcott Humphrey, an old associate of Owen Lovejoy, wanted to add "New York State" to the phrase endorsing equal franchise in Washington. O'Donnell agreed, arguing that "the Union party, as a party, is in favor of equal suffrage." Nicholas La Bau, the Fenton Radical from Richmond County, urged that Negro voting be made a Republican

---

[10] McPherson, *Struggle for Equality*, pp. 227–228; James M. Smith, "The 'Separate But Equal' Doctrine: An Abolitionist Discusses Racial Segregation and Educational Policy during the Civil War," *Journal of Negro History*, XLI (1956), 138–147.

Party test. Among Republican senators only George Andrews, the voice of an older Republicanism, Richard Crowley, a former Know-Nothing who would split openly with Fenton in 1868, Thomas J. Murphy, in the past "always . . . identified with the SEWARD-WEED wing of his party" and another who broke openly with Fenton in 1868, and Charles Stanford, a New York business representative for his California railroading brother Leland, failed to endorse the District suffrage measure. By the spring of 1866, the Democratic Albany *Argus* was referring to New York's Radicals collectively as "the African chorus."[11]

Governor Fenton alluded to his own "feelings" about the issue of legal equality as early as 1865. Adopting an interpretation of the Civil War still useful today, Fenton asserted that Union soldiers had done more than simply preserve the nation; they also "made the Declaration of Independence a living embodiment of the truth that all men are endowed with the inalienable rights of life, liberty and the pursuit of happiness, *without regard to the color of their complexion.* . . . They have not only secured the perpetuity of our institutions, but have made those institutions more sacred than ever before."[12] Inherent in this statement was an abiding Radical belief that the best way to refine society was to reform its institutions. Because an institutional approach had also promised to be politically effective, it underlay the Radicals' entire legislative philosophy. And in the early months of 1867 removal of the discriminatory suffrage requirements from the

[11] Albany *Evening Journal*, March 2, p. 1; 7, p. 1; 9, pp. 1, 2; 10, p. 1; 12, p. 2; 17, pp. 1, 2; April 5, 1866, p. 1; Augustus Kellogg to White, April 4, 1866, White Papers; Harlow and Boone, *Life Sketches of the State Officers*, pp. 91–93, 124–127, 144–147; Stebbins, *Political History*, pp. 160, 310.

[12] *Tribune*, May 22, 1865, p. 8 (italics added).

state constitution promised to be politically effective for at least two reasons.

The first political argument in favor of state franchise reform was tied to the question of national Reconstruction in the South. As the *Tribune* pointed out repeatedly, "Impartial Suffrage" in the defeated Southern states increasingly appeared to be the only solution to the problem facing Congress. The political rights of the freedmen would have to be guaranteed in the South in order to prevent their resubjugation by the very white rebels whom the Union had just spent so much blood and fortune to defeat. It was up to those Northern states which still discriminated against the Negro at the polls to set an example and pave the way for impartial suffrage in the South.[13] A second and more critical consideration involved New York's would-be black voters themselves. The elimination of the $250 property qualification promised to give the ballot to approximately 11,000 Negro voters in New York State.[14] In a state where some 720,000 votes had been

[13] *Ibid.*, Sept. 26, p. 4; 28, p. 4; Oct. 12, p. 4; 20, p. 4; 25, p. 4; Nov. 12, 1866, p. 4.

[14] This was the figure commonly used in the subsequent convention debates (see, for example, *Constitutional Debates*, p. 258). During the congressional debates over the Fifteenth Amendment, George S. Boutwell estimated that 10,000 Negroes would be enfranchised by removing the property qualification in New York (*Congressional Globe*, 40th Cong., 3d sess., 1869, p. 561). *The Census of the State of New York for 1865* (Albany, 1867), p. 17, recorded 20,806 colored males in New York State, but not all of them, of course, were twenty-one years old. *The Ninth Census of the United States, 1870* (Washington, D.C., 1872), I, 51, gives the total "Free Colored" population of New York State (both sexes) as 52,081. William E. Gillette, *The Right to Vote: Politics and Passage of the Fifteenth Amendment* (Baltimore, 1965), p. 82, Table 1, gives the press estimate of disfranchised Negroes as 8,167, but by taking one-fifth of the total black population, he estimates the vote to be 10,416. James M. McPherson,

cast for governor in 1866 and some 850,000 would shortly be cast for President in 1868, 11,000 may not seem like a particularly significant number. Yet Fenton's majority in 1864 had been just over 8,000 votes and his majority in 1866, which was considered a "Radical year," had been under 14,000. Since virtually every one of the Negro voters could be presumed to vote for Radical Republicans, an extra cushion in excess of 10,000 votes was hardly to be ignored in such an evenly divided state.[15] Perhaps most alluring of all to Fenton and his allies was the fact that the bulk of the new Negro voters would be located in New York City and Brooklyn, the very metropolitan areas where the Radicals had been striving for three years to improve their political fortunes. Suffrage reform promised to be a more effective vote-getting measure in those districts than any of the other reforms already passed by the Radical coalition.[16]

The Negro's Civil War (New York, 1965), p. 272, estimates that "about 21 per cent" of New York's adult male blacks on a state-wide basis already qualified under the $250 rule.

[15] Blacks who already voted in New York supported the Radicals. "The twelve thousand colored votes of the State of New York sent Governor Seymour home and Reuben E. Fenton to Albany," wrote the black leaders of Virginia in their 1865 "Address to the Loyal Citizens and Congress of the United States of America" (reprinted in Richard N. Current, ed., *Reconstruction* [Englewood Cliffs, N.J., 1965], pp. 19–20). There had been a colored Republican club in Brooklyn since before the war (McPherson, *Negro's Civil War*, p. 10).

[16] Of the 20,806 colored males listed in the 1865 state census, 4,129 resided in New York County (Manhattan Island), 2,113 in Kings County (Brooklyn), and 1,538 in Queens County (present borough of Queens). These three normally Democratic strongholds thus had by far the heaviest concentrations of Negroes in the state. The federal breakdown by county bears this out: of the 52,081 Negroes (both sexes) in the state, 13,071 were in New York County, 5,653 in Kings, and 3,791 in Queens. Of the remaining fifty-seven counties in the

II

If the Radicals were to eliminate New York's racially discriminatory suffrage requirements and at the same time correct the other weaknesses in the state constitution, they would
have to guide a bill through the legislature authorizing both
a convention and an election to select its delegates. Despite
the large Radical majority in the legislature, this did not prove
to be a routine matter. While there was general agreement
among the Republicans on the desirability of constitutional
reform, there were serious disagreements on questions of form.
These questions were crucial, for they would greatly influence the political cast of the convention itself. How many
delegates should be elected, for example, and when and where
should they meet? The number of delegates would influence
the relative efficiency of the convention and also tend to give
either more or less weight to party (as distinct from personal
or individual) positions. The date of the convention would
determine to some extent whether members of the current
legislature could be delegates. The place of meeting would
affect the character of the outside pressures to which the delegates would doubtless be subjected. Should the delegates be
elected by assembly district or by senate district? The former
might give a break to the Democrats, since they customarily

---

state only Dutchess (2,113), Orange (2,524), and Westchester (2,513)
had over 2,000 blacks. Furthermore, the state census, p. 17, noted that
roughly 9,000 of the 10,000 Negroes living on Manhattan Island resided in households where no taxes were paid, which meant that nobody voted in those households (the constitution had exempted
nonvoting Negroes from taxation, an incentive against even trying to
qualify for the vote). The *World*, March 16, 1867, p. 1, though it had
every reason to make the existing requirements look reasonable, estimated that only 300 "men of color" voted in New York City under
the provisions of the 1846 constitution.

elected a higher percentage of assemblymen than senators.[17] Who should be allowed to vote for delegates to the convention? The existing constitution stipulated the requirements for the election of "state officers," but said nothing on the subject of franchise qualifications for a constitutional convention.

The Fenton Radicals began to hammer out answers to these questions during the early weeks of the 1867 legislative session. First, the assembly decided officially that a convention would be called when L. Harris Hiscock, a Radical from Syracuse and a leading proponent of constitutional revision, reported on behalf of the Judiciary Committee "that in their opinion a sufficient number of votes were cast for such purpose." This effectively overruled the objection of those who argued that the size of the November majority was not obligatory on the legislature.[18]

Next, the assembly turned to the question of the size of the convention. Although the Judiciary Committee proposed 128 delegates, one from each assembly district, a motion was made and eventually carried to piggyback what was called the "32-at-large" plan on top of this number, thereby increasing the total to 160 members. This plan, endorsed by Governor Fenton in his annual message in January, allowed for an additional 32 delegates to be elected in a state-wide vote, rather than standing as candidates in any specific district.[19] Each voter in the state would be allowed to cast a ballot for only his first 16 choices. If Republicans voted for the 16 Republi-

[17] *World*, April 4, 1867, p. 4.

[18] *Assembly Journal, 1867*, pp. 41, 42, 58–59, 63–64, 95, 191; *Assembly Documents, 1867*, II, No. 34, p. 1; No. 36. Hiscock was another former Free Soil Democrat, having bolted in 1856, and was mentioned as a Radical candidate for Speaker by the *Tribune* (Harlow and Boone, *Life Sketches of the State Officers*, pp. 266–269).

[19] "Annual Message," 1867, *Assembly Journal, 1867*, p. 313.

can nominees and Democrats voted for the 16 Democratic nominees, the effect would be to guarantee the election of 16 hand-picked delegates from each party. It made no difference which slate of 16 ran ahead; all 32 would be elected.

When the Democrats joined in support of the 32-at-large plan, their motive was apparent. Under the Judiciary Committee plan, the political make-up of the convention would naturally approximate present party strength in the assembly, and the Democrats could expect to find themselves at a two-to-one disadvantage. The 32-at-large plan offered them an opportunity to elect 16 delegates of their own choosing on a parity basis with the Radicals. Though several of Fenton's close associates in the legislature felt he should not concede the Democrats this opportunity, the Governor apparently believed that the convention would appear too baldly partisan if elected solely on the basis of existing assembly districts.[20] The Democrats could retire to their tents, sit out the convention, and then play the role of spoilers when it came time to ratify the final document. The Governor, of course, hoped to avoid this.[21] Second, several outstanding Radical spokesmen, Horace Greeley among them, stood little chance of election in their home districts. An at-large slate made these men certain winners. Finally, in any given area the Republican voters might defer to one of the party's older and not necessarily Radical statesmen. An at-large slate assured the presence of sixteen dependable Radical leaders, since Fenton's allies controlled the state machinery which would choose them.

The bitterest and most politically sensitive struggle by far, however, was waged over the question of who should be allowed to vote for delegates to the convention. In debating

[20] Albany *Evening Journal*, Feb. 14, p. 2; 15, 1867, p. 1.
[21] *World*, March 1, 1867, p. 8.

the merits of the Fourteenth Amendment during January, Radical spokesmen like John Parker and Orson Stiles, the latter of whom represented the Governor's home district, had re-emphasized their commitment to full civil and political rights for blacks. Assemblyman Palmer Havens stated flatly, "I will never by my voice or vote consent that one rule shall be applied to the imported Celt, and another to the home-bred African." James Barnett, debating a senatorial resolution of thanks for the District of Columbia Equal Suffrage Act, appealed to his colleagues this way: "Let us now take by the hand our black brother . . . put him in possession of his civil rights . . . [and] above all . . . put in his hand the ballot."[22] Consequently, it came as no surprise when the Radicals injected the possibility of New York's Negroes participating on a nondiscriminatory basis in the election for convention delegates.

On February 27, 1867, Charles S. Hoyt, a paradigmatic Fentonite from Radical Yates County, offered an amendment to the assembly convention bill.[23] "Every male citizen of the age of twenty-one years, without distinction of color . . . shall be entitled to vote," he suggested, "but no person shall vote at such election who shall . . . have been engaged in rebellion against the United States."[24] In order to make his secondary proposal operative, he suggested that any voter who was challenged should be required to swear a loyalty oath to the Union. Hoyt's amendment formalized the issue of resolute pro-Unionism, upon which the Radicals had been

[22] Albany *Evening Journal*, Jan. 11, p. 1; 17, p. 1; 24, p. 1; Feb. 8, 1867, p. 2.

[23] Harlow and Boone, *Life Sketches of the State Officers*, pp. 274–276. Hoyt served in the 1852 assembly as a "Radical Democrat," was a former teacher turned physican, and now chaired the Committee on Charitable Institutions.

[24] *Assembly Journal, 1867*, p. 438.

campaigning since the war, as well as the question of Negro suffrage.

The issue of loyalty was the more easily resolved. The assembly approved an oath requirement by a vote of 67 to 52.[25] The question of equal franchise for the Negro proved far stickier. John Parker argued that "the question of the extension of the franchise is one of supreme importance, and the Republican Party is fully committed," and Hoyt claimed that he "would not vote to raise a Convention unless his proposition was incorporated in the bill." Nevertheless, a number of Republican assemblymen were not yet convinced that they should take a firm stand on impartial suffrage, and an even greater number opposed taking that stand on the question of voting for convention delegates. Hiscock, for example, though he claimed to represent "a locality that is understood to be very radical upon this question," could not support what he considered an unconstitutional call for a constitutional convention.[26] Others of like mind recognized the advantage of a few more months in which to gauge the political winds on the black suffrage issue.[27] The Democrats, of course, vehemently opposed equal suffrage at every point in the debate and eventually voted unanimously against Hoyt's amendment. This combination of cautious Radicals and adamant Democrats blocked open franchise by a vote of 33 in favor to 90 opposed.[28]

The assembly version of the convention bill, then, as it finally emerged in early March, provided for the election of 160 delegates, 128 by assembly district and 32 at large, a loy-

[25] *Ibid.*, p. 439.

[26] Albany *Evening Journal*, Feb. 15, p. 1; 26, p. 2; March 2, p. 1; 5, p. 1; 6, p. 1; 12, p. 1; 20, 1867, p. 1.

[27] *World*, Feb. 16, pp. 4, 8; 27, 1867, p. 8.

[28] *Assembly Journal, 1867*, pp. 439–440.

alty oath, and the existing suffrage requirements. Negroes would continue to be discriminated against in the vote for delegates. Although several Radical members wished to give the Judiciary Committee a chance "to perfect the bill" and report it again, this version of the proposal was approved on March 5 by a vote of 88 to 6, and it was sent over to the senate.[29]

The senate during all this time was working on a convention bill of its own, and in a series of lengthy debates had already faced most of the questions raised in the lower house.[30] The senate's answers, however, differed substantially from the ones just agreed upon by the assemblymen. Where the latter provided for the election of delegates by assembly districts, the former favored a complex system based on senatorial districts. Where the lower house opposed racially equal suffrage in the election of delegates, a Radical majority in the upper house, led by O'Donnell, Gibson, La Bau, and White, boldly endorsed that concept.[31] O'Donnell put the Radical position most forcefully: "We shall have fierce partizan [*sic*] conflicts in the Convention. And those conflicts will arise upon the question of suffrage. The Democratic party holds that suffrage is a franchise. The Republican party holds that it is a natural right."[32] The senators also rejected the 32-at-large principle in drafting their version of the convention

[29] *Ibid.*, pp. 442, 497–498, 500, 532–533.

[30] *Senate Journal, 1867*, pp. 216, 227, 238, 256, 264, 269, 293–294. The senate held seven debates on their own proposed convention bill. The subjects included the 32-at-large plan, equal Negro suffrage, equal female suffrage, loyalty oaths, and the allocation of delegates to the various senatorial districts (also see *World*, Feb. 16, p. 8; 28, p. 5; March 1, 1867, p. 8).

[31] *Senate Journal, 1867*, pp. 296–297. Albany *Evening Journal*, Feb. 16, pp. 1, 2; 27, p. 2; 28, p. 1; March 1, p. 1; 6, 1867, pp. 1, 2; *World*, March, 11, 1867, p. 5.

[32] Albany *Evening Journal*, Feb. 27, 1867, p. 2.

bill.[33] Several upstate Radicals hesitated to give the Democrats an artificial advantage, and the Whiggish senators, now more frequently labeled the "Canal Ring" because of their deep involvement in the state's waterway finances, opposed any plan that guaranteed the Radical Governor a sixteen-man cadre of hand-picked lieutenants in the convention.[34] The inclusion of a loyalty oath was the only important provision in the senate bill that conformed with the assembly version.

In a massive amendment, the senate substituted its own convention bill for the assembly's.[35] When the senators then concurred in the assembly bill "with amendments," they were in effect returning a counterproposal. When the assembly, in turn, refused to concur in the senate's amendments, a conference was agreed upon.[36] The conference committee met, worked out a compromise, and reported back to the two houses within a single day. The compromise proposal retained the equal suffrage clause of the senate bill, the election of delegates by senatorial districts as also called for by the senate, the 32-at-large plan recommended by the assembly, and a standard wording for the loyalty oath which had been approved in principle by both houses.[37] The senate concurred in this conference draft of the convention bill on March 19, but the assembly was not scheduled to vote until the 21st.[38] That day the assembly decided to vote on each clause of the

[33] *Senate Journal, 1867*, pp. 312–313.

[34] *World*, Feb. 16, p. 8; 28, 1867, p. 5.

[35] *Senate Journal, 1867*, pp. 309–312.

[36] *Ibid.*, p. 328; *Assembly Journal, 1867*, pp. 576–579, 623; Albany *Evening Journal*, March 7, p. 2; 8, p. 2; 12, 1867, p. 2.

[37] *Assembly Journal, 1867*, pp. 798–801; *Senate Journal, 1867*, pp. 390–393; *World*, March 15, 1867, p. 8.

[38] *Senate Journal, 1867*, pp. 409, 413. The vote in the senate was 22 in favor to 8 opposed (Albany *Evening Journal*, March 18, 1867, p. 1).

compromise separately. The newly worded loyalty oath was agreed to by a vote of 65 to 52. The election of delegates by senatorial districts was rejected, however, and so, despite the efforts of Hoyt, was the equal suffrage provision.[39]

The assembly action necessitated a second conference if the convention bill stood a chance of passing at all in 1867. Both houses agreed to another joint committee, which met on March 22.[40] On the following day the members reported back to their respective houses with a new compromise draft. The key to this proposal lay in the senate's retreat from unrestricted suffrage. The clause, "all persons entitled by law to vote for Members of the Assembly shall be entitled to vote at such election," was substituted for the nondiscriminatory franchise provision of the first conference bill. The assembly, on its part, agreed to permit the election of delegates to the constitutional convention by senatorial rather than assembly districts. Both the 32-at-large plan and the loyalty oath were retained from the previous compromise measure.[41] The special election was set for April 23, 1867, and the constitutional convention was scheduled to assemble in Albany on the first Tuesday of June 1867. In this form both houses of the New

[39] *Assembly Journal, 1867,* pp. 853–856; Albany *Evening Journal,* March 19, 1867, p. 1.

[40] *Assembly Journal, 1867,* p. 887; *Senate Journal, 1867,* pp. 463–464.

[41] Albany *Evening Journal,* March 22, p. 2; 28, 1867, p. 1. Under the final plan each senatorial district was allotted four delegates regardless of the number of assembly districts contained within it. Coupled with the 32 delegates-at-large, this retained a total of 160 delegates in the convention. The text of this second compromise draft is in *Assembly Journal, 1867,* p. 909. The New York State Supreme Court later declared the loyalty oath section of this law unconstitutional (but not until after the election had taken place) in Green v. Shumway, 39 N.Y., 418, June 1867, on the grounds that the legislature might relax existing franchise requirements, but not add to them (Stebbins, *Political History,* p. 213n).

York State legislature finally concurred in the same version of the bill, and on March 29, 1867, Governor Fenton signed into law "an act to provide for a Convention to revise and amend the Constitution."[42] At the same time the congressional Radicals in Washington were enacting the legislation that they hoped would alter significantly the political institutions of the South, New York's Radicals were setting in motion a process that they hoped would do the same for their own state.

III

Less than two weeks before the special election, the Republicans held a nominating convention in Syracuse to choose their sixteen at-large candidates.[43] Included among the sixteen, whose nomination assured their election to the convention, were such Radical luminaries as Horace Greeley, the outspoken editor of the *Tribune;* Waldo Hutchins, who was Governor Fenton's chief lieutenant and leading political troubleshooter; George Opdyke, whose celebrated libel case against Thurlow Weed epitomized the venomous feelings engendered by the Radicals' rise to power; Martin I. Townsend, an oratorically fiery abolitionist campaigner from Rensselaer County in the Hudson Valley; and William A. Wheeler, then among the most dignified and widely respected members of the Radical wing of New York's Republican Party and later Vice-President of the United States under Rutherford B.

[42] *Assembly Journal, 1867*, pp. 972–974, 976, 1862; *Senate Journal, 1867*, pp. 518, 549–550, 1147.

[43] *World*, March 22, 1867, p. 5. Despite the time factor, the Radical-dominated Republican state central committee decided to call a convention rather than choose sixteen men itself. This may be indicative of the Radical devotion to democratic forms and machinery.

Hayes. Most of the Republican candidates in the various senatorial districts around the state were little-known politicians
on the rise, though they were joined by a handful of veteran
Radical state legislators willing to lend their organizational
and parliamentary skills to the anticipated Radical majority.
Some of Fenton's local allies were so confident that they
wanted to reschedule their town elections to run simultaneously with the contest for delegates.[44]

The April special election went almost exactly as predicted.
The Democrats had carried senatorial districts one through
nine, fourteen, and thirty-one in November 1866, and they
were expected to do so again in April 1867. They also hoped
to rebound in the normally Democratic tenth and thirteenth
districts where the Republicans had won razor-thin majorities the last time.[45] On the other hand, the Democrats in five
upstate districts did not even bother to run candidates against
the Fenton men, thus conceding 20 seats without a fight.[46]
The pre-election estimate of 96 Republicans (twenty senatorial districts of 4 delegates each, plus their 16 delegates-at-
large) to 64 Democrats (twelve senatorial districts of 4 delegates each, plus their 16 delegates-at-large) turned out to be
within one delegate of the actual result. In the fifth district,
a New York City district, the voters returned the only split
delegation in the state by electing Norman Stratton, thereby
producing a final convention total of 97 Republicans and 63

[44] Fenton to Greeley, Jan. 8, 1867, Horace Greeley Papers, New
York Public Library.

[45] *World*, March 20, 1867, p. 4. The Republicans had carried the
tenth district (the counties just north of New York City) by only
146 votes and the thirteenth (Albany) by 213 votes. These totals are
derived from adding the votes in the various assembly races in those
districts in 1866.

[46] *Tribune*, April 24, 1867, p. 1; *World*, April 23, 1867, p. 4.

Democrats.[47] The *Times* had little comment, observing only that the results were "very strongly Republican, and that of the Radical type"; the *Tribune* was enthusiastic and anxious to get on with the work of revision; the *World* called the outcome of the special election a "fiasco" and a fitting prelude to the partisan machinations scheduled to begin in Albany on June 4.[48]

The constitutional delegates began to gather in Albany prior to the convention's formal opening. The Republicans met in caucus June 2 and 3 to select a candidate for president of the convention and to organize themselves in advance of the first sessions. The Fentonites were clearly in control and agreed upon William A. Wheeler for president of the constitutional assemblage over Thomas J. Alvord, the former lieutenant-governor whom the Radicals had dropped from the state ticket in 1866. Alvord had since gravitated toward the Whiggish or "Canal" wing of the Republican Party, and his overwhelming defeat was a measure of Radical control in the Republican caucus. Luther Caldwell, another Fenton man, was tapped for the job of secretary to the convention. Even the *World* was impressed with the strength and efficiency of the Radicals, not only in organizing the caucus but also in avoiding serious rifts within the party.[49]

The convention assembled officially at eleven o'clock in the morning, June 4, 1867. Wheeler was easily elected president, receiving 100 of the 149 votes cast, and Caldwell was installed as secretary.[50] Little else was accomplished, though a heated

[47] *Tribune*, April 24, 1867, p. 1; *World*, April, 24, p. 4; 25, p. 1; 26, 1867, p. 4.
[48] *Times*, April 24, 1867, p. 4; *Tribune*, April 24, 1867, p. 1; *World*, April 24, 1867, p. 4.
[49] *Tribune*, June 4, 1867, p. 5; *World*, June 3, p. 8; 4, 1867, p. 8.
[50] *Constitutional Debates*, p. 19.

debate concerned whether the sergeants-at-arms could perform their official duty of repelling "invasion from abroad" and still double as mailmen![51] In a strange way this petty squabble was something of an omen, for the constitutional convention was destined to be plagued throughout its existence with a seemingly endless string of extraneous questions that constantly intruded upon the time and energy of the delegates. In later weeks, for example, a vehement debate over whether to open the windows in the morning was not uncommon. These constant delays were the reason why Horace Greeley, never especially long on patience, rather quickly began to sour on the convention for its apparent dawdling.[52]

An even more foreboding omen was the bizarre affair that occurred as the delegates returned to their hotels after this first day's session. George W. Cole, a wealthy lumber dealer from Syracuse and a brevet general of cavalry in the Union army during the war, walked up to and shot L. Harris Hiscock, the Radical assemblyman from Syracuse, now a delegate to the convention he had worked hard to bring into existence. Cole and Hiscock had been close friends in Syracuse for many years, and the former had left his wife in the care of the latter when he went off to war. Cole had since become convinced that Hiscock tried to make advances toward Mrs. Cole while the General was away at the front, and that when she resisted, Hiscock attempted outright rape. Now, after almost three years in which the friendship between the two men had apparently been resumed as before, Cole had come to Albany to murder the representative from Syracuse. Hiscock died within an hour of Cole's attack, and the General surrendered himself to authorities in Albany.[53] The convention could

[51] *Ibid.*, pp. 20–25.
[52] Van Deusen, *Greeley*, p. 364; Alexander, *New York*, III, 184–185.
[53] *Tribune*, June 5, 1867, p. 5; *World*, June 5, 1867, p. 1; *Times*,

hardly have begun with a more symbolically somber event than the murder of one of its chief architects by his ostensible best friend.

An adjournment followed Hiscock's death, and the convention did not reconvene until June 11, when rules were agreed upon. In addition to the judicial and financial questions singled out by Governor Fenton in his annual message, the delegates faced proposals concerning new legislative districts, longer terms for state senators, and a need to tighten public control over canal contracts. Other issues would certainly be considered. Yet most of them were relatively insignificant or reasonably mechanical alterations of the organic law. Furthermore, there was wide agreement on the vast majority of the revisions likely to be entertained by the convention; most of the issues were not bitterly partisan. Even a question as complex and potentially disruptive as the state judiciary system, for example, could be handled in a remarkably nonpartisan fashion.[54] But the question of racially equal suffrage, which had generated partisan divisions in the state legislature even while the convention was being set up, promised to be the subject of a bitter party battle.[55]

Horace Greeley was made chairman of the Committee on the Right of Suffrage and the Qualifications to Hold Office. Joining him on that committee, which would recommend franchise revisions to the full convention, were four upstate Radicals and two Democrats, one from Brooklyn and the other from Albany.[56] No Democrat from New York City

June 5, 1867, p. 1. The victim's brother, Frank Hiscock, eventually replaced him at the convention. See *Tribune*, June 12, 1867, p. 8, and *Constitutional Debates*, p. 232.

[54] *Constitutional Debates*, p. 2288.

[55] *Times*, June 5, 1867, p. 5.

[56] *Constitutional Debates*, p. 95; *Documents of the Convention of the State of New York, 1867–'68* (Albany, 1868), I, No. 17, p. 2.

was on the committee, even though that city contained approximately 20 percent of the Negroes in the state. The Democratic press was livid and already building the issue of suffrage reform into the most important political question of the year.

The tension over franchise reform increased during the week and a half that the suffrage committee held hearings. Negro suffrage was not the only significant consideration before the committee. There were disputes about residence requirements, about the naturalization of immigrant voters, and about the possibility of granting the vote to women.[57] But the racially discriminatory clause of the old constitution held the focus of attention for the committee, for the convention as a whole, and for the entire state. Petitions by the hundreds poured into Albany and were referred to the suffrage committee. The petitions seemed overwhelmingly to favor universal male suffrage without distinction as to color.[58] By the end of June, Greeley's committee was prepared to go before the convention, and the delegates braced themselves for what they knew would be their most politically significant fight.

The majority report, presented by Greeley and signed by the other Radical committee members, proposed the elimination of all references to race and color in the suffrage clause. The only qualifications on the right of any twenty-one-year-old male to vote in New York State would be one year of state residency, thirty days of district residency, and thirty

[57] *Constitutional Debates*, pp. 178–179, 218, 364–372, 537, 547; *Convention Documents*, I, No. 15, pp. 6–7; Van Deusen, *Greeley*, p. 362.

[58] These petitions are far too numerous to cite individually. Ezra Graves, for example, submitted 37 petitions in one session. They are indexed in *Journal of the Convention of the State of New York, Begun and Held at the Capitol, in the City of Albany, on the 4th day of June, 1867* (Albany, [1868]) (hereafter cited as *Convention Journal*). Also see *Tribune*, June 27, 1867, p. 4.

days of United States citizenship. Criminals and paupers both forfeited their right to vote. In explaining their recommendations, the Radical majority came immediately to the most crucial point:

1st. Strike out all discriminations based on color. Slavery, the vital source and only plausible ground of such invidious discrimination, being dead, not only in this State, but throughout the Union, as it is soon to be, we trust, throughout this hemisphere, we can imagine no tolerable excuse for perpetuating the existing proscription. Whites and blacks are required to render like obedience to our laws, and are punished in like measure for their violation. Whites and blacks were indiscriminately drafted and held to service to fill our State's quotas in the war whereby the Republic was saved from disruption. We trust that we are henceforth to deal with men according to their conduct, without regard to their color. If so, the fact should be embodied in the Constitution.[59]

The Democratic minority on the suffrage committee submitted a separate report. Though the Democrats objected strongly to lengthening the citizenship requirement from the existing ten days to the proposed thirty days, their key point likewise dealt with the racial question.[60] The minority report urged retention of the 1846 franchise requirements for black New Yorkers, unless the people of the state approved an alter-

[59] *Convention Documents*, I, No. 15, pp. 1–4.

[60] The seemingly innocuous extension of the citizenship period from ten to thirty days had important short-run implications for the presidential election of 1868. Naturalization took two years. The 1846 constitution required that a person be a citizen for at least ten days in order to vote. Consequently, ten days prior to each election the Democrats customarily issued a huge number of preliminary citizenship papers to immigrants, thereby insuring that they could vote two years later. By extending the citizenship period to thirty days, the Republicans would bar from the polls in 1868 all those immigrants whom the Democrats had processed ten days before the 1866 election.

native article submitted separately from the rest of the constitution. The minority's primary argument in favor of separate submission was historical: that was the way it was done in 1846 and again in 1860. "It would be unfair to the people to declare: that, whereas, they have again and again refused to accept this change, therefore, we will incorporate it into the Constitution and compel them either to repeal that instrument or to accept this measure." To make racially impartial suffrage "dependent upon the fate of financial articles or of changes in the judicial structure, or of innovation[s] of doubtful popularity," the Democrats continued, "would be unjust to the class who solicit this extension of privileges."[61]

The Radicals must have found this last argument particularly galling, for the Democratic strategy was clearly not one of separating Negro suffrage in order to give it a better chance of ratification. Both the Radicals and the Democrats believed that the equal suffrage article would instead be rendered more vulnerable if isolated from the rest of the constitutional revisions. Arguments against Negro suffrage and appeals to race prejudice would surely be more telling in isolation than in the context of many other nonpartisan constitutional improvements. It was not surprising, therefore, that the long-anticipated debates on black voting in New York came to a head over the question of separate submission.

Henry C. Murphy, the recognized leader of the Democratic delegation, set the great debate in motion with a frank admission: he favored separate submission because he hoped to see nondiscriminatory franchise defeated. Murphy, who had spoken out in Congress against Northern free blacks at the time of the Wilmot Proviso,[62] opposed Negro voting "for

[61] *Convention Documents*, I, No. 16, pp. 3–4.
[62] Leon F. Litwack, *North of Slavery: The Negro in the Free States, 1790–1860* (Chicago, 1961), pp. 47–48.

political reasons" as a Democrat and because he considered it "morally and socially wrong." Political equality for the black man would lead to social equality. Social equality, in turn, would result in a "confounding" of the races to the detriment of whites. Furthermore, Murphy explicitly drew the logical implications for national politics from the proposed action of New York. He predicted that the adoption of racially equal suffrage in New York would give backbone to Congress in trying to implement its own recently enacted Reconstruction program in the defeated Southern states. This, of course, could hardly be disputed by the Radicals; they had cited as one of the reasons for franchise reform the need to clean their own house before cleaning those in the South.

Before closing his speech, Murphy proved himself an able debater by denying in advance one of his opponents' primary arguments: the relevancy of the Declaration of Independence in a discussion of voting rights. Many delegates had already alluded to that document while addressing questions other than Negro suffrage; Murphy could certainly anticipate that the champions of equal suffrage would cite it as well. Governor Fenton, after all, had linked the Declaration to institutional equality as early as 1865. Murphy's position was deceptively simple; he distinguished between restrictions on the power of government and the privilege of exercising that power. The American manifesto of 1776 listed certain civil rights which those who governed could not abrogate, but this did not mean that every person consequently had the right to help rule. If the right to govern was among the inalienable rights of every human being, then there could be no legitimate grounds for restricting the franchise at all: no property qualifications, no residency regulations, no citizenship stipulations, no sexual discriminations, and no age requirements. "The right to vote," Murphy summarized, was not a natural right but one "conferred by society—a franchise to be exercised for the purpose of good government. Such are my views of this question, and with such convictions have I presented this argument."[63] Having fired most of the heavy guns in the antisuffrage arsenal, he withdrew to await a counterattack.

Rising to defend the principle of racially impartial suffrage was Martin I. Townsend.[64] In a long series of rambling and rhetorically strained remarks—his references ranged from classical Greek government to Robert Peel and English reform—Townsend made two substantive points. The first was his belief that whenever injustice was imposed upon a minority, it invariably tended to degrade the majority which worked the injustice. He never really defended this proposition; he merely asserted it. More intriguing, however, were his views on the relationship between political rights and social rights. Townsend clearly favored the former for Negroes but opposed the latter; when questioned from the floor, he declared himself unabashedly opposed to what he termed "the mingling of the races," and absolutely against intermarriage. But unlike Murphy, Townsend argued that black equality at the polls would not be a first step toward black equality in social matters. Those who opposed social contact, in fact, ought to concede the black man political equality, because that would give the Negro a sense of dignity and erase the drive to add white blood to his line. "Sir," replied Townsend to one of his

[63] *Constitutional Debates*, pp. 236–237.

[64] Martin Ingham Townsend, fifty-one years old, was yet another transplanted New Englander and former Free Soil Democrat now turned Fenton Republican. Before the war he had been one of the leading antislavery spokesmen in the Hudson Valley. He was later a member of the New York State Board of Regents and served two terms in Congress as a regular Republican, 1875–1879 (*National Cyclopaedia of American Biography* [New York, 1895], IV, 489; *Biographical Directory of the American Congress, 1774–1961* [Washington, D.C., 1961], p. 1724).

Democratic cross-examiners, "there is no danger of the intermingling of the race by a man who respects his own blood."[65]

Horace E. Smith took a somewhat different position in defense of the majority report. Although he was willing to agree with Murphy that the Declaration of Independence did not apply in the present debate, and that the franchise was a political rather than a natural right, Smith believed every member of society should be granted the right to participate in government unless some negative quality in that person, mental incompetency for example, made it impossible for him to comprehend "the best interests of society." Color manifestly did not disqualify a man from perceiving the truth. Therefore, argued Smith, the allocation of political rights on the basis of race was impractical and actually deprived the state of a source of strength. Having taken this stand, however, Smith somewhat lamely hastened to add that he was not advocating the elimination of color as a social determinant, only as a political determinant.[66]

The distinction between social equality and political equality continued to be a central theme in many of the subsequent speeches made by the Radical defenders of impartial suffrage. Several of them, in fact, became so bogged down in categorizing various sorts of rights that they seemed to lose whatever cogency they might have had. Occasionally an orator would broach a new argument, a fresh idea, or a different viewpoint. Stephen D. Hand, for example, came close to a modernistic notion when he argued that the sociological circumstances of the country had changed so dramatically in the years since the last state constitution was drafted that its franchise requirements no longer fit the actual situation. Above all else, slavery had been blotted out. Its elimination cost the nation

[65] *Constitutional Debates*, p. 241.
[66] *Ibid.*, pp. 243–244.

"a bloody war" and "sent sorrow into every household," but it permitted the people of the United States to see the Negro for what he was: a man like any other man and not a piece of chattel. "The color of his skin is the merest accident in his organism, and is of no consequence," declared Hand.[67]

Both Nathan G. Axtell and Edward A. Brown observed that the question of Negro suffrage was a matter of degree. The black New Yorker had already been granted the right to vote; the issue was whether a property qualification was still necessary. Brown tried to point out the political nature of this question when he reminded the convention that "it took forty-three years [1777–1820] for the politicians of this State to discover the necessity of excluding [Negroes] from the right to vote. Sir," he asked rhetorically, "why was that change made?" Brown was also one of the first to introduce the "reward for services rendered" argument. This point, which received extensive elaboration from subsequent speakers, stressed the fact that black New Yorkers had rallied to the cause of their state and their country in time of mortal danger. The Negro had displayed his loyalty and earned his citizenship; he now deserved his full political rights.[68]

[67] *Ibid.*, pp. 244–245. But color was of consequence socially for Hand, who re-emphasized that the elimination of political distinctions would not eliminate social distinctions: "As to social equality growing out of political equality, I am sorry to hear any man of good sense bring that forward . . . social equality is not a matter of legislation, and never will be."

[68] *Ibid.*, pp. 246–248. Prior to 1821 the criterion of color did not appear in New York State's franchise requirements. On the introduction of constitutional discrimination, see *Reports of the Proceedings and Debates of the Convention of 1821 Assembled for the Purpose of Amending the Constitution of the State of New York* (Albany, 1821); Benjamin F. Butler, "Outline of the Constitutional History of New York, An Anniversary Discourse Delivered . . . November 19, 1847," *Collections of the New-York Historical Society*, 2d ser., II (1849), 62; Charles Z. Lincoln, *The Constitutional History of New York*

On July 12, Henry Murphy responded to the Republican arguments. He made three related points in support of his amendment calling for separate submission. The first was the galling argument which he had first avoided: the franchise article should not be subjected to possible defeat due to flaws in the rest of the constitution. Second, Murphy asserted that enlarging the electorate was a question peculiarly divorced from other constitutional revisions; consequently it should be accorded a separate status. Finally, he pointed out that separate submission "followed the safe line of precedent." There seemed to be no reason for breaking the tradition established by the convention of 1846 and continued in the referendum of 1860.

The Brooklyn Democrat then addressed himself to the larger question, upon which the Radicals had actually concentrated most of their own remarks: the validity of racially impartial suffrage as distinguished from the validity of separate submission. On this score Murphy had done a little homework and was able to cite three appropriate authorities against his Republican opponents. The first was Abraham Lincoln himself. Murphy quoted from the Lincoln-Douglas debates the well-known passage in which Lincoln had elaborated his belief that "a physical difference between the white and black races" would "forever forbid . . . social and political equality" between them. Murphy's second authority was Thomas Jefferson, whom Martin Townsend had earlier claimed as a

from the Beginning of the Colonial Period to the Year 1905, Showing the Origin, Development, and Judicial Construction of the Constitution, 5 vols. (Rochester, N.Y., 1906); Dixon Ryan Fox, "The Negro Vote in Old New York," Political Science Quarterly, XXXII (1917), 252–275; Leo H. Hirsch, Jr., "The Negro and New York, 1783 to 1865," Journal of Negro History, XVI (1931), 417–424; and Chilton Williamson, American Suffrage: From Property to Democracy, 1760–1860 (Princeton, N.J., 1960).

political forebear. Many of the Radicals believed that they had been emulating Jefferson's true spirit by bolting the pre-war Democracy for the new reform party of the Republicans. Murphy chose the section of Jefferson's *Notes on Virginia* which concludes that Negroes were apparently inferior not only because of their subordinate position and lack of training, but also because of inherent biological handicaps.

The third citation was lifted from contemporary scientific thought. Murphy read a paragraph of anthropological data from a treatise by the political scientist Francis Lieber, who was a prominent member of the Union League Club of New York City. Through a comparison of skull types, Lieber had argued that all men, despite the ringing phrases of American political philosophy, were most assuredly not equal. Furthermore, there were not simply different kinds of men, but superior and inferior kinds on a color scale. At the top of the scale stood the white civilizations of the west; at the bottom rested the darkest-skinned societies of the earth, the "Boushmannes" (Bushmen) and the "Papous" (Papuans).[69] Reference to Lieber's data eventually led to a lengthy debate between Murphy and Professor Theodore W. Dwight, the state's most eminent legal scholar.[70] For a whole day these two titans of their respective delegations flailed one another with the data of the social sciences and the logic of the law.[71]

[69] *Constitutional Debates*, pp. 254–256.

[70] Dwight, a frequent intellectual spokesman for the Radical cause, was an expert on prison reform, had published a law book on charity cases (1863), and coauthored an extensive report on prison systems in the United States and Canada for the state legislature (1866). On his earlier career and legal reputation, see Allen Johnson and Dumas Malone, eds., *Dictionary of American Biography*, V (New York, 1930), 571–573.

[71] *Constitutional Debates*, pp. 263–272, 312–316. Dwight's most telling point received little emphasis: Murphy would have the Negro

But the high point of the convention debates over impartial suffrage had been reached before they began.

Patrick Corbett, a lawyer from the Radical bastion of Syracuse, rose after Murphy's rebuttal to deliver probably the clearest, most relevant, and most refreshingly straightforward speech heard during two weeks of debate on the suffrage committee's report. He began by stating openly that every member of the convention, despite all the circumlocution, knew full well that equal suffrage was a partisan issue, that "the word 'white' marked distinctly the dividing line" between the two parties. Corbett also made effectively an argument which others had failed to bring into focus: that the circumstances of the country had changed so dramatically that even Abraham Lincoln had been forced to change with them. "A vast gulf" divided prewar America from postwar America, and the nation could not pretend that life would go on exactly as it had in the past. Significantly, he observed, the Radicals were a party willing to *"use* the results of advancing civilization." In another vein, Corbett drew upon his own experience as an Irish Catholic immigrant to remind the Democrats how recently their present objections against the Negro had provided an underpinning for prejudice against unwanted whites; the point could hardly have been lost on antisuffrage delegates Murphy, Develin, Cassidy, and Collahan. Finally, Corbett was virtually the only speaker to turn the distinction between legal and social equality back upon its defenders. The knife could cut both ways, he suggested, for regardless of whether the convention sanctioned the black man's political equality, his inherent merits as a man—the "quality of a gentleman" which he might possess within himself—could never be crushed out. In conclusion he tied the cause of black

---

barred from voting, not because he was inherently inferior, but because he had not yet accumulated $250.

rights to the younger generation and to the future. Corbett came as close as anyone in the convention to forging a link between America's historic faith in its own preordained progress and the crusade to secure racial justice before the law.[72]

The only political surprise which occurred during the suffrage debate involved Magnus Gross, a Democratic delegate from New York City. Although a loyal Tammany supporter, Gross declared himself in favor of a racially impartial franchise. The *Tribune* probably did not exaggerate when it characterized Gross's statement as "a bombshell [thrown] directly into the camp of his political brethren," but Gross's motives were reasonably transparent.[73] He edited the widely circulated German-language newspaper *Staats Zeitung,* and he seemed to be hinting at a *quid pro quo* with Greeley involving the issues of impartial suffrage and citizenship extension.[74] He would support the former if Greeley would drop the latter. No bargain was struck, however, and the rest of the New York City delegation worked to offset Gross's apostasy. Abraham B. Conger moved that Negroes be barred from voting whether they could meet the property qualification or not; John E. Burrill would limit the franchise to Negroes born in the state of New York; William Cassidy advocated a five-year residency requirement for blacks.[75]

Years of public persuasion, months of legislative politics, and weeks of convention debate culminated finally on the evening of July 17, 1867, when Murphy's amendment for separate submission of the Negro suffrage clause was finally called to a vote. By a count of 29 in favor to 78 opposed the

[72] *Ibid.,* pp. 257–258; Albany *Evening Journal,* July 13, 1867, p. 2; Corbett to White, March 7, 1865, White Papers.
[73] July 18, 1867, pp. 1, 4.
[74] *Constitutional Debates,* p. 316.
[75] *Ibid.,* pp. 480–481, 496, 500–501.

Murphy amendment was rejected.[76] The Radicals had triumphed. Franchise requirements without distinction of race or color were to be included as an integral part of the proposed new constitution for the state of New York. The Radical *Tribune* was gleeful over the result. "The defeat of Mr. Murphy's amendment," it blissfully predicted, "should secure the speedy adoption of the majority report, and we may consider the suffrage question as virtually settled."[77] Seldom has there been a more premature statement of victory.

[76] *Ibid.*, p. 349.
[77] July 18, 1867, p. 1.

8

The Fall of Franchise Reform

I

In retrospect, the vote of the constitutional convention on July 17, 1867, in favor of racially impartial suffrage represented the high-water mark of the Radicals' reconstruction at home in New York. The Fenton Republicans appeared confident, united, and successful in pushing ahead with the most ambitious project yet in what had been a steadily enlarging program of civil and institutional reform. But before the week was out hints in the popular press suggested that below the surface all was not well. As the summer of 1867 wore on, it became increasingly obvious that some members of the Radical coalition which passed the urban and educational reforms of 1865, 1866, and 1867 were beginning to have serious doubts about their commitment to franchise revision. These doubts, in turn, began to dissolve the union of idealism and political efficacy which had sustained the Radical alliance.

The first evidence of serious unrest among Republicans appeared less than a week after the constitutional delegates defeated Murphy's call for separate submission of the franchise article. The *Times*, whose consistent defense of Greeley's report to the convention had revealed the remarkable degree of party unity and policy control achieved by the Radicals during the late spring and early summer of 1867, began to reverse its position and to urge a reconsideration of separate submission. Though still professing to believe in the political equality of the Negro, an editorial claimed that the question of black civil rights was the only one "to be dealt with by the Convention which derives its cogency, and even its propriety, from the revolution produced by the rebellion, and the people ought to be privileged to say whether they are prepared to carry out, in their own State, the principle which the majority of their representatives in Congress have helped to fasten upon the South. A change so radical, so significant in its origin and so interwoven with the policy of the nation, should not be tacked as a makeweight to the general provisions of the Constitution." According to the *Times*, a number of loyal party men were beginning to fear that the questions of race and civil rights might not be worth the risks they entailed.[1]

One important factor in the willingness of these Republicans to consider a retreat on the issue of impartial suffrage at home was a crescendo of Democratic rhetoric. The opposition had begun hammering away at the black question back in March, as soon as it became apparent that the Radicals were serious about revising the state's franchise requirements. At that time the *World* published a "survey" of the Negro population of New York City. Some impression of the *World*'s campaign against Negro suffrage was conveyed on the front page of this survey under the heading "Colored Morals." The paper quoted an unidentified police captain whose opinion seemed to be "the most terse and at the same time true" summation of the subject: "The negroes as a race will lie, but will not swear; will drink when they get a chance, but will

---

[1] July 22, 1867, p. 4.

seldom get drunk; are not addicted to violence, but take to stealing (the only great crime in vogue among them being assaults upon white women); while all will gamble or play policy whenever or wherever they can find or make an opportunity." The story concluded that editorial comment seemed unnecessary: "The facts given in this article will enable each reader to draw his own conclusions."[2] Subsequent stories throughout the spring and summer of 1867 left no doubt that the reader should conclude that Negro New Yorkers should not be allowed to exercise the high responsibilities of running a democratic government; at least the vast majority of them should not.[3] The "great mission" of the Republican Party, maintained the Democrats' leading paper, was "to erase the word *white* from the vocabulary of politics"; the *World* clearly believed that its own mission was to prevent the Republicans from doing so.[4]

[2] March 16, 1867, pp. 1–2. This "survey" placed the total number of Negroes in New York City at 9,948 and included an occupational survey in which waiters and cooks (2,000) headed the list, followed by coachmen (500), laundresses (500), whitewashers (400), and caterers (300). The next two largest categories were thieves, male and female (250), and prostitutes (200). Under "Education" the *World* noted that Negro pupils "possess more than average ability for 'short' tasks, but are not generally capable of long continued steady exertion." Only the handful of families under the heading "Rich Negroes" received any praise—a fairly obvious attempt to show the benefit of retaining the $250 property qualification. The only point made by the *World* which seemed out of keeping with the rest of the article was the frank assertion that "miscegenation in this City, like hydrophobia, has been more written of than experienced." They believed that no more than eighty families were "miscegenating."

[3] *World*, April 4, p. 4; 13, p. 6; 15, p. 4; June 14, p. 4; 20, p. 5; 29, p. 4; July 1, p. 4; 5, p. 4; 23, 1867, p. 4.

[4] *Ibid.*, July 6, 1867, p. 4. Philip D. Swenson. "The Midwest and the Abandonment of Radical Reconstruction, 1864–1877" (Ph.D. dissertation, University of Washington, 1971), pp. 98–105, argues that

The Democrats also re-emphasized the striking parallel between national Reconstruction and the situation in New York State. The Fentonites in Albany were "attempting to introduce into this State the same general scheme for securing perpetual Republican majorities which Congress has forced upon the South. The essence of the scheme is, to enfranchise all the negroes and disfranchise as many as possible of the whites."[5] The *World* had a good case. Eliminating the $250 property qualification would gain the Republicans several thousand black votes in New York City and Brooklyn; lengthening the citizenship period would temporarily deprive the Democrats of several thousand more. The New York Democracy was finding the role of surrogate Southerner more and more frustrating, and the tone of their racist campaign had become shrill by midsummer of 1867.

Yet all-out opposition from the Democrats was to be expected. Regardless of how loudly they screamed or how racist their appeals became, the Republicans would almost certainly have persevered as long as franchise revision seemed politically effective. The municipal measures of the past three years demonstrated clearly the Radicals' willingness to undertake bitterly partisan reforms. But there was a second and more crucial reason for the growing Republican uneasiness: the slowly accumulating evidence that equal suffrage at home risked alienating more white voters than it could compensate for with new black ones.

When Fenton called for a constitutional convention in his annual message of January 2, 1867, over a year and a half had

---

racist voting was a function of the ability of the Democrats to elicit it, rather than of the inherent racism of the population. New York's Democrats worked hard to elicit racist reactions throughout the summer and fall of 1867.

[5] *World*, Aug. 1, 1867, p. 4.

passed since any Northern state had rejected Negro suffrage. Furthermore, the crisis over national Reconstruction had burst fully into the open; President Andrew Johnson had been repudiated at the polls in the fall of 1866; and the Radical reformers had succeeded in making their programs the policy of the Republican Party. Even the cautious *Evening Journal* had seen Negro suffrage as a wave of the future during the spring of 1867. Discussing Connecticut's approaching referendum on the subject, it had maintained that "public sentiment has undergone a great change upon this question within a twelvemonth; and thousands who, in 1866, doubted the expediency of extending the suffrage, now adopt it as an essential article in the advanced creed of the party."[6] These were the circumstances in which the Radicals had decided to add franchise revision to their postwar program of civil and institutional reform in New York.

The first setback, however, had occurred while the state legislature was still debating the final form of the convention bill, and it may have been influential in persuading the senate to accept the assembly's more guarded position on black suffrage in the special election. This was the defeat of the Radicals in neighboring Connecticut. Labor leader Ira Steward suggested that the Republicans surrendered the Nutmeg State by allowing the Democrats to become sole champions of the eight-hour idea there.[7] Although this argument probably encouraged a portion of the Fentonites to go along with the pending eight-hour bill, most writers in the popular press disagreed with Steward's analysis. What he attributed to the eight-hour controversy, they attributed to the issue of Negro suffrage.

The *World* cried loudly that black suffrage had undone

[6] Albany *Evening Journal*, Jan. 26, 1867, p. 1.
[7] *Tribune*, April 4, 1867, p. 4.

the Republicans in Connecticut and gratuitously counseled New York's Radicals to reconsider their own support of that principle.[8] Connecticut, after all, appeared politically similar to New York, with significant numbers of immigrant voters in the downstate areas, pockets of traditional New England antislavery sentiment in the interior counties, and an incumbent Republican Party dominated by Radicals who had also decided that impartial suffrage was a wave of the future. Nor was the *World* the only paper to attribute the Republican defeat in Connecticut to the race question. Other interested and influential journals, including three Republican giants— the Providence *Journal*, the Springfield *Republican*, and the Philadelphia *North American*—all saw the defeat in the same way.[9] What many editorials labeled the "Lesson of Connecticut" seemed clear: slow down on Negro suffrage.

The *Tribune* had drawn a very different lesson indeed. Republicans should not apply the brakes, but rather accelerate the drive toward equal political rights for the Negro. Treachery and cowardice had defeated the party in Connecticut, not its courageous stand on the valid principle of impartial suffrage. A national senator from that state had actually bolted the Republican Party and gone over to the Democracy on the eve of the April election. "The experience of all parties is, that cowardice is the worst policy," trumpeted the *Tribune:* "Agitation, progress, constant advances, are as necessary to [the Republican Party's] purity and strength as sea currents and salt are to the purity of the ocean. When a great principle is at stake, we cannot gain a half victory. Such victories are surrenders; for we either concede that our enemy is right, or that we are weak. No party can live without answering its mission." There was no need either to apologize for or to play

[8] April 4, 1867, p. 4.
[9] *World*, April 8, 1867, p. 4.

down their forthcoming Albany convention, the *Tribune* urged the Radicals: "*The battle is now for Universal Liberty and Impartial Suffrage.* Let the word be passed along the line."[10]

As soon as this word reached the editorial office of the *Times*, however, it stopped. The *Times* found this cry for what it called the further "Radicalizing" of the party most unsatisfactory. It preferred instead to note:

Even in New-England, which has hitherto taken the lead in the "progressive political movement," grave doubts begin to be felt whether the triumph thus far achieved may not prove to be more showy than solid—temporary and short-lived rather than permanent and enduring. And there are a good many others, both in New-England and out of it, who are not a little anxious as to the effect of the new crusade which seems to be threatened by the extremists and ultraists of the day.[11]

Republicans had won a position of great power under the existing franchise regulations, even if the geographical basis of their support seemed perilously off balance. To be sure, franchise revision would help dramatically to right that balance by giving the substantial Negro population in New York City and Brooklyn a ballot now largely withheld. But if the effort to secure franchise revision cost the Republicans a significant portion of the upstate majority they could already count on, then its value would be questionable at best. Perhaps it was better to stick with a sure thing; the Radicals in Connecticut had lost votes even in old antislavery counties.

Though these initial misgivings had been overcome during the late spring and early summer, the reintroduction of similar doubts in late July soon produced a sense of hesitancy

[10] April 5, 1867, p. 4.
[11] April 9, 1867, p. 4.

among the delegates themselves. Despite the fact that the convention bill had been drafted with the assumption that a new constitution would be submitted to the people at the November elections of 1867, the *Times* began to allude to the possibility that the delegates might not finish their work quickly enough to meet the November deadline. Moreover, the *Times* implied that the delegates were slowing their deliberations consciously. The Radical Republicans, who ultimately controlled the pace of the convention, were apparently no longer certain that they wished to carry a revised constitution with them to the polls.[12] What appeared to be a probable asset in January had begun to look like a possible liability by midsummer.

In early September more evidence arrived. It was in the form of election results, and it seemed to bode ill for the cause of Radical reform in general and Negro suffrage in particular. The first results were from Vermont. Although Vermont was for all practical purposes a one-party state, the incumbent Republican governor lost a significant portion of the overwhelming majority which he had captured in 1866.[13] More telling would be the returns from Maine and California. Politicians throughout the North waited anxiously for the September contests on the coasts; perhaps they might give some hint of the national mood.

The celebrated saw laid to rest in this century by James A. Farley had some validity during the post-Civil War years; the Union really did tend to vote the way Maine voted. And in Maine, a Republican stronghold since the 1850's, the Republicans had the additional advantage of an extremely popular candidate for governor in the person of Joshua L. Chamberlain. Nevertheless, early returns indicated that the Republi-

[12] *Times*, July 30, 1867, p. 4.
[13] *Tribune*, Sept. 4, 1867, p. 4.

cans had done considerably worse in September 1867 than they had in September 1866. A majority of 27,500 in 1866 was pared to 13,500 in 1867, and many analysts believed only Chamberlain's immense personal popularity had saved the day.[14]

Paired with the election in Maine was the September contest in California. Californians voted tremendous Republican majorities in each of the war years and in each of the postwar elections through 1866. But as the 1867 returns trickled across the country, the eastern newspapers slowly became aware that the Democracy had actually captured the state. Henry H. Haight, who left the Republican Party to rejoin the Democrats, was elected governor over George C. Gorham by a convincing margin. Exact figures were difficult to determine from three thousand miles away, but the result was certainly unsettling in a state where the totals had been three-to-two Republican since 1863.[15]

Interpretations of the September results were offered by each of the leading papers in New York. The *World*, as might be expected, gloated over the returns and predicted a Democratic resurgence across the United States. The outcomes signaled an impending "reaction" against Radical extremism. With little to celebrate for nearly five years, the Democrats in New York took full advantage of the opportunity afforded them by the strong showing in Maine and the victory in California.[16]

For leading Republican organs the results of early Septem-

[14] *Times*, Sept. 10, 1867, p. 5; figures are rounded off to the nearest 500.

[15] *Ibid.*, Sept. 6, p. 8; 7, p. 5; 27, 1867, p. 1; *Tribune*, Sept. 23, 1867, p. 4.

[16] *World*, Sept. 3, p. 4; 6, p. 4; 7, p. 1; 9, p. 4; 10, pp. 1, 4; 11, 1867, p. 4.

ber were sobering. On the one hand, they wished to explain
the setback in Maine and the defeat in California as being
unique and as isolated as possible, while on the other hand,
they wanted to draw from the results the customary "lessons"
that they hoped their adherents in New York State might
heed. The *Times* attributed the defeat in California to intraparty struggling, and consequently read the results as "a warning . . . to political manipulators in other states." This warning was plainly aimed at Governor Fenton and his allies.[17] As
for the setback in Maine, the *Times* once again placed primary blame on a completely local issue: the prohibition of
liquor. The Radicals in Maine, to a far greater extent than
the Radicals in New York, had become closely identified with
the prohibition issue, and it apparently hurt them badly. The
New York Republicans had flirted with this reform in 1866,
but had since dropped it in light of the reaction it evoked in
New York City. Party infighting on one coast, then, and the
liquor question on the other made the two situations unique;
the poor Republican showings were not part of a trend. Significantly, however, the *Times* did not stop with these peculiarly local explanations. According to a major editorial, the
elections did have a larger "Moral":

There is a warning in the case. . . . by which Republican leaders
in other States should not fail to profit. With all its strength, the
party cannot afford to be made responsible for irrelevant issues,
or to be saddled with the odium which attaches to all the theories
and crotchets of zealous but intolerant minorities. The motives
which lead to concession on the part of majorities are usually
good. They are threatened with divisions and yield to preserve
party unity. Their experience in Maine will not be too dearly
purchased if it suggest [*sic*] to extremists the wisdom of forbear-
ance and moderation, and to the great body of the Party the peril

[17] Sept. 7, 1867, p. 4.

of tampering with the authorized standard of national policy in obedience to the local demands of an aggressive minority.[18]

The "warning" could hardly be more obvious. When a Radical minority—such as the Fenton coalition—tries to foist a dangerous local issue—such as franchise revision—upon the Republican Party, against the better judgment of a hesitant majority, then the Radical minority should be resisted. In short, it was time for all those party members who had steadfastly supported the Radical reform program for the last three years to reconsider their intraparty commitments.

The *Tribune* could not permit this sort of logic to invade the Radical ranks without a challenge. The very next day it answered the *Times* with an editorial "lesson" of its own. Earlier in the week the *Tribune* had agreed that the poor showings were the direct result of local and consequently unique circumstances; here the two most influential voices of New York Republicanism could hardly disagree.[19] But the voice of the Radicals saw the outcomes in Maine and California as perfect examples of what could happen now that the party was left without a strong leader at the national level. President Johnson's abandonment of true Republicanism left each local organization to struggle on alone. Naturally, then, the various state parties became embroiled in petty questions, lost their sense of purpose, and began to backpedal shamelessly whenever they felt the least bit unsure about a controversial policy. The only way to compensate for the lack of a national leader was to rally the party's disparate forces and "advance the whole line." The Republican Party's historic mission was the elimination of all vestiges of slavery in the United States, and that goal could finally be reached with

18 Sept. 11, 1867, p. 4.
19 *Tribune*, Sept. 7, p. 4; 9, 1867, p. 4.

a guarantee of nondiscriminatory suffrage in every state. No middle ground was tenable; the fall of the National Union Party, now "so much carrion lying in a ditch," demonstrated that.

All who are timid or time-serving should be allowed to go to the rear. We want no compromise coalitions, no "People's party movements," no temporary political makeshifts. Better be fairly and squarely defeated on the principle of universal freedom and universal suffrage than gain a victory that will leave one man, no matter what color, without every political right. Honorable defeat is a hundredfold more precious than dishonorable victory. We have to meet the cries of "nigger supremacy," and "America for the white men," and other degrading appeals to popular prejudice. Well, we heard these cries in 1856, under Fremont, and in 1860 and 1864, under Lincoln. . . . We triumphed. . . . Let us spend the few remaining weeks in organization. Let us above all things surrender no principle—make no concession. Then our triumph will be righteous as well as sublime.[20]

Although the *Tribune* insisted upon "no concession," the confidence of the Republicans at the Albany constitutional convention, which had been dragging on all this time while the delegates awaited indications of the popular mood, had been seriously shaken by the September elections. The Radical majority began to show signs of losing its nerve.

II

The rapid series of events that took place during the last weeks of September and the first weeks of October 1867 dramatically influenced the subsequent history of the Republican Party in New York State. On September 18 the *Times* came out openly for adjourning the constitutional convention until after the elections in November, rather than submitting revi-

[20] *Ibid.*, Sept. 12, 1867, p. 4.

sions at that election. Ostensibly the reason was lack of time, but clearly the *Times* considered a graceful retreat on suffrage reform the only prudent course.[21]

That same evening, September 18, the Republican delegates to the Albany convention called a caucus to discuss the possibility of adjournment. The question split the Radicals badly. Prominent politicians like William Wheeler, Charles Folger, and Martin Townsend were among those who advocated adjournment and retreat. Delegates of equally high standing, however, like the idealistic reform politicians M. Lindley Lee, Ezra Graves, and James A. Bell, argued for completing the work of the convention in time to submit the new constitution for popular ratification in November. Following hours of sharp debate, the latter group prevailed. The Radical caucus resolved to finish the new constitution by October 10 and submit it at the general election.[22]

On September 20, only one day after the caucus decision, still another piece of disheartening evidence appeared, and since the *Tribune* was the only major paper to highlight the story, the Radicals in Albany could hardly have missed it. Maryland was voting on a new organic law in late September, and according to the *Tribune,* the intent of its constitution makers was almost exactly opposite to that of the Radicals in Albany: "The Civil Rights bill was to be ignored, as it had been time and again outlawed by decisions of Maryland judges; the nigger, and especially the nigger who fought for the Union, was to be 'reduced to his normal condition,' or at least shut out from the ballot and such other civil privileges

---

[21] *Times*, Sept. 18, 1867, p. 4.

[22] *Ibid.*, Sept. 19, 1867, p. 5; *Tribune*, Sept. 19, 1867, p. 5. The former gave the caucus vote as 41 to 21 and the latter as 46 to 21. For information on Lee, Graves, and Bell, see Brockway, *Fifty Years*, pp. 86–91, 247–252; and *Biographical Directory of Congress*, p. 1206.

as he could safely be deprived of."[23] Nonetheless, available returns were unequivocal: the new constitution was winning ratification in a landslide. The impact on the delegates in Albany must have been more than negligible.

On the following day, September 21, the *Times* once again came forward with a plea to adjourn the convention. No longer caring whether the retreat looked graceful, the *Times* admitted that adjournment "may look like failure." But "even this will be preferable to the promulgation of a crude and clumsy piece of work, satisfying nobody, and destined to defeat at the polls."[24] The last phrase, of course, was the operative one. If you campaign on impartial suffrage, the *Times* warned wavering Republicans around the state, you are certain to be defeated. Back off and play safe.

On Tuesday, September 24, the constitutional convention resumed business following a long weekend. George William Curtis, a Radical delegate-at-large, called from the table his resolution, "that on Tuesday, the 24th of September, at 12 o'clock noon, this Convention will adjourn until the second Tuesday of November, at the same hour."[25] Three procedural votes followed quickly, in which the convention defeated a motion by Democratic delegate-at-large Smith M. Weed to adjourn until the first Tuesday of May 1868, and then defeated a motion by another Democratic delegate-at-large, Francis Kernan, to submit the already completed judiciary and suffrage articles by themselves at the November election.[26] Finally, by a vote of 78 to 40, the constitutional convention adjourned itself until after the fall elections.

[23] Sept. 20, 1867, p. 4.
[24] Sept. 21, 1867, p. 4.
[25] *Convention Journal*, p. 626; *Constitutional Debates*, pp. 1951, 1955.
[26] *Convention Journal*, pp. 626–630.

The political alignment on the vote to adjourn was striking. Every Republican who voted cast a ballot for postponement of further deliberations until after the fall canvass; Republicans accounted for all but 4 of the 78 votes to adjourn. Even Radicals like Lindley Lee, Ezra Graves, and James Bell, the three who had led the caucus fight against adjournment, now switched to vote in favor of delay. Horace Greeley himself cast an aye vote for the Curtis resolution. Many Republicans, according to the Albany *Evening Journal*, "object to raising this question now, because they fear that 'the public mind is not prepared for it,' and that we should 'excite prejudices that might result in a defeat at the polls.' This," chastised that paper, "is the argument of a base timidity."[27]

The Democrats voted overwhelmingly against adjournment; all 40 of the no votes were Democratic. As a thoroughly disgusted *Tribune* pointed out, the Democrats had previously voted at every opportunity in favor of delays and hindrances. They were largely responsible for the long weekends customarily enjoyed by the delegates, and they seldom showed up to help raise a quorum even while the convention was in session.[28] Nevertheless, the Democrats, who vehemently opposed franchise reform and whose only interest in constitutional revision was to free New York City from the metropolitan commissions imposed by the Radicals from Albany, now went on record in favor of pushing ahead with the work of the convention. Yet this vote was not entirely a charade. Suffrage reform had suddenly begun to look like a fine issue for the Democrats, and they no doubt sincerely hoped that the Republicans could be forced to run on their franchise article at the November election. At the very least, the

[27] Sept. 24, 1867, p. 2.
[28] Sept. 25, 1867, p. 4.

Democrats wanted to make it as embarrassing as possible for the Radicals to dump their constitutional project.

Back in March, while groping for arguments against the wisdom of calling a constitutional convention, the *World* had suggested that the Radicals in the state legislature might some-day have cause to regret ever initiating the drive for constitutional revision.[29] That wishful thought had now come to pass. With an insight sharpened by its own partisan motives, the *World* tried to reconstruct what had happened:

The popular vote last fall did not, according to the present constitution, require a convention to be called this year. But the Republicans, by a strained interpretation, nevertheless, called one. They saw that a change of less than seven thousand votes would lose them the State, and calculated that, in so close a contest, the negro vote must save them. To secure suffrage for the negroes was the main reason why the Convention was called. The Republican State Convention for nominating delegates at large thought this alone worthy of special mention among the reforms for which the Convention was called. The stiff and obstinate refusal of the Republicans to submit this to the people as a separate proposition, shows that they have no faith that it can be carried on its merits.

Furthermore, continued the *World*, even less dramatic constitutional reforms had come back to haunt the Radicals.

They hoped to buoy [suffrage reform] up and float it through on other reforms. But the progress of discussion has pretty well extinguished all hope of adoption of the constitution as a whole. The canal interest will oppose it because it does not provide for the enlargement [of the state's waterways]. The liquor interest

[29] March 25, 1867, p. 5. The *World* had based this hope on what happened in 1846, when Democratic Governor Silas Wright insisted on constitutional revision which ended up hurting his own party. A man with four aces, the wags quipped, should not insist on a new deal.

will oppose it if it authorizes prohibition, and the temperance interest if it does not. One powerful and active set of men will oppose it if it does, and another if it does not, adopt Mr. Harris's report on municipal government. There is hardly a question which has been vehemently discussed in the Convention on which the beaten party will not oppose the adoption of the new constitution. Each section of citizens and each local interest cares more for its own special views than for the whole body of other changes. . . . These various dissenting sections will amount, in the aggregate, to a majority of the votes, even without the opponents of universal negro suffrage. . . . the Republicans are sick of the whole project and would gladly back out.[30]

By late September 1867, constitutional revision in general and franchise reform in particular had become a nightmare for the Radicals. What promised in January to bolster their alliance had turned out instead to be a political Pandora's box. The convention debates had brought into the open a host of relatively petty but divisive questions that now plagued the always delicate relationships within the Radical coalition. The Fenton coalition of reforming idealism and political efficacy was being strained to its breaking point.

When the *Times* first broached the idea of adjourning the constitutional convention until after the election, it counted on "the sheer force of popular apathy" to allow the Radicals to back out of their commitment to suffrage reform. "By-and-by," an editorial had predicted, the public "may cease to think of the [constitutional] body altogether."[31] At least since the September results in Maine and California, however, the Democrats had evidently decided that opposition to impartial suffrage was probably their best single issue for 1867, even if the Republicans would not commit themselves to it.

[30] Sept. 20, 1867, p. 4.
[31] July 30, 1867, p. 4.

Consequently, the *World* was not about to permit the question to slip quietly out of public view. Calling the whole convention a "fiasco," it urged that the Radicals' abortive attempt to revise the state constitution "be brandished in their faces!" and "thrust into their entrails!"[32]

The rapid flow of events was in no way retarded by the fact that the Republican state convention was scheduled to assemble at Syracuse on September 25, the day after the constitutional convention voted to adjourn until mid-November. Most of the Republican delegates to the constitutional convention set out immediately for the party meeting in Syracuse. Their decision in Albany, however, left the Radical majority facing a difficult dilemma: they had backed down on the question of impartial suffrage in New York State, but their political identity still depended upon support of congressional Reconstruction at the national level. And congressional Reconstruction had increasingly come to imply impartial suffrage for freedmen in the South. The Syracuse convention would have to find some way around this inconsistency.

There was no question that the Radicals still controlled both the party organization and the state convention. A delegation from New York City organized jointly by Fenton's ubiquitous lieutenant, Waldo Hutchins, and one of the Governor's original nominees for fire commissioner, Martin Brown, was seated in place of a delegation headed by Thurlow Weed, who was apparently ready to return to his old party. The Fenton men forgave neither Weed's support of Hoffman in 1866 nor the epithets rained upon them in the past by Weed's Whiggish allies.[33] The old "Dictator" was turned away. Not-

[32] Sept. 25, p. 8; 26, 1867, p. 4.
[33] *Tribune*, Sept. 24, 1867, pp. 1–2, reminded the convention of Weed's old description of the Fenton coalition: "Radicals, Jacobins,

withstanding some degree of personal and geographical jealousy, Roscoe Conkling, New York's new senator, was elected president of the party convention. Several incumbent officers who had become linked to the "Canal Ring" within the party were dropped from the state ticket and replaced with Radicals loyal to Governor Fenton and his coalition.[34] But a large problem still remained. How should the state platform treat the issue of Negro suffrage?

Andrew White, who declined to run for a third term in the state senate in order to devote his full time to Cornell University, chaired the resolutions committee of the convention. He and his colleagues labored to fashion a plank that would meet the Radicals' problem in the approaching election: "Resolved, That, as Republicans of the State of New-York, recognizing the obligations of consistency and straightforwardness in support of the great principle we profess, we unhesitatingly declare that suffrage should be impartial; that it is a right which ought not be limited by property or by color."[35]

At first glance this appeared wholly inconsistent with the action just taken by the party at Albany; it seemed to be a ringing endorsement of the idea that the Radicals had apparently abandoned the day before. Upon closer examination, however, the plank was carefully drafted in conditional words, like "should" and "ought," and did not mention precisely where suffrage should be impartial. This would later provide

---

and negro-worshippers." Five thousand copies of this issue of the *Tribune* were brought to Syracuse for distribution to the delegates, and Charles S. Spencer read aloud from it to the convention during the debate over seating the rival New York City delegations.

[34] Stebbins, *Political History*, pp. 159–168; Albany *Evening Journal*, Sept. 26, p. 2; 27, 1867, p. 2; *Tribune*, Sept. 25, p. 1; 26, 1867, p. 1; *Times*, Sept. 26, 1867, p. 4; *World*, Sept. 27, p. 4; 28, 1867, pp. 4, 5.

[35] *Tribune*, Sept. 26, 1867, p. 1.

a loophole for the Republican press to squeeze through, but
for the time being the Radical majority within the party had
decided not to alter its ultimate goal, at least in principle.
Pressures within the party and within the state, especially following the September returns in other Northern contests, had
forced a temporizing withdrawal in the Albany convention.
The controversy over national Reconstruction and the possibility that the political winds might yet shift, however, convinced the Radicals gathered in Syracuse to delay burning
their bridges completely. Instead, they chose White's ambiguity. More Northern state elections were scheduled for
early October, and perhaps they might help the Radicals off
the horns of their dilemma.

"The result of the elections which take place to-day in
Pennsylvania, Ohio, and Iowa," wrote the *World* on October
8, "will be regarded by men of all parties throughout the
country as signifying the people's verdict on the party in
power."[36] This was certainly true in New York State, for regardless of the significance attributed to the September elections in Maine and California, not only as symbolic omens
but also as early indications of possible trends, their importance paled in comparison with the October elections in
Iowa, Pennsylvania, and especially Ohio. Iowa had long been
a Republican stronghold, and the election in Pennsylvania involved no major offices, but there were a number of reasons
to watch Ohio closely.

New York's Radicals had some affinity with Ohio's Radicals. The old Barnburners and Free Soilers among them had
worked together closely when they were all younger. While
the New Yorkers battled Seymour, their Ohio brethren
fought Clement Vallandigham; when dissatisfaction with Lincoln's leadership came to the surface in 1864, Ohio and New

[36] Oct. 8, 1867, p. 4.

York Radicals together took the initiative which resulted in the short-lived candidacy of John C. Frémont. There were also important parallels in the political situations of the two states. Like New York, Ohio had its Radical districts along the Great Lakes plain and in the Western Reserve. It also had its traditionally Democratic areas in the downstate river counties. Like New York, Ohio had been under Radical control during the postwar years, though the state remained politically close. The Democracy there had proved itself almost as resilient as it was in New York. But of supreme importance to the Fentonites in New York was the fact that their Ohio counterparts were committed to what the Albany Radicals had backed away from: presenting the voters with a constitutional amendment authorizing impartial Negro suffrage.[37]

The early returns from Iowa, Pennsylvania, and Ohio on the morning of October 9 all told the same story: the Radicals were in trouble. In neighboring Pennsylvania the Democrats won the only state-wide office at stake, a judgeship, and they were in the process of gaining at least a standoff in the previously Republican legislature.[38] In Iowa, Colonel Samuel Merrill would apparently defeat his Democratic opponent, Charles Mason, for governor, but the Democrats had made remarkable gains in a state which had been a Republican sanctuary for a decade.[39] To confuse the Republicans further, the party in Iowa appeared to have been saved rather than hurt by the

[37] The proposed amendment would have eliminated color as a voting requirement, thus enfranchising Negroes, and would also have disfranchised anyone who deserted from the Union army or dodged the Union draft (Eugene H. Roseboom, *The Civil War Era, 1850–1873,* Vol. IV of *The History of the State of Ohio* [Columbus, 1944], p. 462).

[38] *World,* Oct. 9, pp. 1, 4; 10, p. 1; 11, 1867, p. 1; *Tribune,* Oct. 9, 1867, p. 1; *Times,* Oct. 7, 1867, p. 1.

[39] *Times,* Oct. 7, p. 1; 9, p. 1; 21, 1867, p. 5.

prohibition issue. This made it more difficult in retrospect to write off the election in Maine as only a local fluke. Township elections in Connecticut and city elections in New Jersey had also gone to the Democrats, according to the press.[40] But the focus of attention was on Ohio. There the race for governor was so tight that both parties were claiming victory on the basis of early telegraph information.

General Rutherford B. Hayes, later elected eighteenth President of the United States in another disputed canvass, was locked in a political cliffhanger with Democrat Allen G. Thurman. For three days the outcome of this gubernatorial race was uncertain in New York City. Only on the 11th of October did the press reach a consensus that Hayes had been elected with a majority of something less than 2,000 votes out of a total of just under half a million.[41] This margin was down from a state-wide Republican advantage of nearly 30,000 votes in 1865, and over 40,000 in 1866. Furthermore, the state legislature in Ohio had actually slipped under Democratic control.

What decimated the ranks of Ohio Radicals appeared obvious: the villain was the suffrage referendum. Despite the closeness of the gubernatorial race, there was absolutely no question concerning the popular verdict on the proposed franchise amendment in Ohio. The very first returns indicated that it was beaten; by the time Hayes's victory was known, defeat of the suffrage proposal had become a rout. Even the Radical press was forced to put it bluntly: "The negro suffrage amendment is dead."[42] The final vote against franchise revision in Ohio stood 216,987 in favor to 255,340 opposed.[43]

[40] *World*, Oct. 9, pp. 1, 4; 10, 1867, p. 4.
[41] *Times*, Oct. 11, 1867, p. 1; *World*, Oct. 11, 1867, p. 1; *Tribune*, Oct. 12, 1867, p. 5.
[42] *Tribune*, Oct. 10, 1867, p. 4.
[43] Roseboom, *Civil War Era*, p. 462.

The *Tribune* tried desperately to put the best face on the Ohio results and to prevent the conclusion which almost every other political analyst was reaching, namely, that the Negro suffrage referendum had led Republicans to the slaughter:

We shall of course have the old cry renewed—"See how Ohio has voted down Equal Manhood Suffrage—hadn't we better drop the nigger, and take care of ourselves?" The answer is ready: Ohio on Tuesday gave more votes, and a larger proportion of her Republican strength for Manhood Suffrage, than any other State has ever given—more by thousands than *she* would ever have given till now. Say that one Republican in every twenty went straight over to the enemy on this question, and one weak brother voted the Republican ticket but failed to vote for Manhood Suffrage, what of it? New-York, twenty-one years ago, gave but 85,406 votes for Equal Rights; in 1860 she more than doubled this, giving it 197,503; and still it was heavily beaten, though Lincoln carried the State at that election by 50,000 majority. The next time, it will have at least 300,000; and, if beaten by a handful, its enemies will scream and fire guns for their glorious victory. So it will be in other States; while the vital principle of genuine Democracy marches on through seeming defeats to its inevitable and conclusive triumph.

The point here was that the Radicals' earlier assessment of the suffrage issue was still valid—the principle was still gaining ground among white voters, not losing it. But the *Tribune*'s rhetoric had become strained, its tone almost hysterical, and its evidence little more than incantation. Those Republicans "whose hearts [were] with the adverse hosts" should be driven from the party while the true believers continued to fight for "the arduous but inevitable achievement of Equal Rights for all citizens."[44]

Few politicians possessed the messianic faith of the *Tribune*.

[44] Oct. 10, 1867, p. 4.

As an answering editorial in the *Times* pointed out, the logic of intentionally alienating all of one's marginal allies, and forcing them into the camp of the enemy, seemed politically suicidal.[45] The *Times* had a quite different "lesson" for its readers: the Republican Party had grown too successful for its own good. In the wake of the war it enjoyed so much political success that it "became presumptuous" and careened heedlessly down paths of extremism. The returns from other states indicated that the American people chose not to risk "peace, order and prosperity . . . for the profit of partisans or the pleasure of political theorists." Only by abandoning its quixotic adherence to a minority crusade and exercising instead a "greater prudence in the management of party interests" might the Republicans of New York "still remedy these evils and retain the State."[46] This debate, now fully and openly joined in the press, reflected the political agonizing within the minds of individual members of New York's Radical coalition. Their resolution of the debate would have a profound influence on the future of Republicanism in the Empire State.

"Honor to Ohio," responded one of the most ringing editorials ever to appear in the *Tribune*. Ohio Radicals had consciously chosen to submit the principle of manhood suffrage to their constituents, knowing full well that they might be sacrificing votes, rather than "stand still" and enjoy a comfortable majority. What made this so heroic was the conscious factor; in Ohio the Radicals "deliberately chose to be right rather than safe. They chose to fight a doubtful battle for a great and good end, rather than accept a cheap and certain but relatively unimportant success."[47] A century later this rhetoric sounds noble indeed. To the Fentonites in New York,

---

[45] *Times*, Oct. 11, 1867, p. 4.
[46] *Ibid.*, Oct. 10, 1867, p. 4.
[47] Oct. 12, 1867, p. 4.

however, it may have sounded somewhat hollow; the Democratic press explained why.

"This is as canting a piece of moral coxcombry as we remember to have seen," wrote the *World*. The Ohio Republicans had proposed their amendment during the first months of 1867, in the full flush of the Radical victories of November 1866. When the Ohio legislature placed the amendment on the ballot, few doubted that it would be an asset rather than a liability. To Greeley's assertion that "they deliberately chose to be right rather than safe," the *World* replied, "they had the fullest confidence that they were safe; a confidence that seemed, at the time, to have a solid basis."[48] That was the same time the New York Radicals passed their convention bill. But the Radicals in New York differed from those in Ohio, the Democrats believed, because the former could still back out after the September elections indicated that a retreat was in order. This was impossible in Ohio; they were already fully committed. Furthermore, the *World* reminded Republicans, the author of the *Tribune*'s noble sentiments had himself voted for adjourning the constitutional convention and against submitting any articles already completed.[49] These considerations certainly blunted the cutting edge of the *Tribune*'s appeal.

Although the arguments of the *Tribune* may have made some impression on the sensibilities of the Fentonites despite the efforts of the *World*, that impact did not seem to outweigh the Radicals' apparently stronger desire for political advantage. A majority of them preferred "a certain but relatively unimportant success" to martyrdom. The question was not whether to retreat but whether they could retreat fast enough or far enough to salvage a victory in November. To summarize Republican thinking in New York as well as in

[48] Oct. 14, 1867, p. 4.
[49] Oct. 21, 1867, p. 4.

other Northern states at this time: "Ohio was the acid test and the answer was negative."[50]

Within days of learning the final outcome in Ohio, the *Times* sounded a keynote for the remainder of the campaign. The Republicans would stand by the tenets of congressional Reconstruction and even defend the principle of impartial suffrage in the South. But they would ignore the Negro in New York and abandon the principle of impartial suffrage at home. Groping for rationalizations, the *Times* came up with a "different circumstances" theory. The suffrage plank in the Syracuse platform, it contended, was meant to apply only to the Negro voter in the South. The question was no longer one of consistency; it was now purely a "practical" matter:

Ohio refused to admit negroes to the suffrage on equal terms with the whites; but there are practical reasons for allowing negroes to vote in the South, which do not prevail in the North,—and in spite of the loud demands made in the name of universal freedom and equal justice by the apostles of "progress," *practical* considerations have, and always will have, much more weight than abstract principles in determining the result of an election.

The *Times* labeled impartial suffrage a necessity in the South because of the numbers of people involved, the likelihood of abuse of freedmen by former slaveholders, and the danger that political power would revert to rebel hands in the absence of black votes. Republicans would not need to change their "fundamental principles or aims"; they needed only "a better temper and a calmer mind—less intolerance and greater moderation." There was no need to abandon the basis of Reconstruction in the South, counseled the *Times*, only to abandon it at home.[51]

The primary alternatives open to the Radicals were thus

[50] Gillette, *Right to Vote*, p. 26.
[51] Oct. 14, 1867, p. 4.

clearly outlined in the press. On the one hand, the *Tribune* urged a continuation and perhaps even an acceleration of the reform program which had carried the Radicals to the political summit they now occupied. If this course of action, which hinged upon pushing ahead with franchise revision, had the effect of purging the Radical coalition of all those politicians who were only fellow travelers, then so much the better. The crusading army would be purified. Even if the party slipped temporarily at the polls, the good fight should be fought. On the other hand, the *Times* advised moderation, compromise, even outright retreat. Although this meant giving up, at least temporarily, the postwar program of civil and institutional reform, it promised to afford the Republican Party as a whole a better chance of retaining the political power it now held in New York State. As it turned out, most of the leading Radicals ultimately agreed with the second analysis. The growing doubts of the summer and the cautious backward steps of late September became a headlong retreat by mid-October following the Ohio results. Constitutional franchise reform got trampled in the rush.

Perhaps Governor Fenton himself best captured the general mood of the Radicals. In a letter addressed to a large Republican rally in New York City's Cooper Union the Governor reluctantly acknowledged his belief that nondiscriminatory suffrage, at least in New York State, seemed doomed. The flame which had burned down in the Albany convention, and then flickered back up at the Syracuse convention, now seemed completely out. Instead, caution and racism were aglow. "It is perhaps too much to expect," he wrote with regret, "that long-rooted prejudice, skillfully enflamed by ambitious leaders, will give way in a day."[52]

Regardless of how reluctantly it may have been made, how-

[52] Fenton to the Cooper Institute Republican Rally, *Times,* Oct. 17, 1867, p. 1.

ever, Fenton's assessment of the voters' political temper was
very probably correct. Racism had surfaced frequently in
New York's recent political past. Prejudice played as large a
part as party in defeating the suffrage referendum of 1860;[53]
the anti-Negro horrors of the 1863 draft riot were still vividly
remembered; blacks had been barred from Lincoln's funeral
procession when it passed through New York City in 1865.[54]
Moreover, many of the Radicals themselves had indulged in
racist rhetoric during their prewar careers, especially the former Democrats now so prominent in the successful postwar
coalition.[55] Perhaps their own past arguments intensified the
anxiety felt by an increasing number of Radicals over the
issue of Negro suffrage. And Fenton was correct when he
accused the opposition of "skillfully enflaming" the voters'
well-documented prejudice.[56]

But even if the Governor's assessment was incorrect, even
if New York's prejudice might have been overcome in November of 1867, few among Fenton's followers—not to mention his opponents both within and without the party—were
prepared to run the political risk that such an effort would
involve. Some Radicals were leery of the project to begin
with, and the spring results in Connecticut strengthened their
doubts. Others feared the September indicators in California
and Maine, especially when coupled with the Maryland constitutional ratification. Most of the rest found Ohio to be the
clincher. The drive to revise the state's franchise qualifica-

[53] Stanley, "Majority Tyranny," pp. 426–429.
[54] *Tribune*, April 24, 1865, p. 4.
[55] Foner, *Free Soil*, p. 267; Foner, "Racial Attitudes of the New
York Free Soilers," *New York History*, XLVI (1965), pp. 311–329.
[56] *World*, Oct. 18, 1867, p. 4, for example, on the day following the
rally to which Fenton wrote, blared out that no matter how far or
how fast the Radicals retreated, they would still be "bound hand and
foot to their African idol."

tions, initiated by the Radicals in January, had ground to a full stop on the eve of the November elections.

III

Both the election of 1867 and the subsequent history of franchise reform in New York State were anticlimactic. In the November canvass the Republican Party ran more poorly than it had in any year since Seymour's election in 1862. Every state-wide office being contested in 1867 went to the Democrats, from secretary of state down to prison inspector. The Democratic margins of victory ranged from a 39,927 majority for state engineer to a 50,277 majority for canal commissioner; Fenton's majority for governor in 1866 had been 13,789 votes.[57] The resurgent Democracy captured surprisingly firm control over the state assembly, winning 73 seats to the Republicans' 55. Even in the gerrymandered state senate, Republicans emerged from the election with a scant two-seat majority, 17 to 15.[58] The new senator from New York City's fourth district was William Marcy Tweed himself; the Democrats had returned to Albany with a vengeance.

The Republicans had been hurt badly by canal frauds, the threat of a stronger liquor law, fraudulent voting in New York City, and some remarkably ill-chosen candidates.[59] Nevertheless, the exultant Democrats frankly attributed their success to the single issue of racial equality. Even though fran-

[57] *The Tribune Almanac and Political Register for 1868* (New York, [1867]), p. 49.

[58] *Tribune*, Jan. 7, 1868, p. 7.

[59] *Times*, Oct. 11, p. 4; Nov. 18, 1867, p. 5; *World*, Oct. 16, p. 4; 22, p. 4; 23, p. 4; 24, p. 4, Nov. 19, 1867, p. 6; Albany *Evening Journal*, Nov. 2, 1867, p. 2; Alonzo B. Cornell to White, Sept. 28, 1867, White Papers; Alexander, *New York*, III, 179–188; Stebbins, *Political History*, pp. 193–211; Van Deusen, *Greeley*, pp. 365–366.

chise reform was not on the ballot, its influence, according to the *World*, swung the election:

Here in New-York, this late dominant party [the Radical Republicans] decreed in the Constitutional Convention that the negroes should be placed on equality at the polls and in the jury box with the whites. Their nominating conventions pledged the party to carry out that decree and also to insist upon its establishment in all other sections of the State. The election has been held, and the people called upon to give their verdict upon that question. The result is now seen by the Republican majority of thirteen thousand of last year being swept away, and a Democratic majority of from thirty to forty thousand substituted. Thus it is in every section of the country where this question has been made an issue and Radicals insisted upon the people doing homage to their ebony idol, defeat and disaster have followed.[60]

Both the Albany *Evening Journal* and the New York *Commercial Advertiser*, a paper which had brought Weed back into the editorial arena, likewise attributed the Republican defeat to the party's identification with Negro rights in New York.[61] So, of course, did the *Times*.[62] Alone among the major newspapers was the *Tribune*, which insisted the defeat was due, not to the party's short-lived commitment to impartial suffrage, but to the Radicals' ultimate cowardice on that issue: "We are beaten by Republicans this year."[63] Since the Radicals had lost despite their retreat from reform, argued the *Tribune*, they might as well have gone down fighting for the measure that would have been the capstone of their program. They could hardly have done worse.

[60] Nov. 7, 1867, p. 4.
[61] Albany *Evening Journal*, Nov. 6, p. 2; 7, 1867, p. 2; *World*, Nov. 8, 1867, p. 5.
[62] Nov. 11, 1867, p. 4.
[63] Nov. 6, 1867, p. 4.

Perhaps the *Tribune* had a valid point; there is no way to determine how well the Republicans might have run with the proposed franchise revision held aloft rather than tucked away. Suffice it to say, however, that the Radicals themselves had lost faith in the measure prior to the election; afterward they never revived the question. Within a week after the electoral debacle, the *Times* declared that suffrage reform at home was dead. The exultant *World* rephrased the argument: "The negro has been covered up and laid away under Democratic majorities amounting to nearly one hundred thousand in Ohio and New-York."[64]

The constitutional convention which reconvened November 12, 1867, was a chastised body. Although its legal status was unchanged, the voters had apparently repudiated the reform spirit that created it. Six Democratic delegates to the convention had run for other public offices on the previous Tuesday; all were elected. Three of the seven Radical delegates who attempted the same thing were defeated. The state comptroller, who had been defeated, doubted whether he had the legal authority to continue the delegates' per diem allowance without further legislative action. Although the Republican majority resolved once again to persevere and to submit a constitution to the people, their sense of purpose, their faith that they were riding a righteous wave of the future, and especially their belief in the political efficacy of their proposed constitutional revisions had been all but completely sapped by the results of the election.[65]

Through the ensuing months, the convention moved as tortuously as ever. Lack of a quorum was chronic; vacillations, uncertainties, and procedural hassles marked what progress

---

[64] Nov. 16, 1867, p. 4.
[65] Albany *Evening Journal*, Nov. 9, p. 2; 24, 1867, p. 2; *World*, Nov. 12, p. 1; 13, p. 4; 14, p. 4; 16, 1867, p. 4.

was made. The debates grew still more turgid than they had been during the previous summer. Not until the last week in February 1868 did the delegates finally near the end of their deliberations.[66]

On February 21 a special Committee on Submission of the Constitution offered its report to the convention. Despite its Republican majority, the committee was willing to settle for a tripartite submission: the judiciary article, the suffrage article, and the remaining body of the constitution, each to be voted upon separately.[67] For a week the convention debated this report. Some delegates believed that the judiciary article should be incorporated into the body of the constitution and that the suffrage question alone was worthy of separate submission. Very few still argued that the constitution should be submitted in its entirety. Some argued that a special ratification election should be called, while others preferred to place the proposed new organic law on the ballot at the next general election.

The statement of Seth Wakeman, a member from a district where the Democratic Party had not even bothered to run a slate of candidates in the election for convention delegates, probably best summarized the evolution of Radical thinking on the politics of suffrage reform. Wakeman, a veteran Republican officeholder, was a perfect example of a Radical torn over the question of continuing the reconstruction at home. He had originally established his substantial political position upon antislavery idealism, and he believed personally in the franchise revision at hand. Though a former Whig, he identified himself with Fenton's coalition after the war, since it

[66] For the plodding progress of the convention between November 1867 and February 1868, see Lincoln, *Constitutional History*, II, 241–422; and *Constitutional Debates*, pp. 1970–3971.

[67] *Convention Journal*, p. 1132; *Convention Documents*, No. 180.

seemed to embody the same political approach that he had used so successfully for nearly fifteen years. Now, however, that fortuitous mix of genuine reform and political success had broken down, and Wakeman had to decide whether he would jeopardize his political standing by continuing to hold tightly to his personal ideals.[68]

It will be recollected, perhaps, by some, that in the early part of this session, when the suffrage question was under consideration, I took strong ground in favor of allowing the colored men the same rights at the ballot-box we granted to the white man. I took the ground at that time that there should be no distinction between colored men and white men upon this subject. I believed at that time that popular opinion demanded that action at our hands. I believed then, sir, that it was but carrying out what public opinion demanded. We were sent here for the purpose of framing a Constitution for the people of this State, and adapting it to the sense of the people. We have since had public opinion expressed upon this subject, not only in our own State but in the Western States, that are more radical than our own, and shall we entirely disregard that public sentiment so as to allow the Constitution we shall frame to be voted down by the people? I came here for one [*sic*] for the purpose of helping to frame a Constitution for the people of this State, not only upon the suffrage, but upon other questions important to the people of this State. I believe, in my heart, that by inserting this provision the entire Constitution will be voted down by the people. Shall I perform my duty if I adhere to what I insisted upon last summer? It seems to me not. I came from a county which has always been republican, and I trust always will be; every town in our county is republican, represented by republican supervisors; the board of supervisors unanimously, and without one dissenting voice, passed

[68] *Biographical Directory of Congress,* p. 1762; Stafford E. North, ed., *Our Country and Its People: A Descriptive and Biographical Record of Genesee County, New York* (Boston, 1899), p. 349.

a resolution in favor of the separate submission of this question to the people. I am not governed by that alone; but I have taken some pains to get the expression of the will of the people at home; and I tell gentlemen here, that men there who are truly loyal, and who will vote in favor of colored suffrage every time it comes up, are in favor of a separate submission of this question. Shall we now hazard all our work here by insisting upon what we have heretofore advocated under different circumstances? I for one am not prepared to do so, although I would vote to-morrow and next day, if I had a chance, to place colored men upon equal terms with their white neighbors. . . . Notwithstanding what I said last summer, I shall vote in the discharge of my duty in favor of the separate submission of this question.[69]

Wakeman chose what he considered the politically sagacious course, and it is worth noting that he was subsequently elected to the House of Representatives for the Forty-second Congress. Although 29 Radicals registered their enduring opposition to separate submission of the franchise article, a motion to reverse the July vote on that proposal carried with 82 votes in its favor. Of the 82 aye votes, 44 were cast by men like Wakeman, withdrawing their earlier support of New York Radicalism's most ambitious project.[70] The political events of the fall of 1867 hung heavily indeed over the constitutional convention.

After additional debate failed to resolve the question of when to offer the constitutional revisions to the people, the delegates decided to dump the whole matter into the lap of the state legislature. Accordingly, the convention approved a final draft of its proposals on February 28, 1868, without stipulating a date for ratification. The Republicans united for the last time in favor of the constitution, and the Democrats ac-

[69] *Constitutional Debates,* pp. 3886–3887.
[70] *Ibid.,* p. 3891; *Convention Journal,* pp. 1186–1187.

counted for all of the votes against it.[71] That same evening the New York State Constitutional Convention of 1867 voted to terminate its inglorious existence.

The politically divided legislature of 1868 never did reach an agreement on when to submit the proposed constitution to the people. The convention itself had voted to "recommend," but not to order, ratification at the general election of November 1868, but both major parties shied away from injecting the state constitution into the politics of a presidential year. Not until 1869 was the proposed constitution resurrected by yet another session of the state legislature, the third one to be involved with the matter. Though this legislature voted to place the revisions on the November 1869 ballot for popular ratification, it also decided to subdivide the constitution even further: an article dealing with powers of taxation was plucked from the body of the document and joined the judiciary and franchise articles as separate referendums.[72]

On November 2, 1869, the people of New York State accepted the new judiciary article, but rejected both the taxation article and the body of the proposed constitution. The provision to eliminate racially discriminatory suffrage was also defeated; 249,802 people voted for the two-and-a-half-year-old project of a coalition that no longer existed, while 282,403 favored retention of the property qualification for Negro voters in New York. Significantly, the Republican state platform remained entirely silent on the franchise question.[73] Only the Fifteenth Amendment to the Constitution of the United States, ratified by one session of the New York legislature in 1869, then rejected after the fact by another in

[71] *Constitutional Debates*, pp. 3947–3948; *Convention Journal*, pp. 1256–1257.

[72] Lincoln, *Constitutional History*, II, 414–419.

[73] *Ibid.*, pp. 419–420; Stebbins, *Political History*, p. 265.

1870, finally realized the Radicals' goal in the state.[74] What was designed to have been the crowning achievement of the Radicals' postwar program of civil and institutional reform had instead brought to the coalition doubt, dissension, and defeat. Although Reuben Fenton served on through 1868, the reconstruction in New York did not survive November 5, 1867.

[74] Gillette, *Right to Vote*, pp. 84–85, 115. Gillette contends, p. 50: "The pattern of the framing and passage of the Fifteenth Amendment indicates that the primary objective was to make Negro voters in the North; the secondary objective, to keep Negro voters in the South." The political circumstances in New York State support this conclusion. The Rochester *Democrat* (a Republican paper), according to the *Times*, Oct. 14, 1867, p. 4, had begun to call for a national amendment to secure Negro votes in the North on the day following the Ohio election in October 1867.

9

Epilogue

Reform served the Radicals in New York very well from 1865 to 1867. It hindered their Democratic opponents; it offered a reasonable hope of offsetting traditional Republican weaknesses in the state's largest urban centers; it appealed to the idealistic preconceptions of those men who, since the antislavery crusade, had envisioned the Republican Party as a vehicle of progress; it provided purpose and direction on the state level at a time when the party was without a decisive national leader; it gave long-eclipsed elements within the party an opportunity to determine policy. The Fenton coalition in New York State demonstrated a tendency to centralize power for the general welfare, and, by 1867, had taken significant legislative action in the fields of urban safety, public health, housing standards, and popular education. Moreover, substantial evidence suggests that the Fentonites intended to continue this reform program had they maintained their political ascendancy.

During 1866, for example, Radical legislators had authorized a special investigation of the state's prison system and commissioned a comparative study of penal institutions in other states and in Canada.[1] Although these reports were com-

[1] *Senate Journal, 1866*, pp. 349, 408; *Assembly Journal, 1866*, pp. 644,

pleted early in 1867, the legislature adjourned before the recommendations could be incorporated into a bill and guided
through the two houses. As a result, prison reform was put
off until the next session. What was intended as a one-year
postponement, however, turned out to be an indefinite delay
following the Radical defeat in November of 1867.

A similar situation existed regarding public welfare institutions. In his annual message of 1867, Governor Fenton made
a cogent appeal for legislative action in this area. The state,
he pointed out, was granting substantial sums of money to
various local and private charitable institutions, but refusing
to strike out against the deplorable conditions which existed
in some of them. The Governor believed that the state had a
legitimate right, indeed a duty, to demand certain minimum
standards from those organizations receiving public funds.[2] In
response to Fenton's suggestion, the Radical legislature of
1867 created the Board of State Commissioners of Public
Charities, the first of its kind in New York State history.[3]
The board was to inspect each of the facilities receiving state
aid and to recommend legislation establishing the standards
which they should be required to meet. Yet, by the time these
recommendations came back, the character of the legislature
was changed. The coalition that inaugurated the process of
welfare reform had been broken and defeated. Consequently,
even though the Board of Charities was slightly expanded in
1873, it was not until 1890 that subsequent legislators focused
enough attention on this subject to adopt the elementary rec-

---

702, 835; *Assembly Documents, 1867,* II, No. 35. The report on
prisons in the United States and Canada, 574 pages long, was coauthored by Theodore W. Dwight and E. C. Wines.

[2] "Annual Message, 1867," *Senate Journal 1867,* pp. 15–16.

[3] *Assembly Journal, 1867,* pp. 200, 431, 481, 704, 868, 935, 958, 1764,
1850; *Senate Journal, 1867,* pp. 544, 801, 1000, 1004, 1020, 1134.

ommendation of removing the insane from public almshouses and placing them in separate institutions.[4]

Even more dramatic possibilities existed. Albany and Buffalo, for example, both large cities by national standards, had already received police commissions from the state legislature. Albany's Capital Police District was created in 1865 by the same alliance which passed the Metropolitan Fire Department Act; the legislators who established the Metropolitan Board of Health in 1866 also set up Buffalo's Niagara Police District.[5] These actions had fit perfectly into the Fentonite reform pattern, and the Radicals' characteristically mixed motives were as obvious in these as in the metropolitan reforms: Albany and Buffalo contained the most substantial pockets of Democratic strength upstate. Rochester, by comparison, which was nearly as large as Albany, but somewhat more dependably Republican, received no police commission. It is reasonable to assume that the Radicals would eventually have restructured some of the other antiquated social institutions of Albany and Buffalo, just as they had tried to do in New York and Brooklyn, and thereby force, regardless of the ever-present partisan reasons for doing so, safety, health, and housing reforms on the state's second rank of cities a generation earlier than they were actually undertaken.

[4] David M. Schneider and Albert Deutsch, *The Road Upward: Three Hundred Years of Public Welfare in New York State* (Albany, 1939), pp. 32–33.

[5] *Assembly Journal, 1865,* pp. 1335, 1584; *Senate Journal, 1865,* pp. 979–980; Albany *Evening Journal,* Jan. 26, p. 2; 31, p. 2; Feb. 16, p. 2; 17, p. 2; 23, p. 2; 24, p. 2; 25, p. 2; March 2, p. 2; 16, p. 3; 21, p. 3; April 21, pp. 2, 3; 22, p. 2; 27, 1865, p. 1; *Assembly Journal, 1866,* pp. 1095–1096; *Senate Journal, 1866,* pp. 738, 1076; E. G. Spaulding to White, April 1, 1866, White Papers; Albany *Evening Journal,* March 22, p. 2; 30, 1866, p. 2; Harlow and Boone, *Life Sketches of the State Officers,* p. 319; Raymond B. Fosdick, *American Police Systems* (New York, 1920), p. 79 and n.

But all of these projects—prison reform, welfare reform, and secondary urban reforms—had to await an entirely different political era. The Radical program had depended all along upon a union of idealism and political efficacy; indeed, the latter had given a cutting edge to the former. During 1867, however, the reconstruction at home, like the national Reconstruction, became bound up with the question of race. This question proved politically disastrous; reform was discredited and the reformers defeated. With the fall of the Fenton coalition the surge of postwar reform stopped abruptly. The Negro was not the only victim of race politics in New York. What had been a promising attempt to deal with some of the most glaring problems engendered by the emerging forces of urbanization and industrialization lost its momentum.[6]

Reform in New York not only failed to advance after 1867, but was actually driven backward when the Democrats nullified its impact. In November of 1868 a Tammany man, John T. Hoffman, was elected to succeed Fenton as governor, and in November of 1869, for the first time since the formation of the Republican Party, the voters returned both a Democratic assembly and a Democratic senate to serve under him.[7] Tweed's allies thus controlled the state government as securely in 1870 as Fenton's had controlled it in 1867. One of the principal results was passage of the so-called "Tweed Charter" that year. By the provisions of this document, state commis-

[6] For the impact of Northern race politics in 1867 on national Radicalism see Trefousse, *Radical Republicans*, pp. 372–373, 404.

[7] Alexander, *New York*, III, 227–228. These successes were partially attributed to voting frauds in New York City. Tammany was so blatant that they brought upon themselves a full-scale congressional investigation. The results of this investigation, which represent a close look at Tammany methods during Tweed's most flagrant days, are contained in *Reports of Committees of the House of Representatives*, 40th Cong., 3rd sess. (Washington, D.C., 1869).

sions imposed upon the metropolitan district reverted to local control under the mayors and the city councils of New York and Brooklyn. Although the fire department continued to function primarily "above politics" and in the public interest, the cutting edge of the health board's sanitary regulations was dulled considerably, and enforcement of the recent Tenement House Law ceased altogether.

II

The events of 1867 cost the Radicals not only their continued control over state legislation, but their ascendant position within the Republican Party as well. Indeed, the electoral results of 1867 cost the Fentonite coalition its very existence. The municipal and educational reforms had failed to produce the political advantages anticipated by many of the legislators who voted for them. As the *Evening Journal* archly observed in the wake of the 1867 debacle, reform commissions in the metropolitan district, those "Brandreth's pills" for Radical ills in New York City, seemed to be the wrong political prescription. They did not "achieve desired results at the ballot box."[8] When suffrage reform subsequently brought outright defeat, the idealism of most of the Radicals proved insufficient to outweigh their political circumspection. Consequently, a large majority of the politicians who had supported Fenton's coalition since the end of the war began to search for more promising sources of political influence to replace the program of civil and institutional reform.

Chief among the political alternatives sought by members of the Radical coalition after the defeat of 1867 were business backing and federal patronage. The first provided a stable source of campaign funds, which made it especially attractive

[8] Nov. 6, 1867, p. 2.

to those who aspired to higher office. The Governor himself turned to this ready source of political aid in 1868, when he signed the infamous Erie Railroad bill. For three years Fenton had consistently vetoed all of the railroad legislation which managed to find its way through the legislature. But in 1868, with his old coalition crumbling around him, he evidently could not resist accepting support from one of the state's two major railroad interests. The alliance was a new one for him, but he needed all the allies he could enlist if he wished to remain both a serious vice-presidential possibility and the leading contender for Edwin Morgan's seat in the United States Senate.[9]

The second source of political influence which became more attractive to the Radicals after 1867 was federal patronage. From the very beginning of their rise to power the Fentonites had largely done without federal patronage; after their open break with President Johnson, in fact, they made a virtue of disdaining it. But they could afford this luxury because they were partially compensating themselves with the new commission jobs that fell to the governor's disposal in the course of their reconstruction at home. Beginning in 1868, however, this source of compensation was completely cut off. Democratic success at the polls guaranteed that the legislature

[9] Fenton was widely mentioned for the second spot on a Grant ticket in 1868, and at least since 1867, when Conkling replaced Ira Harris, Fenton was thought to be after Morgan's senate seat, which expired in 1869 (*World*, Jan. 12, 1867, p. 5; Alexander, *New York*, III, 192–194; Stebbins, *Political History*, pp. 309–321). For signing the Erie bill, Fenton was reputed to have received $20,000 for his campaign coffers (Alexander, *New York*, III, 220). The state senate later investigated the Erie business, and its findings, though little more than a whitewash, are contained in *Documents of the Senate of the State of New York at Their Ninety-Second Session, 1869* (Albany, 1869), V, No. 52.

would create no additional positions for the governor to fill, and to make matters worse, the Democrats and the anti-Fenton "Canal Republicans" had enough votes in the senate to block confirmation of the appointments to which the governor was already entitled.[10] In light of this situation, many Radicals took a long second look at the possibilities of regaining some federal patronage. Roscoe Conkling was now in the United States Senate, and he was one of their own.[11] Accepting political favors from Conkling was hardly the equivalent of accepting political favors from the Johnson administration. Conkling's subsequent rise to power within the New York State Republican Party provided a rough index of the renewed importance of federal ties among the Radicals.[12]

III

The political careers of the Republicans who had made up the postwar Radical coalition followed no particular pattern after its defeat and dissolution in 1867. Fenton himself, a politician to his marrow, managed to muster just enough support to be elected to the United States Senate in January 1869. There he almost immediately collided with Conkling and came off second best when the latter won Grant's support. At the Syracuse convention of 1870, Conkling's forces wrested formal control of the New York State Republican Party from the forces of their erstwhile ally and former chieftain, Reuben

[10] The divided senate of 1868 blocked every one of Fenton's major appointments. Seven anti-Fenton Republican senators voted consistently with the Democrats against the Governor's selections (*Times*, April 29, p. 5; 30, 1868, p. 5; *World*, April 29, p. 6; 30, 1868, p. 4).

[11] A. K. Bailey to White, Nov. 30, 1866, White Papers.

[12] David M. Jordan, *Roscoe Conkling of New York: Voice in the Senate* (Ithaca, 1971), pp. 85–165; Depew, *Memories of Eighty Years*, pp. 35–77.

Fenton.[13] As a result, Fenton and several of his old lieutenants, including Waldo Hutchins, cast their lots with the Liberal Republicans in 1872. Perhaps they saw this movement as
a possible means of reviving the kind of alliance of idealism
and political efficacy that carried them to power during the
years immediately after the war. But following the disastrous
Greeley candidacy, Fenton returned once again to the regular
Republican Party.[14] Other members of Fenton's postwar coalition never left the regular organization. They adhered to
the state machinery under Conkling, and they served the
policies of Grantism just as unswervingly as they had adhered
to the machinery under Fenton and pursued the reconstruction at home. Still others, including a large percentage of the
unsuccessful legislative candidates in 1867, simply dropped
out of New York State politics.

Following the breakup of Fenton's coalition and the political shifting of the period 1868 to 1872, the Republican Party
took on a fundamentally different character in New York
State. Though it continued to style itself "Radical," the party
was on a new tack.[15] After regaining power under Conkling
and Platt, these "New Radicals" seemed to re-embrace the
ghosts of their more Whiggish ancestors; sound money, pa-

[13] Brockway, *Fifty Years,* pp. 317–318, 342–350; Rawley, *Morgan,*
pp. 231–232; Alexander, *New York,* III, 219–222, 250–264.

[14] For Fenton's part in the Liberal bolt of 1872, see Earle Dudley
Ross, *The Liberal Republican Movement* (New York, 1919), *passim*
and especially p. 103n. The *Tribune,* May 2, 1872, p. 5, lists New
York's delegation to the Liberal convention; included among the
names are such prominent former Radicals as James R. Allaben, E. C.
Topliff, and Augustus F. Allen.

[15] David Donald, *Charles Sumner and the Rights of Man* (New
York, 1970), p. 350, has recently revived in new terms the distinction
between Old Radicalism and New Radicalism suggested over thirty
years ago by Louis M. Hacker in *The Triumph of American Capital-
ism* (New York, 1940).

tronage broking, and friends who could fill a campaign chest became the hallmarks of New York Republicanism during the next decade.[16] This transformation at the state level prefigured a similar process at the national level and terminated the reconstruction of New York even more quickly than it ended the Reconstruction of the nation.

IV

This study has concentrated exclusively on New York State, and it would be presumptuous to generalize about the postwar period of political activity in other Northern states. The suspicion remains, nevertheless, that a considerable amount of reinterpretation may be in order if the Republicans in other states reacted during the years immediately following the Civil War in a fashion similar to the Radicals of New York. In such key states as Massachusetts and Ohio, for example, Republicans also undertook significant reform programs. In Massachusetts they passed civil rights laws, reorganized the state police, created a board of prison commissioners, a board of railroad commissioners, and a board of health during the immediate postwar years.[17] In Ohio the Radicals tackled labor problems, created a state board of charities, and brought badly needed metropolitan police reform to Cleveland. As in New York, the Ohio reforms were undone following the Radicals' defeat over equal suffrage.[18] Republicans in Missouri were reported by the New York press to be consciously adopting the

[16] Jordan, *Conkling, passim;* Alexander, *New York,* II, 187–188, III, 32–33. Shortreed, "Radicals," pp. 65–67, 71–74, suggests that many former Whigs among even the early Radicals never lost their Hamiltonian preconceptions.

[17] Albert Bushnell Hart, ed., *Commonwealth History of Massachusetts* (New York, 1930), IV, 584–615.

[18] Roseboom, *Civil War Era,* p. 252; Fosdick, *American Police Systems,* p. 93.

Fentonite strategy of imposing urban reforms on St. Louis; Illinois Republicans were striving in the same way to make Chicago more habitable; and Democratic Detroit also received a Republican-dominated metropolitan police force.[19] Educational reform was widespread throughout the North during the immediate postwar period.[20] Likewise, Radicals in almost every Northern state entertained the possibility of securing suffrage equality for the Negroes within their borders.[21] The list of parallel activities could easily be lengthened. Still, it is beyond the scope of the present study to answer the question of whether there was a substantial "reconstruction" undertaken all across the North by Radical organizations at the state level. The Radical Republicans in New York, however, did attempt a reconstruction of their own at home.

[19] *World*, March 7, 1867, p. 4; Bessie L. Pierce, *A History of Chicago*, II (New York, 1940), 303–354; Fosdick, *American Police Systems*, pp. 92–93.

[20] Ellwood P. Cubberley, *The History of Education: Educational Practice and Progress Considered as a Phase of the Development and Spread of Western Civilization* (Boston, 1920), p. 686, noted that Vermont (1864), Connecticut (1868), Rhode Island (1868), and Michigan (1869) also eliminated rate bills from their public schools during the postwar era. "Superintendent's Report, 1868," pp. 48–49, noted that Pennsylvania, Wisconsin, Kansas, Maine, Maryland, Vermont, Nebraska, and Indiana all added significantly to their teachers' training colleges during the Reconstruction era.

[21] Gillette, *Right to Vote*, p. 26; Leslie H. Fishel, Jr., "Northern Prejudice and Negro Suffrage, 1865–1870," *Journal of Negro History*, XXXIX (1954), pp. 8–26.

Selected Bibliography

Manuscripts and Personal Papers

Conkling, Roscoe. Library of Congress, Washington, D.C.

Fenton, Reuben. Fenton Historical Society, Jamestown, New York.

——. New-York Historical Society, New York.

——. New York Public Library, New York.

——. New York State Library, Albany.

Folger, Charles J. New-York Historical Society, New York.

Gilman, Daniel C. Johns Hopkins University Library, Baltimore.

Greeley, Horace. Library of Congress, Washington, D.C.

——. New York Public Library, New York.

White, Andrew Dickson. Cornell University Libraries, Ithaca, New York. Microfilm.

Government Documents

New York State, Assembly. *Documents,* 87th through 91st sessions, 1864–1868. Albany.

——. Assembly. *Journal,* 88th through 91st sessions, 1865–1868. Albany.

——. Convention of 1821. *Reports of the Proceedings and Debates of the Convention of 1821 Assembled for the Purpose of Amending the Constitution of the State of New York.* Albany, 1821.

——. Convention of 1846. *Debates and Proceedings in the New-York State Convention for the Revision of the Constitution.* Albany, 1846.

——. Convention of 1867–1868. *Documents of the Convention of the State of New York, 1867–'68.* Albany, 1868.

——. Convention of 1867–1868. *Journal of the Convention of the State of New York, Begun and Held at the Capitol, in the City of Albany, on the 4th day of June, 1867.* Albany, [1868].

——. Convention of 1867–1868. *Proceedings and Debates of the Constitutional Convention of the State of New York Held in 1867 and 1868 in the City of Albany.* 5 vols., paged consecutively. Albany, 1868.

——. Metropolitan Board of Health. *Annual Report, 1866.* New York, 1867.

——. Secretary of State. *The Census of the State of New York for 1865.* Albany, 1867.

——. Senate. *Documents,* 78th, 88th, and 90th through 91st sessions, 1855, 1865, 1867–1868. Albany.

——. Senate. *Journal,* 88th through 91st sessions, 1865–1868. Albany.

United States, Congress. *The Ninth Census of the United States, 1870.* Washington, D. C., 1872.

——. Congress, House. *Congressional Globe.* 40th Cong., 3d sess. Washington, D.C., 1869.

——. Congress, House. *House Documents,* 40th Cong., 3d sess., Nos. 31 and 41. Washington, D.C., 1869.

——. Congress, House. *House Executive Documents,* 43d Cong., 2d sess., XIII, No. 95. Washington, D.C., 1875.

Almanacs, Handbooks, and Encyclopedias

Bardeen, C. W. *Dictionary of Educational Biography.* Syracuse, n.d.

Biographical Directory of the American Congress, 1774–1961. Washington, D.C., 1961.

California Blue Book. Sacramento, California, 1967.

The Evening Journal Almanac, 1864–1867. Albany, 1864–1867.

Johnson, Allen, and Dumas Malone, eds. *Dictionary of American Biography.* Vol. V. New York, 1930.

National Cyclopaedia of American Biography. Vol. IV. New York, 1895.

The Tribune Almanac and Political Register for 1868. New York, [1867].

Newspapers

Albany *Evening Journal.*

New York *Times.*

New York *Tribune.*

New York *World.*

Periodicals and Magazines

Harper's Weekly.

New York *Weekly Tribune.*

Reminiscences and Autobiographies

Breen, Matthew P. *Thirty Years of New York Politics Up-to-date.* New York, 1899.

Brockway, Beman. *Fifty Years in Journalism, Embracing Recollections and Personal Experiences, with an Autobiography.* Watertown, N.Y., 1891.

Depew, Chauncy M. *My Memories of Eighty Years.* New York, 1922.

Platt, Thomas C. *The Autobiography of Thomas Collier Platt.* Ed. Louis J. Lang. New York, 1910.

White, Andrew Dickson. *Autobiography of Andrew D. White.* 2 vols. New York, 1905.

———. *The Diaries of Andrew D. White.* Ed. Robert M. Ogden. Ithaca, 1959.

Biographies

Bannan, Theresa. *Pioneer Irish of Onondaga*. New York, 1911.

Brown, Francis. *Raymond of the Times*. New York, 1951.

Conkling, Alfred R. *The Life and Letters of Roscoe Conkling, Orator, Statesman, Advocate*. New York, 1889.

Donald, David. *Charles Sumner and the Rights of Man*. New York, 1970.

Dorf, Philip. *The Builder: A Biography of Ezra Cornell*. New York, 1952.

Harlow, S. R., and H. H. Boone. *Life Sketches of the State Officers, Senators, and Members of the Assembly of the State of New York in 1867*. Albany, 1867.

Jordan, David M. *Roscoe Conkling of New York: Voice in the Senate*. Ithaca, 1971.

Lynch, Denis T. *"Boss" Tweed*. New York, 1927.

McJimsey, George T. *Genteel Partisan: Manton Marble, 1834–1917*. Ames, Iowa, 1971.

McMahon, Helen Grace. "Reuben Eaton Fenton," Master's thesis, Cornell University, 1939.

Pearson, Henry Greenleaf. *James S. Wadsworth of Geneseo*. New York, 1913.

Peters, Harry T. *Currier & Ives, Printmakers to the American People*. Garden City, N.Y., 1942.

Rawley, James A. *Edwin D. Morgan: Merchant in Politics*. New York, 1955.

Simkin, Colin, ed. *Currier and Ives' America*. New York, 1952.

A Sketch of the Life of Governor Fenton. New York, 1866.

Van Deusen, Glyndon G. *Horace Greeley: Nineteenth Century Crusader*. New York, 1953, 1964.

——. *Thurlow Weed: Wizard of the Lobby*. Boston, 1947.

Monographs and Special Studies

Alexander, DeAlva Stanwood. *A Political History of the State of New York*. 3 vols. New York, 1909.

Andreano, Ralph, ed. *The Economic Impact of the American Civil War.* Cambridge, Mass., 1962, 1967.

Atkins, Gordon. *Health, Housing and Poverty in New York City, 1865–1898.* Ann Arbor, 1947.

Becker, Carl L. *Cornell University: Founders and the Founding.* Ithaca, 1943.

Benson, Lee. *The Concept of Jacksonian Democracy.* New York, 1964.

———. *Merchants, Farmers, and Railroads.* Cambridge, Mass. 1955.

Bishop, Morris. *A History of Cornell.* Ithaca, 1962.

Blake, Nelson M. *Water for the Cities.* Syracuse, 1956.

Bonadio, Felice A. *North of Reconstruction: Ohio Politics, 1865–1870.* New York, 1970.

Bowditch, Henry I. *Public Hygiene in America: Being the Centennial Discourse Delivered before the International Medical Congress, Philadelphia, September, 1876.* Boston, 1877.

Bradley, Erwin S. *The Triumph of Militant Republicanism: A Study of Pennsylvania and Presidential Politics, 1860–1872.* Philadelphia, 1964.

Brearley, Harry Chase. *The History of the National Board of Fire Underwriters: Fifty Years of a Civilizing Force.* New York, 1916.

Brock, W. R. *An American Crisis: Congress and Reconstruction, 1865–1867.* New York, 1963.

Chambers, J[ohn] S[harpe]. *The Conquest of Cholera.* New York, 1938.

Citizens' Association of New York. *Report by the Council of Hygiene and Public Health of the Citizens' Association of New York upon the Sanitary Condition of the City.* New York, 1865.

Clune, Henry W. *The Genesee.* New York, 1963.

Cole, Arthur C. *The Era of the Civil War, 1848–1870.* Chicago, 1922. Vol. VIII of *The Centennial History of Illinois.* Ed. Clarence W. Alvord.

Cox, John, and La Wanda Cox. *Politics, Principle, and Prejudice, 1865–1866: Dilemma of Reconstruction America.* New York, 1969.

Cross, Whitney R. *The Burned-over District: The Social and Intellectual History of Enthusiastic Religion in Western New York, 1800–1850.* New York, 1950, 1965.

Cubberley, Ellwood P. *The History of Education: Educational Practice and Progress Considered as a Phase of the Development and Spread of Western Civilization.* Boston, 1920.

Curti, Merle, and Roderick Nash. *Philanthropy in the Shaping of American Higher Education.* New Brunswick, N.J., 1965.

Donald, David. *The Politics of Reconstruction.* Baton Rouge, La., 1965.

Donovan, Herbert D. A. *The Barnburners.* New York, 1925.

Draper, Andrew Sloan. *Origin and Development of the Common School System of the State of New York.* Syracuse, 1905.

Duffy, John. *A History of Public Health in New York City, 1625–1866.* New York, 1968.

Dunning, William A. *Reconstruction, Political and Economic, 1865–1877.* New York, 1907, 1962.

Earle, Thomas, and Charles T. Congdon, eds. *Annals of the General Society of Mechanics and Tradesmen of the City of New York, from 1785 to 1880.* New York, 1882.

Fenton, Reuben E. *Speech of Hon. Reuben E. Fenton, of New-York, delivered in the House of Representatives, February 16, 1860.* Pamphlet in Special Collections of Butler Library, Columbia University.

Finegan, Thomas E. *Free Schools: A Documentary History of the Free School Movement in New York State.* Albany, 1921.

Fitch, Charles E. *The Public School: History of Common School Education in New York from 1633 to 1904.* Albany, 1905.

Flick, Alexander C., ed. *History of the State of New York.* 10 vols. New York, 1933–1937.

Foner, Eric. *Free Soil, Free Labor, Free Men: The Ideology of the Republican Party before the Civil War.* New York, 1970.

Fosdick, Raymond B. *American Police Systems.* New York, 1920.

Franklin, John Hope. *Reconstruction after the Civil War.* Chicago, 1961, 1967.

Frasier, George Willard, and Frederick Lamson Whitney. *Teachers College Finance.* Greeley, Colo., 1930.

Gates, Paul W. *The Wisconsin Pine Lands of Cornell University: A Study in Land Policy and Absentee Ownership.* Ithaca, 1943.

Gillette, William E. *The Right to Vote: Politics and the Passage of the Fifteenth Amendment.* Baltimore, 1965.

Hart, Albert Bushnell, ed. *Commonwealth History of Massachusetts.* Vol. IV. New York, 1930.

Hedrick, Ulysses Prentiss. *A History of Agriculture in the State of New York.* New York, 1933, 1966.

Hesseltine, William B. *Lincoln and the War Governors.* New York, 1948.

Hewett, Waterman T. *Cornell University: A History.* 4 vols. New York, 1905.

Katz, Michael B. *The Irony of Early School Reform: Educational Innovation in Mid-Nineteenth Century Massachusetts.* Cambridge, Mass., 1968.

Limpus, Lowell M. *History of the New York Fire Department.* New York, 1940.

Lincoln, Charles Z. *The Constitutional History of New York from the Beginning of the Colonial Period to the Year 1905, Showing the Origin, Development, and Judicial Construction of the Constitution.* 5 vols. Rochester, 1906.

Litwack, Leon F. *North of Slavery: The Negro in the Free States, 1790–1860.* Chicago, 1961.

Lubove, Roy. *The Progressives and the Slums: Tenement House Reform in New York City, 1890–1917.* Pittsburgh, Pa., 1962.

McKitrick, Eric. *Andrew Johnson and Reconstruction.* New York, 1960.

McManus, Edgar J. *A History of Negro Slavery in New York.* Syracuse, 1966.

McPherson, James M. *The Negro's Civil War.* New York, 1965.

———. *The Struggle for Equality: Abolitionists and the Negro in the Civil War and Reconstruction.* Princeton, N.J., 1964.

Mandelbaum, Seymour J. *Boss Tweed's New York.* New York, 1965.

Mayer, George H. *The Republican Party, 1854–1966.* New York, 1967.

Melvin, Bruce L. *Rural Population of New York, 1855 to 1925.* Memoir 116, in the publications of Cornell University Agricultural Experiment Station. Ithaca, 1928.

Miller, Nathan. *The Enterprise of a Free People: Aspects of Economic Development in New York State during the Canal Period, 1792–1838.* Ithaca, 1962.

Montgomery, David. *Beyond Equality: Labor and the Radical Republicans, 1862–1872.* New York, 1967.

Morris, Lloyd. *Incredible New York, 1850–1950.* New York, 1951.

Nevins, Allan. *The State Universities and Democracy.* Urbana, Ill., 1962.

North, Stafford E., ed. *Our County and Its People: A Descriptive and Biographical Record of Genesee County, New York.* Boston, 1899.

Patrick, Rembert W. *The Reconstruction of the Nation.* New York, 1967.

Pierce, Bessie Louise. *A History of Chicago,* 3 vols. New York, 1937–1957.

Potter, David M. *People of Plenty.* Chicago, 1954.

Rayback, Joseph G. *A History of American Labor.* New York, 1966.

Roosevelt, Theodore. *New York.* Cambridge, Mass., 1891. In *Historic Towns* series. Ed. Edward S. Freeman and William Hunt.

Roseboom, Eugene H. *The Civil War Era, 1850–1873.* Columbus, 1944. Vol. IV of *The History of the State of Ohio.*

Rosenberg, Charles E. *The Cholera Years.* Chicago, 1962.

Ross, Earle Dudley. *The Liberal Republican Movement.* New York, 1919.

Schneider, David M., and Albert Deutsch. *The Road Upward: Three Hundred Years of Public Welfare in New York State.* In the series Social Welfare Today in New York, No. 1. Albany, 1939.

Shallcross, Cecil F., and Thomas A. Ralston. *The History of the New York Board of Fire Underwriters.* New York, 1917.

Smillie, Wilson G. *Public Health: Its Promise for the Future, A Chronicle of the Development of Public Health in the United States, 1607–1914.* New York, 1955.

Smith, Stephen. *The City That Was.* New York, 1911.

Stebbins, Homer A. *A Political History of the State of New York, 1865–1869.* New York, 1913.

Steward, Ira. *A Reduction of Hours Is an Increase of Wages.* Boston, 1865. Reprinted in John R. Commons, *et al.,* eds. *A Documentary History of American Industrial Society,* Vol. IX. Cleveland, 1911. Pp. 284–301.

Sullivan, James, *et al.,* eds. *History of New York State, 1523–1927.* 5 vols. New York, 1927.

Swenson, Philip D. "The Midwest and the Abandonment of Radical Reconstruction, 1864–1877." Ph.D. dissertation, University of Washington, 1971.

Swift, Fletcher Harper. *Federal and State School Finance.* Place and date unknown.

——. *History of Public School Funds in the United States.* New York, 1911.

Trefousse, Hans L. *The Radical Republicans: Lincoln's Vanguard for Racial Justice.* New York, 1969.

Veysey, Lawrence R. *The Emergence of the American University.* Chicago, 1965.

Whitney, Frederick Lamson. *The Growth of Teachers in Service.* New York, 1927.

Williamson, Chilton. *American Suffrage: From Property to Democracy, 1760–1860.* Princeton, N.J., 1960.

Wilson, James Grant, ed. *The Memorial History of the City of New York.* 4 vols. New York, 1892–1893.

Wright, Alfred Hazen. *The New York People's College.* Ithaca, 1958. No. 21 in the *Cornell Studies in History* series.

——. *The New York State Agricultural College.* Ithaca, 1958. No. 20 in the *Cornell Studies in History* series.

Zeller, Belle. *Pressure Politics in New York: A Study of Group Representation before the Legislature.* New York, 1937.

Zilversmit, Arthur. *The First Emancipation: The Abolition of Slavery in the North.* Chicago, 1967.

Articles

Adams, Charles Francis, Jr. "A Chapter of Erie," *North American Review,* CIX (July 1869), 30–106.

——. "An Erie Raid," *North American Review,* CXII (April 1871), 241–291.

Adams, Henry. "The Gold Conspiracy," *Westminster Review,* XCIV (October 1870), 411–436.

Biggs, Hermann M. "An Address: Sanitary Science, the Medical Profession, and the Public," *Medical News,* LXXII (1898), 44–50.

Bogue, Allan G. "Bloc and Party in the United States Senate: 1861–1863," *Civil War History,* XIII (1967), 221–241.

Brieger, Gert H. "Sanitary Reform in New York City: Stephen Smith and the Passage of the Metropolitan Health Bill," *Bulletin of the History of Medicine,* L (1966), 407–429.

Brown, Ira V. "Pennsylvania and the Rights of the Negro, 1865–1887," *Pennsylvania History,* XXVIII (1961), 45–57.

——. "William D. Kelley and Radical Reconstruction," *Pennsylvania Magazine of History and Biography,* LXXXV (1961), pp. 316–329.

Butler, Benjamin F. "Outline of the Constitutional History of New York, An Anniversary Discourse Delivered . . . November 19, 1847," *Collections of the New-York Historical Society,* 2d. ser., II (1849), 9–75.

Fehrenbacher, Don E. "Disunion and Reunion," in John Higham, ed., *The Reconstruction of American History.* New York, 1965. Pp. 98–118.

Fishel, Leslie H., Jr. "Northern Prejudice and Negro Suffrage, 1865–1870," *Journal of Negro History*, XXXIX (1954), 8–26.

Foner, Eric. "Racial Attitudes of the New York Free Soilers," *New York History*, XLVI (1965), 311–329.

Fox, Dixon Ryan. "The Negro Vote in Old New York," *Political Science Quarterly*, XXXII (1917), 252–275.

Glad, Paul W. "Progressives and the Business Culture of the 1920's," *Journal of American History*, LIII (1966), 75–89.

Gray, John C. "Remarks on Cornell University," *Proceedings of the Massachusetts Historical Society*, XI (1869–1870), 85–92.

Hirsch, Leo H., Jr. "The Negro and New York, 1783 to 1865," *Journal of Negro History*, XVI (1931), 417–424.

Katz, Michael B., "The Emergence of Bureaucracy in Urban Education: The Boston Case, 1850–1884," *History of Education Quarterly*, VIII (1968), 155–188, 319–357.

——. "From Voluntarism to Bureaucracy in American Education," *Sociology of Education*, XLIV (1971), 297–332.

Kramer, Howard C. "Early Municipal and State Boards of Health," *Bulletin of the History of Medicine*, XXIV (1950), 503–517.

Link, Arthur S. "What Happened to the Progressive Movement in the 1920's?" *American Historical Review*, LXIV (1959), 833–851.

McKitrick, Eric. "Party Politics and the Union and Confederate War Efforts," in William Dean Burnham and William Nisbet Chambers, eds., *The American Party Systems: Stages of Political Development.* New York, 1967. Pp. 117–151.

Montgomery, David. "Radical Republicanism in Pennsylvania, 1866–1873," *Pennsylvania Magazine of History and Biography*, LXXXV (1961), 439–457.

Nicklason, Fred. "The Civil War Contracts Committee," *Civil War History*, XVII (1971), 232–245.

Payne, Aaron H. "The Negro in New York Prior to 1860," *Howard Review*, I (1923), 1–64.

Pessen, Edward. "The Workingmen's Movement of the Jacksonian Era," *Mississippi Valley Historical Review*, XLIII (1956), 428–443.

Richardson, James S. "Mayor Fernando Wood and the New York Police Force, 1855–1857," *New-York Historical Society Quarterly*, L (1966), 5–40.

Shortreed, Margaret. "The Antislavery Radicals: From Crusade to Revolution, 1840–1868," *Past and Present*, XVI (November 1959), 65–89.

Smith, James M. "The 'Separate But Equal' Doctrine: An Abolitionist Discusses Racial Segregation and Educational Policy during the Civil War," *Journal of Negro History*, XLI (1956), 138–147.

Stanley, John L. "Majority Tyranny in Tocqueville's America: The Failure of Negro Suffrage in 1846," *Political Science Quarterly*, LXXXIV (1969), 412–435.

Veiller, Lawrence. "Tenement House Reform in New York City, 1834–1900," in Robert W. DeForest and Lawrence Veiller, eds., *The Tenement House Problem*. New York, 1903. Pp. 69–118.

Index

*The Radical Republicans and Reform
in New York during Reconstruction*

Designed by R. E. Rosenbaum.
Composed by York Composition Co., Inc.,
in 11 point linotype Janson, 3 points leaded,
with display lines in Weiss italic.
Printed letterpress from type by York Composition Co.
on Warren's 1854 text, 60 pound basis,
with the Cornell University Press watermark.
Bound by Vail-Ballou Press
in Interlaken book cloth
and stamped in All Purpose foil.

Library of Congress Cataloging in Publication Data
(For library cataloging purposes only)

Mohr, James C
   The Radical Republicans and reform in New York during Reconstruction.

   Bibliography: p.
   1. New York (State)—Politics and government—1865–1950. 2. Republican Party. New York (State).
I. Title.
F124.M73   320.9'747'04   72-12404
ISBN 0-8014-0757-5